TECHNOLOG[barcode]
WOMEN'S V

THE EDITOR

Cheris Kramarae is Professor of Speech Communication, University of Illinois at Urbana-Champaign, where she teaches courses in interpersonal communication, feminist theory and sociolinguistics. She is the author of over 30 articles on language and gender, and author, editor or co-editor of seven books on communication and feminist theory, including *A Feminist Dictionary* (Pandora Press, 1986), *Language and Power* (Sage, 1984), *Language, Gender and Society* (Newbury House, 1983), *The Voices and Words of Women and Men* (Pergamon Press, 1980) and *Women and Men Speaking* (Newbury House, 1981).

TECHNOLOGY AND WOMEN'S VOICES

KEEPING IN TOUCH

Edited by

Cheris Kramarae

ROUTLEDGE & KEGAN PAUL
New York and London

First published in 1988 by
Routledge & Kegan Paul Inc.
in association with Methuen Inc.
29 West 35th Street, New York, NY 10001

Published in Great Britain by
Routledge & Kegan Paul Ltd
11 New Fetter Lane, London EC4P 4EE

Set in Bembo 10/12 & Optima
by Belgrave Phototypesetting Ltd., Scarborough
and printed in Great Britain
by Billings Ltd., Worcester

Library of Congress Cataloging in Publication Data

Technology and women's voices.
Includes index
1. Women in Technology.   2. Technology—Social
aspects.   I. Kramarae, Cheris.
T36.T43 1988 303.4'83'088042 87-12861

British Library CIP Data also available
ISBN 0-7102-0679-8

CONTENTS

CONTENTS

ILLUSTRATIONS

PREFACE

'I feel like asking my boss, "What do you think I am—an extension of the machine?".'
(Comment by a clerical worker quoted in *Race Against Time* 1980, 12)

Women's speech and technology may seem to have nothing in common—but, as the authors of this collection detail, they are richly interconnected. We quite obviously do not address all technologies of importance to all women. What we offer are illustrations in several areas which suggest the importance of the general project.

Some topics (e.g. women and computers, telephones, typewriters, printing) have an obvious relevance to discussions of past and current work and social structures. Other topics (e.g. sewing machines, washing machines, microphones) have been chosen precisely because they have not been discussed as social processes with relevance to women's social lives. Most of the research and examples come from the US, Canada and England. This volume is just a beginning for all the international work needed on this topic. For example, an extension of this volume would include discussion of the technological processes imposed on people in the Third World, particularly the effects of the processes on women's resources and social relationships and the meaning of those effects for people elsewhere. These essays are a contribution to communication and gender research, and a challenge and invitation to malestream researchers to question, for example, the assumption that men in the West have a location which is separate and adequate for theorizing about communication and technology without consideration of the origin of the imposed hierarchical social divisions of such polar terms as female/male, East/West, and Black/white.

In addition to the topics in this collection we could construct lists of numerous other technological processes important to women's interaction. For example, initial plans for this book included an essay on the language of reproductive technology which would argue that the terminology used by the 'experts' in reproductive

ix

technology has, through the years, helped organize the ways women think about their lives, including their relationships to other women and to men. An illness prevented the author from finishing the essay in time for this publication.

All technological developments can usefully be studied with a focus on women's social interactions, even those developments which would initially seem to have little to do with women's lives. For example: girls' and women's uses of bicycles. I have been fascinated by nineteenth century feminists' accounts of the bicycle as a mechanical device which changed women's movement through their communities. (Elizabeth Cady Stanton declared in 1895 that 'many a woman is riding to the suffrage on a bicycle' [Kramarae and Treichler 1986, 69].) Early feminists told stories of the ways women were discouraged (bottles and insults thrown their way) from riding bicycles. In some families bicycles and motor bikes are still considered more suited to boys' than girls' lives—and boys are often allowed more freedom as to when and where they ride. (One of the contributors for this collection tells me that her brothers were allowed to learn to ride at an earlier age than she was, and that even now her father discourages her, a postgraduate student, from riding her bicycle to work.) But in general in Western countries the bicycle is no longer considered only a male mode of transport.

The situation is much different in other parts of the world. In Delhi I asked friends why I saw many men and *no* women pedalling bicycles or steering motorcycles—only some women getting rides on the cycles. I was told that even if a woman could afford a bike or motorcycle, she couldn't use it for fear of ridicule; those are men's modes of transportation. Besides, the woman's sari would make bike riding very difficult. (In the US, women's interest in bicycle riding was early linked to arguments for 'rational dress,' that is, women's clothing styles which did not require yards and yards of skirt material.) Millions of women in India daily walk many miles hauling water for their families; procuring water is a woman's duty just as riding a bicycle is a man's activity (Rami 1985). Women seldom use bicycles for such activities as getting water, visiting relatives, or taking their homemade lace to collection points for selling. Men with bicycles market the products of women lace makers (Mies 1982). Thus gender-differentiated technology deepens women's economic and social dependence. In this and other cases, we can see that the genderizing of transport affects women's talk, including when and where it occurs, the topics, and the perceived value of the talk by women and men.

I have enjoyed working with the women and man whose essays are included in this collection. They are educators and activists who have very busy schedules, yet who became willing contributors to this cooperative effort. The focus and ideas for specific contents of the volume grew out of my discussions with Lana Rakow and Jan Zimmerman, both of whom have written valuable feminist critiques of technology and communication research. I thank Dale Spender for the many discussions (about women's interactions, and feminist history and theory) which we have had over the past dozen years. And I thank Brinlee Kramer, Ann Russo and Barrie Thorne for their many critiques and encouraging comments on this and other projects. Philippa Brewster and Candida Lacey have been very patient and helpful editors who have done much to support this and much other interdisciplinary feminist research. I also thank Elizabeth Taylor who read the manuscript so carefully and Victoria Leto who spent many hours proofreading, assisted by Jim Jackson and Dale Kramer.

Cheris Kramarae, January 1987
University of Illinois-Urbana-Champaign

REFERENCES

Kramarae, Cheris and Paula Treichler, with the assistance of Ann Russo. 1986. *A Feminist Dictionary*. New York and London: Pandora Press.

Mies, Maria. 1982. *The Lace Makers of Narsapur: Indian Housewives Produce for the World Market*. London: Zed Press.

Rami, Prabha. 1985. 'Just one more queue: women and water shortage in Tamil Nadu.' In Madhu Kishwar and Ruth Vanita, eds. *In Search of Answers: Indian Women's Voices from Manushi*. London: Zed Books, 104–14.

CHERIS KRAMARAE

GOTTA GO MYRTLE, TECHNOLOGY'S AT THE DOOR

'The perfect secretary should forget that she is a human being, and be the most efficient aid at all times and on all subjects ... She should respond to [her boss's] requirements exactly as a machine responds to the touch of lever or accelerator.'

(Emily Post, 1945, 548)

A few women were talking together after hearing a public lecture on common beliefs about the ways women and men talk. A young woman said she thought it was 'nice' that many people realized and appreciated that women talk differently, often smoothing things over and making people feel better. An older woman responded something like this:

'It's nice? Well, I don't know. If women are supposed to take care of making everyone easy in social situations, how come we're not given tax breaks for cars and gasoline to scoot around helping people out? And how come we're not given training in microphone use, and special classes to help us take care of crowds? What about giving us special phones with cross-country networks connections so we can keep in touch and know who needs help and where? How are we supposed to exercise these 'nice' social skills we're supposed to have without some help here? How come we're not given control of those communications satellites up there so we'd have the necessary equipment to help keep everyone talking with each other?'

Indeed, how come? Her questions raise many more questions. In Western cultures women are expected to be unpaid facilitators of others' talk. Women write the thank-you notes and letters to relatives, call the sick, keep family photos and histories, and discuss interpersonal relationships. When, where, and how do they do this? What are the living arrangements, travel systems, devices or tech-

1

niques which facilitate, restrict, and structure women's interaction? Do women have distinctive speaking skills and if so how are they developed? Do these skills make them more effective telephone operators and receptionists? Are women really born physically and psychologically better structured to be receptionists than are men, as some men say? If women and men have differing access to others and work with different technological processes, what does this mean for the way we interact with women and with men? For the way the world operates? These concerns seem both essential and basic—critical to our understanding of human history and, more particularly, to our understanding of the stereotypes, actualities and evaluations of girls' and women's talk and writing.

Technological processes developed by men for men are nearly always interpreted by women in ways other than those intended by men. While there are many topics to be considered under a general heading Technology and Women, we have focused on a specific, important, and generally ignored subject: technological processes have lasting impact on women's communication, something the creators and developers seldom if ever consider. The articles in this volume trace the operations of several specific innovations (e.g. electricity, telephone, washing machine, bus, printing press, computer) and their effects on Western social interaction. The histories of these specific innovations can lead to a general discussion of how all technological practices—including innovation, creation, production, maintenance and use—affect the ways, places, times and content of talk, writing and publishing.

One of our contributions to discussions of *technologies* is to consider them not as machines, but as social relations; all technological systems (e.g. transportation and washing processes) can be seen as communication systems. (This is not a new concept—although it is not a widely used approach. What *is* new is the serious consideration of these social relations as involving women as well as men.) One of our contributions to discussions of *social relationships* is to consider them as organized and structured by technological systems which allow or encourage some kinds of interactions and prevent or discourage other kinds.

One start is by looking at existing analyses of technology. It *is* a way to start—but one which will disappoint, because histories of technology have almost nothing to say about women. One author of a book on technology told me, 'When women get involved in technology, then we'll write about them.' When women get

involved? Before our exchange that day, I had done the very customary activities of using, in a building constructed of wood,
metals and plastics, the running water fixtures, heating system, re-
frigerator, toothbrush, ready-made clothing (which I had slightly
altered by use of needle, thread and scissors), telephone, electric
lights, pen, typewriter, tampon and lotion. A friend had given me a
ride in a car to the building where the conference was held. (At
home I usually use a bicycle to get to work and to buy pasteurized
milk, and food transported from other parts of the country.) I rode
an elevator and during the day I used hundreds of other items or
processes which are not just heaven- or hell-sent outgrowths of the
soil. I and all other women I know around here are heavily 'involved' with technology.

I knew what he was likely thinking, of course, when he made that
statement, because many others have declared that women have not
been very 'technological' or inventive; that is, we have not created
many of the items called technology. His work is focused on men's
activities; he perhaps does not know about the many inventions of
women, documented in the growing literature on their innovations.
(He could read Trescott [1979] and Warner [1979] for a start on this
literature.) Women have not, it is true, designed the majority of
devices which are used in homes (supposedly women's most natural
place) or in offices and factories where many women spend many
hours. Rather than dismissing women as non-inventors, that scholar could be asking why men have considered women the 'mere'
users, but not appropriate creators, shapers and producers, of technology.

The analyses in this collection can also help explain women's
specific interactions in specific contexts. Consider a weekly gathering of young, suburban mothers who have 'chosen' to have children
in their twenties, 'taking time off work' for several years to care for
their children. How are their interactions influenced by the architec-
tural designs of their homes and neighborhoods, local and national
transport systems, household appliances, public service supports,
their clothing, food preservation, infant formulas, heating and
electrical resources? And by the values built into the technologies?

Then we can ask the same questions about the technological systems which impinge on the talk of a gathering of urban, poor,
'unemployed' mothers, gathered in a woman's kitchen. The
answers will be different. And they will help us listen for, appreciate
and explain many of the differences heard in 'the ways women and

men talk' (too often explained as 'sex differences' rather than as largely situational differences). The answers will also help us explain some of the differences in talk *within* that social category *women*, as we learn more about the ways their resources and expectations vary.

What technologies, and what cultural assumptions about those technologies, are present in these women's interaction? How do our descriptions and understanding of the talk differ once we consider technological practices? What are the technological fixes or solutions which women apply and which others apply to women's lives? The answers do not come readily, because they require a consideration of political, social and economic issues of women's lives. But such an approach begins to flesh out what we mean when we now more habitually, but still vaguely, qualify our research statements by stating that of course women's talk differs by age, race, income, ethnic group.... Some of that 'differs' comes from differing technological resources and values. What are the technological resources available and how are they distributed? Who are the experts? The users? Who is doing the washing, cooking, child care and transporting of groceries; and how are they doing it? What is the social status of the differing work they do?

Similar questions can (and should) be asked about men's interaction. And in fact, asking these questions about women encourages our consideration of all communication patterns. But many other scholars *have* been concerned with male involvement with technology. Not perhaps in the ways suggested by this book (and not even explicitly as *men's* experiences and values), but Western history of technology has been basically men's history. In fact, one way of describing what has been traditionally considered as technology is to say it consists of the devices, machinery and processes which men are interested in. (This is a reason why we do not find discussions of child care devices in men's books on technology.)

There are, of course, other definitions of technology. The least helpful are those which refer only to devices and machinery and to the techniques used to make things work. This is similar to the lopsided way of describing housework in terms of dust cloths and cleaning fluids without reference to the social systems which determine who it is who does the dusting and cleaning. The most helpful (at least for our interest in women's social relations) are the definitions which place social practices at the center. For example, Arnold Pacey (1983) describes technology practice as 'the application of scientific and other knowledge to practical tasks by ordered systems that involve people and organizations, living things and machines' (6). David Noble (1977; 1984) introduces technology as the transformation of science into a means of capital accumulation. In these definitions, technology is a human, political and social ac-tivity.

Because they are compact and because they spotlight the basic concerns and assumptions of their writers, definitions are often use-ful. But they are often too cryptic. For the purposes of extended dis-cussions such as contained in this book I would add these points:

—Technology, like all aspects of 'progress,' is usually thought of as a masculine invention and activity. In actuality we are all intensely involved in and affected by technology practices. Official and professional development and evaluation of tech-nology has been done by men who have limited knowledge about women's daily lives and problems, and very limited in-terest in expanding women's economic and social freedom.

—New technological processes are usually considered a part of modernization which many think inevitably leads to the im-provement of the status and well-being of the people involved. Actually, modernization has resulted in women losing tradi-tional roles in agriculture and handicrafts production, and thus losing some of their autonomy, influence, and access to resources (Tiano 1984). This erosion has not, however, 'freed' them to become full-time homemakers and child rearers; women typically have double work loads of familial and other, income-generating responsibilities. Because their domestic tasks are stressed and are considered to be insular activities, men do not consider women to be part of any important com-munication networks.

—Technology is usually considered 'big world' talk, connected in communication research with the 'public' sphere, men, mass media, machines, and market prices. To connect women and technology is to challenge the private/public division present throughout malestream communication theorizing.

—Most Western technological change is linked to traditional, patriarchial work practices. Ironically what seems new for men often turns out to be very much the same old thing for women. Since the industrial revolution—with the separation of men from daily domestic life and the separation of unpaid house and child care work from other work—social hierarchies have

5

remained amazingly consistent. In this sense, much of the seemingly revolutionary technology is actually very conservative. The relationship between change and continuity is one of the topics of this book.

—The concept of technological innovation today has the central significance that theological discussions had in medieval times (see editors' note for essay by Judith McGaw 1982, 798). Many of our current debates about politics, history, change, values, lifestyles and liberation center on concerns about technology.

—The tech-fix, the belief that technology can solve all kinds of problems, even social ones (Bush 1983, 152), has not worked to make a better world for women. This is not to say that women do not use and profit from many innovations. Technological change *can* be positive for women, either through chance benefits resulting from changes introduced primarily by business managers for themselves or from conscious addressing of women's problems. It is just that this has seldom happened. As Arditti *et al.* (1984), writing about reproductive technologies, state, 'Each new technology is born in a mire of complex social issues—issues the technologists, apparently, never stop to debate' (4). Equity in assessment and management of technology would itself be the most major of technological changes.

—Many of the technological developments which are thought of as primarily tools to complement human skills also have critical importance to women's social relations. As Margaret Lowe Benston (this volume) points out, the scientific/technical language and world view is increasingly accepted as the only legitimate model for discussing and interpreting reality—with world- and word-shaking implications for the subject matter and form of discourse.

If technology practices are *human* structures and organizations, how strange that most historians, scientists and social critics haven't included consideration of women's social relations as essential to understanding technology. (Strange—but actually we are not astonished because to many people, technology = science = men; Dale Spender (1982; 1983), Jan Zimmerman (1986), Joan Rothschild (1983), and other feminist theoreticians have given us accounts of how women have been separated from historical and social criticism.)

Technological processes have been studied from the (usually implicit) vantage point of men's experiences. When one puts women at the center of analysis, male biases and masculist ideologies become clearer, and one discovers new questions as well as fresh approaches to old questions. Women and men share some social processes, and there are other lines of differences (e.g. social class) which divide women from women and men from men, and which at times may unite working–class women and men. The challenge is to develop a more inclusive understanding of the social relations and ideologies of technological processes.

How to begin? Some technological practices will be more revealing than others for studying social relations. For example, in Western cultures introduction of the telephone in homes and businesses has altered experiences for both men and women. Upper-class, urban households had telephones long before poor, rural households. But sexual divisions of labor in every institution established different contexts for the uses of the telephone by men and by women. New occupations—e.g. switchboard operators, telephone repairers— were differentiated by gender. Stereotypes emerged of girls gabbing endlessly on the phone. The chapter in this volume on the telephone is by Lana Rakow who is completing the first extensive study of women and the phone, a study which begins with the perceptions and experiences of women rather than with the many jokes about girls' and women's use of the telephone to gossip. As we have discovered through our 1970s and 1980s studies of gender and language, the stereotypes and jokes are misleading, making identification of actual gender-related differences more difficult. Rakow's essay should encourage future studies of the connections of restrictions on girls' movement through their communities, the girls' uses of the telephone, and the types of networks they develop. Studies are needed worldwide on class and geographical differences in girls' and boys', and women's and men's access to, and uses of, the telephone (and other technological processes mentioned and discussed in this volume). As Barrie Thorne (1987) has pointed out, children are ignored or conceptually privatized in most social science research which also, when gender is attended to, tends to compare the separate worlds of boys and girls. Studying telephone uses across age groups can help us listen to gender separation *and* interaction.

Automobiles (and trains and buses) are called transportation, rather than communication, technology; yet a prime function for these resources is the bringing together or dispersing of people. In this volume the essays on the telephone and on the automobile (Virginia Scharff) pay particular attention to the meaning of this equipment to women in non-urban settings who do not see other adult women as frequently as do many urban women. (This is not to say that physical proximity to others is the only factor in determining whether one feels isolated or cut off from others with whom one can feel an affinity. Rural women who live with husbands and children often talk about isolation. Urban women who live in crowded buildings often say that they 'have nobody to talk with.' The suggestion in this volume is that an analysis of the communication systems and patterns can tell us a lot about the resources which women and men have to determine what is communicated, how, when, by whom and with what results.)

Men own more automobiles even though women are more often expected to take care of many projects for which there are not now telecommunication substitutes for travel (e.g. taking food to and visiting the sick, and eating with friends). Yet even public transport is not usually planned with the specific social and economic requirements of women in mind (Genevieve Giuliano 1983, and the essay by the Women and Transport Forum, this volume). Many women employed outside the home are also expected to perform truckloads of transport work each week (e.g. obtaining medical and dental care for family members, transporting children to school and social activities, carting groceries).

Many other technological practices are obviously of major importance to women. This volume includes a section of essays on the typewriter and computer. Margery Davies, who has written a book on women's entry into offices as 'typewriters,' here writes about typists' office interaction, including collective action to change working conditions. From interviews with clerical workers using computers, Anne Machung documents their reactions to the organization of word processing centers; the women's social contact with others has been drastically altered in ways many of the women deplore. Even for women doing computer programming, there is, Sherry Turkle writes, the worry that too close a relationship with a computer will alter their relationships with other people. Judy Smith and Ellen Barker discuss ways feminist computer programs can be used to make the interaction among women with similar interests faster, more frequent, more economical and satisfying.

Other topics are included in this volume to illustrate how we can

8

look with interest and benefit at technology practices which seem initially to have little relationship to women's social relations. The sewing machine, initially advertised to homemakers as a machine to free women from excessive sewing time, did serve some valuable mechanical functions, but the industrial uses made of it meant many women worked long, poorly paid hours in sweatshops. Other women working at home found use of the sewing machine made companionship and information exchange more difficult (Cheris Kramarae this volume).

Victoria Leto's essay on washing technologies deals with what is, in Western culture, usually considered a 'naturally' solitary task. Her historical study looks at the more collective and companionable options which have been available for clothes washing, and at the social and economic forces which have led to the current isolating practices. Many of the household technologies operated by women working alone in the house have not been designed for the home. Clothes and dish washing machines, refrigerators and modern stoves were designed and initially manufactured for commercial launderies, hotels, hospitals and other institutions (Hayden 1984, 73). Yet this machinery, rather than being used for neighborhood or community collective services, was scaled down for individual family use, abetting the isolation of many women. We have growing documentation (Cowan 1983) that the household 'labor-saving' devices have actually *not* made the household easier to run, or freed women for other activities. As the equipment has been introduced into the homes of families which could afford it, the cleaning standards have been raised; and it's still women who are doing the repetitive tasks, mostly performed at home and alone.[1]

While some of the new electrical appliances have not basically changed the ways women work in the home, the use of electricity in the home did prompt other modifications in women's interaction. The twentieth-century introduction of electricity to first urban and then rural homes obviously was a technological innovation of major importance. Leanne Hinton (this volume) traces the impact of electric lights, stoves, air conditioning (and telephone and community water system) on oral traditions, especially as they are practiced by women.[2]

Walter Ong has argued that the microphone is an instrument which has enabled women, in particular, to amplify their voices in order to reach larger audiences. Theoretically the microphone could serve women this way. However, Anne McKay (this volume) finds that non-technical restrictions have been the primary reason that women have not been heard as frequently as are men in public places talking to crowds. Her work supports accounts of the causes and results of men's anxiety about, and control of, women's voices on radio. Although radio (and TV) broadcasting (programming and voices) *could* have been developed to enhance the interaction of the middle-class women who after World War I were encouraged to stay home, much of the paternalistic programming and voices seemed designed to make women more isolated. The topics and male announcers addressed women as wives, homemakers, mothers and sex objects, rather than as people with many personal, social and economic interests (Kramarae 1984; in press). Altered values concerning women's involvement in public affairs will be needed if more women are going to be allowed to amplify their voices through microphones.

Women have been more restricted than men in what they can say and where; they are also restricted as a result of what others say and write. Marilyn French (1985) suggests that literature addressed to women ideologically redefined women in terms of motherhood. Mark Schulman (this volume) argues that the creation of mothering is perhaps the most important effect print has had on women's lives, but he also reviews the history of women as creators, producers and distributors as well as consumers of print.

In this volume, we attempt no simple explanation for the impact of any one technology on women's interaction—but we make an argument for the importance of considering technological processes when discussing women's words and interaction. Machinery is designed and developed by people with assumptions about what makes for necessary, desirable, profitable and important human activity; planners, manufacturers, and systems organizers may consider women's labor and efficiency, but seldom is women's communication with other women and with men considered a necessary part of the planning or evaluation.

The Western technological imperative is frequently explained and justified by the quest for Progress. Yet, as Alice Walker (1983) says, much 'progress' benefits only a few and is built on the low or unpaid labor of others (163). (She writes in particular of white progress built on slavery.) The new technologies may promise additional competencies and control for those who organize the systems, but they may be used for further exploitation of those who don't. Jan Zimmerman (1983) considers the following possible sequestering functions of some innovations called communication technology:

> Women isolated at home, trapped in electronic cages, using ca-
> ble TV, computers, and touch-tone phones for video shopping
> and telephone banking. Women reading *Family Circle* maga-
> zine on the TV screen to see which recipes they should pull
> from their home computer file, while daughter Jane plays with
> her voice-synthesized doll and son Dick plays computer chess.
> Women forced to do data entry or circuit board assembly from
> home for piecework pay, so they can work and care for chil-
> dren at the same time. (4)

And these are the luckier women who are given some means to use
these processes, means often withheld from, for example, older
women, and poor women. All women are judged by the processes
and products of the middle-class machinery. For example, once
washing machines are in middle-class homes, standards of cleanliness based on use of those machines are applied to everyone, whatever their access to washing machines. Further, once washing
machines are in middle-class homes, developers are not likely to improve the more communal washing facilities. At this point almost
any woman responsible for clothes washing will want a home
machine—regardless of whether home washing machines make for
the best overall economic and social system.

It is not that we don't want change. (All workers who challenge
the need for and value of forced technological change—always
defined as progress—are accused of being 'afraid of change,' 'old-
fashioned,' 'selfish,' 'standing in the way of progress,' and [if they
are women who are voicing the concerns and anger] 'strident.') In
fact, what many of us believe is most needed in the world *is*
change—for those who are economically and socially devalued (that
is, in the great majority of cases, women). We want to help make
the decisions—not just have to try to live with the decisions and
changes. We want more egalitarian and creative work and
relationships—which will not come about just through more male-
dominated technology changes, but through a rethinking and then a
restructuring of the social relationships in which technology is embedded.

Many of us are skeptical of technological changes—which are
often designed with our labors (but not our interests, interaction,
health or happiness) in mind. There is widespread concern among

women that unless we become involved in the decision making that is called technological progress, new processes will embody the same old sexism, racism and classism (Rakow 1984). Reviewing the current, seemingly progressive arguments made to encourage women to train for and obtain computer jobs, Berch (1984) states that despite the appearance of new opportunities for women, the new technology represents 'more than anything else the *reconstruction of domination*: new technology bears the sexist/classist imprint of its designers' (42).

Using specific illustrations, these essays assess technological changes in terms of their impact on women's social lives. The issues raised apply to all technological processes, and are important for all women.

NOTES

1   Dolores Hayden (1984) reviews the themes of fear, guilt and pseudo-scientific arguments used in advertisements for privately owned washers, vacuum cleaners and other household appliances (76). Even before the ring-around-the-collar commercials—husband or son criticizing a woman for using a detergent which doesn't rinse away their neck dirt and oil—women were trying to measure up to the increasingly demanding cleanliness standards reported and supported in 'women's magazines.'

2   These accounts are certainly not intended to romanticize the work of women in the past who have spent much more than their share of time waiting in queues at water wells and taps and transporting water. The accounts do argue that women's interaction is affected by technological changes in ways not often considered by planners or evaluators.

REFERENCES

Arditti, Rita, Renate Duelli Klein and Shelley Minden, eds. 1984. *Test Tube Women: What Future for Motherhood?* London: Pandora Press.

Berch, B. 1984. 'For women the chips are down.' *Processed World* 11 (Summer), 42-6.

Bush, Corlann Gee. 1983. 'Women and the assessment of technology: to think, to be; to unthink, to free.' In Joan Rothschild, ed. *Machina Ex Dea: Feminist Perspectives on Technology*. New York: Pergamon Press, 151-70.

Cowan, Ruth Schwartz. 1983. *More Work for Mother: The Ironies of*

Household Technology from the Open Hearth to the Microwave. New York: Basic Books.

French, Marilyn. 1985. *Beyond Power: On Women, Men, and Morals*. New York: Summit.

Giuliano, Genevieve. 1983. 'Getting there: women and transportation.' In Jan Zimmerman, ed. *The Technological Woman: Interfacing with Tomorrow*. New York: Praeger.

Hayden, Dolores. 1984. *Redesigning the American Dream: The Future of Housing, Work, and Family Life*. New York: W.W. Norton.

Kramarae, Cheris. 1984. 'Nachrichten zu sprechen gestatte ich der Frau nicht.' In Senta Trömel-Plötz, ed. *Gewalt durch Sprache*. Frankfurt: Fischer Taschenbuch Verlag, 203–28.

Kramarae, Cheris. In press. 'Censorship of women's voices on radio.' In Sue Fisher and Alexandra Todd, eds, *Gender and Discourse: The Power of Talk*. Norwood, New Jersey: Ablex Publishing.

McGaw, Judith. 1982. 'Women and the history of American technology.' *Signs: Journal of Women in Culture and Society* 7:4, 798–828.

Noble, David. 1977. *America by Design: Science, Technology, and the Rise of Corporate Capitalism*. New York: Alfred A. Knopf.

Noble, David. 1984. *Forces of Production*. New York : Alfred A. Knopf.

Ong, Walter. 1974. 'Agonistic structures in academic: past to present.' *Interchange* 5:4, 1–12.

Pacey, Arnold. 1983. *The Culture of Technology*. Cambridge, Mass.: MIT Press.

Post, Emily. 1945. *Etiquette: The Blue Book of Social Usage*. New York: Funk & Wagnalls.

Rakow, Lana. 1984. 'Feminist approaches to technology: implications for communication scholarship.' University of Illinois, manuscript.

Rothschild, Joan. 1983. 'Introduction: Why machina ex dea?' In Joan Rothschild, ed. *Machina ex Dea: Feminist Perspectives on Technology*. New York: Pergamon Press, ix–xxix.

Spender, Dale. 1982. *Women of Ideas and What Men Have Done to Them*. London: Routledge & Kegan Paul.

Spender, Dale. 1983. *There's Always Been a Women's Movement This Century*. London: Routledge & Kegan Paul/Pandora Press.

13

Thorne, Barrie. 1987. 'Children and gender: constructions of difference.' Paper given at the conference on Theoretical Perspectives on Sexual Difference, Stanford University, February.

Tiano, Susan. 1984. 'The public-private dichotomy: theoretical perspectives on 'women in development.' *The Social Science Journal* 21:4 (October), 11-28.

Trescott, Martha Moore, ed. 1979. *Dynamos and Virgins Revisited: Women and Technological Change in History*. Metuchen, New Jersey: Scarecrow Press.

Walker, Alice. 1983. *In Search of Our Mothers' Gardens: Womanist Prose*. New York: Harcourt Brace Jovanovich.

Warner, Deborah. 1979. 'Women inventors at the Centennial.' In Martha Moore Trescott, ed. *Dynamos and Virgins Revisited: Women and Technological Change in History*. Metuchen, New Jersey: Scarecrow Press, 102-19.

Zimmerman, Jan. 1983. *The Technological Woman: Interfacing with Tomorrow*. New York: Praeger.

Zimmerman, Jan. 1986. *Once Upon the Future: A Woman's Guide to Tomorrow's Technology*. London: Routledge & Kegan Paul.

MARGARET LOWE BENSTON

WOMEN'S VOICES/MEN'S VOICES: TECHNOLOGY AS LANGUAGE

'If it's not appropriate for women, it's not appropriate.'
(Postcard from the International Women's Tribune Centre)

Men and women in our society have very different experiences in nearly every aspect of their lives, so it is not surprising to find that their experiences with respect to technology are also very different. Boys and men are expected to learn about machines, tools and how things work. In addition, they absorb, ideally, a 'technological world view' that grew up along with industrial society. Such a world view emphasizes objectivity, rationality, control over nature and distance from human emotions. Conversely, girls and women are not expected to know much about technical matters. Instead, they are to be good at interpersonal relationships and to focus on people and on emotion. They are to be less rational, less capable of abstract, 'objective' thought. (See Chodorow 1978; Benston 1982; and articles in Rothschild 1983.)

These differences have consequences in two different areas: first, technology itself can be seen as a 'language' for action and self-expression with consequent gender differences in ability to use this 'language.' Second, men's control over technology and their adherence to a technological world view have consequences for language and verbal communication and create a situation where women are 'silenced.'

The ideals for men and women are communicated in a variety of ways and are acted on from early childhood. By my early teens, while boys my age were discovering cars and pinball machines, I discovered books and horses. Later in adolescence, Friday night at the local drive-in would be spent with the boys discussing cars or football and the girls discussing clothes or gossiping about friends. In high school, shop was required for boys and home economics for

15

girls but even if any of the girls had had a choice we would never have ventured into a world of tools and grease.

Unlike most of the girls I knew, however, I liked science in high school and took a chemistry major in college. I was odd enough to enjoy mathematics and theoretical work but still I avoided or skimped labs. In graduate school, as a physical chemist, I was in one of the 'hard' sciences and my husband was in English, yet he was the one who did the plumbing repairs and tuned up the car. We both liked music but he was the one who discussed needle and speaker characteristics endlessly with his male friends; I would simply let them talk while I listened to the records. Still avoiding lab work, I did a theoretical problem rather than an experimental one for my PhD thesis and later, when I switched to computing science, it was to explore the social implications of this new technology.

me too!

There is a clear pattern here. Even though I like mathematics and scientific theory, I have never felt at home around machines and technology. I am not alone in this—it is typical for women. In fact, even with my history of avoidance, I am considerably more at home in the world of machines and equipment than are many women. I have, after all, done laboratory work, however reluctantly, and I do teach technical courses.

Darlene

This is not to say that women do not use tools and machines in our society. *Everyone* interacts with the underlying technological system; technology and society are words for different aspects of the same whole. Sometimes machines or systems are used by both women and men—we both use the same means of transportation and we both use telephones and TVs. But there *are* important differences. First of all, much equipment tends to be gender-typed. There are machines and tools 'suitable' for men—saws, trucks, wrenches, guns and forklifts, for example—and those 'suitable' for women—vacuum cleaners, typewriters and food processors. Even on assembly lines, men make cars and women assemble electronic components or pack fish. Most often, women are excluded from control of large or powerful pieces of equipment. More importantly, women are excluded from an understanding of *technique* and of the physical principles by which machines and tools operate (see, for example, articles in Kelly 1981).

This exclusion is important because technique is often overlooked as a major component of technology. To simply refer to the machines and tools involved is not a sufficient definition of any system of technology; often the underlying knowledge or technique is more important than the actual machines. After all, if all the machines are destroyed, they can still be rebuilt as long as the human beings who built them retain the knowledge that was used to build them in the first place. Technique includes not only this knowledge of how to construct equipment but the knowledge of how to use it. It further includes much basic scientific knowledge, such as that required to control the chemical processes involved in refining or the physical principles involved in electronics. Scientific principles, mathematical techniques and even techniques for organizing production, such as assembly lines, can all be important parts of 'technique' and hence part of technology.

The exclusion of women not only from active practice in scientific and technical fields but from training in basic physical and mechanical principles means that even when women use tools or machines, they are marginal to a male-created and male-dominated technology. (Note: all of this describes the usual situation for most Western women, not the invariable rule for each individual. Some women do well in technical areas and there are large numbers of men who don't know or care about operating dump trucks or understanding computer design. But as far as social norms go, men are assumed to be inside the magic circle and women outside. And, in fact, socialization and education mean that most men do operate well in at least one or two technological areas. Note also that, although this paper is concerned with gender differences in technology processes, it is important to recognize that there are other ways in which access to tools and technique is not equal for everyone. We live in a society of institutionalized hierarchy and sexism; in addition to gender, race and class are also factors in determining such access.)

Besides gender differences in access because of experience and training, there are differences because of the very logic of the tools and techniques of our society. As a social force, technology has moved far beyond a relationship between an individual and their tools. It is now deeply intertwined with major institutions of the society, most notably industry, government and the military. As Dickson notes, 'the institutionalization of technology has meant that the choice of particular machines [and techniques], or at least the control over this choice, remains in the hands of a dominant social class' which exercises fundamental power in the society (1974, 177). This dominant class, which is almost exclusively white and male, operates on a logic of profit and of maintaining their control over society. The technical world view, mentioned earlier, is a

17

straightforward reflection of their world and their interests (though it is also shared by white working-class and minority men who are not so well served by it). The technology developed in our society is developed overwhelmingly by this dominant class and reflects their logic and their interests.

For those of us seeking a more egalitarian, cooperative society, many fundamental tools and techniques—such as those to support democratic decision making and communications—simply do not exist. The telephone system, for example, makes communication between two people easy but it is very difficult to arrange a group discussion. This situation is quite appropriate to an individualistic society but not necessarily in one where cooperation is more highly valued. New computer-based communications open up even more the possibilities for group interaction, and some of this potential is being realized (see other articles in this book), but the commercial uses now being developed serve mostly the dominant group's interests.

The logic of ruling-class men then leads to a technology that reflects ruling-class men's experience and view of reality. As mentioned earlier, this view of reality is, to a large extent, shared by other men in the society. The fact that much of the technology of modern industrial society is more compatible with male habits of mind and experience than it is with those of women thus imposes a second kind of limit to women's access to this technology.

TECHNOLOGY AS A LANGUAGE OF ACTION
Introduction

As Dickson (1974, 176-7) points out, technology can serve as a 'language' of social action. The technology available at any specific time provides a range of options for acting on the world. Dickson's point is primarily that these options function rather like words in a language. In the case of language itself you must use the words as given in attempting to speak; in the case of technology, you must use what tools and techniques are available in any attempt to carry out a particular action.

The direct analogy falters because while one can usually find words and or combinations of words to express new meanings, actions are more constrained by the available technology. We can carry out only those activities where suitable techniques or machines are available. One cannot travel by public transit to places that don't have service, for example, and, as I have painfully learned in doing

18

simple household maintenance, simple jobs become impossible if you don't have a Phillips screwdriver when you need one. Another example: it is impossible for women to combine control over their pregnancies with sexual freedom until an adequate technology for birth control exists.

The 'language' for action provided by the technological options available to a person must be understood then as one that imposes limits on what can be 'said.' The range of options for any person at any given period reflects the characteristics of the society of that period. As we saw above, men and women have different access to training, knowledge and confidence around technology. One result of this difference is that men have access to much more of the technological realm than women have and their potential for action is correspondingly much larger. Men repair cars, make furniture in their basement shops, drive large trucks, operate cranes, build houses, captain ships or operate small boats, use guns, design computers and do scientific experiments. It is not that all men do all of these things but these and actions like them define a male domain that women enter only as exceptions. Women's domain contains fewer and less powerful machines, and women typically do not engage in behavior that changes the physical world or involves much control over it.

A second consideration is that the technology itself may not be suitable for things that women would like to 'say.' Expressions of community through group conversations on the telephone are, as we have seen, nearly impossible. As another example, if one should want to live in some kind of cooperation with nature rather than in a relationship of exploitation and domination, then very little technology exists to help (Dickson 1974; Merchant 1980).

Technology and power

Differences in the ability to act, to express oneself, are not neutral. Use of any of the different options communicates a great deal of information about the one who is acting. Men not only have access to a much wider range of action around technology than women do but that action implies a great deal more control over the physical and social world.

This question of control is, I think, a central one in understanding why the logic of present technology makes it inaccessible to women. Domination over nature, i.e. control over the physical world, is a central feature of much of present day technology. Part of the

technical world view (which is the male norm, remember) is the belief in one's *right* to control the material world. Part of successful socialization as a man in our society involves gathering confidence in
one's actual *ability* to exercise that control. Women generally do not
think they have the right to control the material world and have little confidence in their ability to; as long as they doubt either, it is
very difficult for them to use a technology created by those who accept domination/control as a given.

This does not necessarily mean that women must learn to accept
the technical world view unquestioningly. Increasingly feminists
have been raising the question as to whether or not this kind of
domination over nature *is* in fact legitimate (see Griffin 1978 and
Merchant 1980). From this might follow the development of new
technologies based on different assumptions about the world and on
a changed relationship to nature. Keller (1983), Arditti *et al.* (1980)
and Easlea (1978) all discuss these issues. Such alternates to present
technology could provide a 'vocabulary' that is more compatible
with experiences and issues outside the mainstream technical view
of the world.

In the present situation, however, power is the most important
message that male use of technology communicates. Power over
technology and the physical world is just one aspect of men's domination of this society. Patriarchy in the West means that not only is
it white men (and a minority of these) who hold political power and
the prestige positions but that individual men have control over individual women. Male power over technology is both a product of
and a reinforcement for their other power in society. Even at the
household level, every time a man repairs the plumbing or a sewing
machine while a woman watches, a communication about her help-
lessness and inferiority is made. She doesn't understand or have access to a crucial area of the society and has less control over her physical surroundings than the man does.

Technology as self-expression

A specific machine or tool can be used as an individual statement or
means of expression. For example, men seem to identify with their
cars as expressions of themselves more than women do and often
are explicit in using them as symbols. As one of the most obvious
examples, the very existence of 'muscle cars' and the image these
cars project comes out of a particular ideal of macho masculinity.
(And it would seem that the working-class or Black men who most

20

often drive these cars are using this image as a substitute for the actual power and control over their lives that they lack.)

Ghetto blasters are also obviously used, most often by young males, Black and white, to make a statement that seems to include an aggressive claim to public space and a hostility to any other claims on that space. Guns are widely regarded as symbolic penises, and military technology can be an expression of male potency (a point made graphically in the movie *Dr Strangelove*). The engineering student of precalculator days wore a slide rule on his belt to indicate his (superior) absorption in an esoteric and tough field. The lead guitarist in the local rock band, like the owner of a muscle car or an MX missile, can use his instrument to communicate a particular vision of male sexuality and power. For years, executives expressed their eminence by their *refusal* to use a technology, i.e. executives did not type since the typewriter was a female tool. However, with the advent of electronic office systems, it's now called 'keyboarding' instead of 'typing' and, since a computer is involved, it's okay for executives to do it. In each of these cases, the technology is used by men to express something of their perceived relationship with the social world.

Because of the gender differences discussed above, women use technology much less as a means of symbolic self-expression. Clothes and cosmetics are the traditional means of expressing femininity and an association with anything technological is definitely unfeminine.

Using computers

Even where use is not symbolic and where males and females do have access to the same technology as a means of self-expression, the way in which they use it is often very different. Video games, for example, are played almost exclusively by boys and young men. Part of the appeal of these games seems to be that of control—in this case the possibility of increasing levels of control over a limited, well-defined world (see Weizenbaum 1976 for a related discussion). Given this, more may be involved in making video games attractive to girls than simply substituting Ms for Mr Pacman.

There are also differences in self-expression, graphically shown by Turkle's work (1984). She investigated children's behavior in a 'computer-rich' environment where third- and fourth-grade students had unlimited access to machines and were encouraged to develop their own approaches. The children rapidly became proficient in creating programs for animated designs and cartoons on a computer screen. Some, in fact, developed extremely sophisticated approaches. These approaches varied for different children, however, and Turkle characterizes two important styles. In one, the students conform to our ideas of 'computer people' or engineers: these children were concerned with mastering the technology itself—with developing an orderly, rational, systematic approach to achieving precisely defined goals. Other children were more like artists—the esthetics of the final result were more important than a precise blueprint for how to get there and they often worked by trial and error. Turkle points out that 'programming style is an expression of personality style,' and she goes on to say, 'the [first type] tend to see the world as something to be brought under control.... The [others] are more likely to see the world as something they need to accommodate to, something beyond their direct control' (Turkle 1984, 105–106).

Not surprisingly, girls tend to have the second, 'artistic' sort of approach while those concerned with mastering the technology itself are overwhelmingly male. 'In our culture, girls are taught the characteristics of soft mastery—negotiation, compromise, give-and-take—as psychological virtues, while models of male behavior stress decisiveness and the imposition of will' (Turkle 1984, 108; see also Turkle this volume).

In these cases, we have another example of gender differences in the expression of self through the use of technology. And even though here the direct interaction is between child and machine, both the results and style of that interaction communicate important messages to others. Even though the 'artistic' masters are highly competent, their work does not include the 'male' characteristics of objectivity and control. Girls using this style are not demonstrating their fitness to join the male world—quite the contrary.

As mentioned above, feminist critiques of science and technology have in fact raised the question as to whether the proper approach to these areas may not be to look for new styles that do not include domination and control. Turkle's work provides a practical demonstration that new styles, embodying more of the things women value, may in fact be possible.

EFFECTS OF TECHNOLOGY ON VERBAL COMMUNICATION

Women's silence

Gender differences around technology have consequences for verbal communication as well. In her book *Man Made Language*, Dale Spender (1980) is concerned with differences in the ways that women and men use language. In particular, she introduces Edwin Ardener's concept of women as a 'muted' and men as a 'dominant' group with respect to language, meaning and communication. Ardener (1975) argued that in patriarchal cultures, men create the general system of meanings for the society and then validate those meanings by asking other men if they are correct. Women are muted because they have no part in the creation and validation of meaning. The result is that it is difficult for women to express themselves: the concepts and vocabulary available to them are those that come out of male experience.

Inherent in this analysis is the 'assumption that women and men will generate different meanings, that is, that there is more than one perceptual order, but that only the "perceptions" of the dominant group, with their inherently partial nature, are encoded and transmitted' (Spender 1980, 77).

Men's perceptions are heavily influenced by technology and a technological world view. Men are expected to be rational, objective and able to keep emotions out of most parts of their lives. The characteristics of stereotypical scientists or engineers are only a slight exaggeration of the traits of normal men. It is not clear whether the technical world view with its emphasis on facts, control, rationality, and distance from emotion or personal considerations is a cause or an effect of the definition of normal masculinity but it is clear that the two are deeply interwoven. Even the ideal businessman, operating according to objective logic and the latest principles of scientific management, represents the technical world view in action.

Men and women have access to different vocabularies, experiences and concepts around tools, machines and technique. Women are excluded from education and action in the realm of technology. They do not have the same access to technique or the same experience with concepts and equipment that men do. They are not expected to act from a technical view of the world. Instead, women's world is one of people, nurturance and emotion. Ideal women are expected to be experts in human relations and, in relations with men, to supply emotional depth and insight. The highly technological world of men is one of single cause and effect, of order and control, of rationality; the human world of women is more complicated and less logical. It involves resolution of conflicts between the world of facts and the world of emotion, commitment and responsibility to others. It often involves contradictions arising out of conflicting duties and conflicting loyalties (see Gilligan 1982).

It is the male world that is dominant, however. As a number of critics (among others Dickson 1974 and Easlea 1978) have pointed out, the scientific/technical world view is more and more accepted as the only legitimate model for interpreting reality. Men's acceptance of such a world view, together with their greater familiarity with the technological realm, means that they have generated a perception of the world which women do not share but are required to use, at least in order to communicate with men.

Besides men's control over the creation of meaning, they also have control over styles of communication. Articles in Thorne *et al.* (1983), along with material in Spender (1980), outline a variety of ways in which male control over the terms of communication can lead to women's inability to participate. Of interest for our argument are, first, the insistence, particularly in public discourse, on the separation of the 'personal' from the 'scholarly,' 'scientific' or 'rational,' and second, the emphasis in public styles on verbal competitiveness and dominance.

The terms of the discourse as given by men put women at an immediate disadvantage. Men are *experts*; women are not. The TV images of a male authority figure using pseudo-scientific terms to sell detergent or orange juice or headache remedies to women is merely an exaggeration of the ordinary terms of communication between men and women. Men see themselves as authorities; their real power in society, their scientific/technical world view and the fact that men do have more expertise in a wide variety of 'male' areas make this inevitable. Control over and understanding of technology is only one facet of that expertise but it is an important one in a society increasingly technologically based. The areas of male expertise are defined by them as the only legitimate areas of concern; women's whole realm is dismissed as unworthy of serious notice. The resulting communication between men and women is then largely asymmetric and women's contribution is often mainly that of finding topics that men want to discuss (Spender 1980).

It sometimes happens that areas that previously 'belonged' to women are taken over by male experts and reduced or transformed into acceptable terms. The medicalization of contraception and reproduction is a good example of this—as knowledge in these areas becomes more 'scientific,' women listen to or quote male experts and are left with little to say for themselves. This occurs in spite of the fact that midwives, for example, are highly knowledgeable. Once the 'scientific experts' take over, however, women's knowledge is devalued.

In general male discourse is characterized by 'facts' and by rules, by objects, by technical matters or by matters made technical. As one interesting example of this, note Rosabeth Moss Kanter's point (1977) that exchanges around professional sports constitute *the* common currency for social interactions between men, regardless of differences in status, power, education, etc. In general, women are not so interested in these sports and don't use them in the same way in conversation with either other women or men.

There are a number of reasons why women may not be very interested in professional sports: lack of experience in these sports in school and difficulties with the violence in many of them are probably major factors. But I believe that at least some of the difference between men's and women's approach to sports is due to the technological world view that seems to be necessary equipment for sports fans. The scientific/technical world that men create is, as noted before, one of rules and facts. So is the world of professional sports. Of course, all sports have to have rules but sports fans are not participants; they are spectators participating vicariously in a limited, rule-driven world (Hoch 1972). It is a world of numbers and statistics as well. Baseball especially attracts fans interested in numbers. They typically care about and learn endless statistics about the teams, the players and the game generally.

Communicating about technology

The inequality resulting from male control over the terms of communication can be seen clearly when technology itself becomes the subject matter of the discourse. Men, in general, relate to other men as equals around technology: they exchange information and discuss points of interest. Where men have interests in some common technical area, either at work or as a hobby, such discussion is a way of relating to peers and a common language to share interests and knowledge.

Men and women do not, however, communicate as equals about technology. The information flow is almost entirely one-sided: men may *explain* a technological matter to women but they do not discuss it with them; that they do with other men. The education process in technological fields, for example, is heavily dependent on learning from fellow students and this asymmetry becomes a major problem for women. It is very difficult to discuss technical problems, particularly experimental ones, with male peers—they either condescend or they want to simply do whatever it is for you. In either case, asking a question or raising a problem in discussion is proof (if any is needed) that women don't know what they are doing. Other male students, needless to say, do not get this treatment—whatever it is becomes a joint problem to be solved.

Generally, because they lack knowledge, women do not discuss technology with other women at all. When they do, my experience in scientific work has been that since most women scientists have learned male styles, the discussion is most often conducted in terms indistinguishable from male conversations. Turkle's work however gives an indication that other styles may be possible.

Tunnel vision

The general inequality in communication is unfair to women but it also has consequences for men. Spender points out that men frequently 'don't know what women are talking about' (1980, 96). In part, she says, this results from the kind of *tunnel vision* that comes from total acceptance of the dominant definition of reality. Women must at least recognize that there are different points of view and must know enough of the dominant one to survive within it. When men have uncritically accepted the scientific/technical world view, they tend to view the kinds of issues important to women and the solutions they find to problems as absurd and illogical. With no perception of the assumptions underlying the non-technological world view that comes out of women's experience and women's responsibilities, they are literally unable to understand what is being said.

CONCLUSION

Men and women seem to inhabit different worlds. All too often they speak to each other only across a gulf of misunderstanding or inequality. Women have lost a great deal from this state of affairs: the whole realm of technology and the communication around it reinforces ideas of women's powerlessness. Men lose by this too:

they lose touch with a reality outside their own technical world view. In addition, both men and women lose the chance to develop a technology that would serve other goals than those of a small group of privileged white men.

There is no easy solution to the problem. Yes, women do need to learn more about technology and gain more confidence. Yes, men do need to be more sensitive to other perceptions. But these are only preconditions. Fundamental change can only come about by an attack on all the structures of domination in the society. As a part of this, we will have to change science and technology to give more primacy to the kinds of approaches now considered feminine. If we can do that, the consequences will be new kinds of technology as well as new kinds of people. Both of these will be necessary for ending the barriers that now exist between men and women.

REFERENCES

Ardener, Edwin. 1975. 'Belief and the problem of women.' In Shirley Ardener, ed. *Perceiving Women*. London: Malaby.

Arditti, Rita, Pat Brennen and Steve Cavrak, eds. 1980. *Science and Liberation*. Boston: South End Press.

Benston, Margaret Lowe. 1982. 'Feminism and the critique of scientific method.' In Angela Miles and Geraldine Finn, eds. *Feminism in Canada*. Montreal: Black Rose Books, 47–66.

Chodorow, Nancy. 1978. *The Reproduction of Mothering: Psychoanalysis and the Sociology of Gender*. Berkeley: University of California Press.

Dickson, David. 1974. *Alternative Technology and the Politics of Technical Change*. London: Fontana.

Easlea, Brian. 1978. *Liberation and the Aims of Science*. London: Chatto & Windus.

Gilligan, Carol. 1982. *In a Different Voice*. Cambridge Mass.: Harvard University Press.

Griffin, Susan. 1978. *Women and Nature: The Roaring Inside Her*. New York: Harper & Row.

Hoch, Paul. 1972. *Rip off the Big Game*. New York: Anchor.

Kanter, Rosabeth Moss. 1977. *Men and Women of the Corporation*. New York: Basic Books.

Keller, Evelyn Fox. 1983. *A Feeling for the Organism*. New York:

27

Freeman.

Kelly, Alison. 1981. *The Missing Half: Girls and Science Education.* Manchester: Manchester University Press.

Merchant, Carol. 1980. *Death of Nature: Women, Ecology and the Scientific Revolution.* San Francisco: Harper & Row.

Rothschild, Joan, ed. 1983. *Machina Ex Dea: Feminist Perspectives on Technology.* New York: Pergamon.

Spender, Dale. 1980. *Man-Made Language.* London: Routledge & Kegan Paul.

Thorne, Barrie, Cheris Kramarae and Nancy Henley, eds. 1983. *Language, Gender, and Society.* Rosley, Mass.: Newbury House.

Turkle, Sherry. 1984. *The Second Self.* New York: Simon & Schuster.

Weizenbaum, Joseph. 1976. *Computer Power and Human Reason.* San Francisco: Freeman.

MARGERY W. DAVIES

WOMEN CLERICAL WORKERS AND THE TYPEWRITER: THE WRITING MACHINE

'Of the woman who took down his instructions in shorthand before typewriting them he knew absolutely nothing. To him she was merely a part of the typewriting machinery, and the glazed pigeon-hole might have been a great gulf dividing them, instead of what it was.'
                                                      (Ellen Ada Smith, 1898)

'Shortly before Mr Sholes's death a daughter-in-law remarked to him what a wonderful thing he had done for the world [in inventing the typewriter], and this was his ... reply, "I don't know about the world, but I do feel that I have done something for the women who have always had to work so hard. It will enable them more easily to earn a living". ' (Heath 1944, 272)

Whether or not Christopher Latham Sholes, often cited as the inventor of the typewriter, actually said this, many other writers since Sholes have said much the same thing. And they are all wrong—on all counts. Sholes was not the first person to invent the typewriter; scores of people before him had devised writing machines. Sholes's renown comes more from the fact that his machine was sold to the Remington Company, the first mass manufacturer of typewriters in the United States. Nor did the typewriter cause the employment of women in clerical work in the United States; women were drawn into the office because of the mushrooming demand for clerical labor occasioned by the expansion and consolidation of the capitalist economy at the end of the nineteenth century. In fact, those very structural changes in capitalism underlay the successful manufacture of the typewriter, for not until accounting, correspondence and record keeping increased along with governments and firms did the usefulness of a writing machine become self-evident.

Nonetheless, there are ways in which the typewriter affected the employment of women in offices. Because the typewriter was a new machine, it was 'sex-neutral' and did not have a history of being associated with men. In the absence of this association, women seeking work as typists did not face the obstacle that typing was 'men's work,' even though there were many who maintained that the office in general was not a suitable place for a woman. Although there is nothing intrinsic to the typewriter which dictates that it be operated hour after hour by the same person, it is true that typing fast and accurately are skills that take some time to develop. Thus the very existence of the machine helped to justify a division of labor within office work where some people did nothing but type all day long. As the work of typing came quite rapidly in the United States to be identified as 'women's work,' a larger and larger percentage of typists was female. The typewriter was a factor in the concurrent feminization and proletarianization of the clerical labor force.

Insofar as the typewriter was a facilitating factor in the employment of women in clerical work, it helped to move women out of work in the home and family and into work in the labor force. Given the feminization of clerical labor in general and, to an even greater extent, typing in particular, it is tempting to conjure up the image of women, cast together in large groups through their common work as typists, forming strong workplace bonds of communication, friendship and support—bonds which might grow into organizing campaigns, union drives and successful united efforts to wrest better wages and working conditions from employers. Up until the 1970s, such was seldom the case, even though attempts to organize office workers in the United States date back to the efforts of the Women's Trade Union League in the early twentieth century. Although there were many firms that had large typing pools, these pools were often divided and divided again into finely graduated hierarchies and small promotional steps which could often lead to a competitive rather than a cooperative climate. Furthermore, many clerical workers, even if they worked at large companies, were in relatively small working groups once they actually got to their desks in the departmental divisions and subdivisions. This was certainly true for private secretaries. Many clerical workers, in addition, worked in small companies and institutions. The small size of the actual clerical work unit, not to mention the competitiveness virtually inherent in a finely graduated promotional hierarchy, mitigated against the development of a coherent clerical class.

This is not to say, of course, that clerical workers did not form close personal ties or supportive communities in the workplace. There was clearly a lot of personal communication among women (and no doubt men) in the office. The evidence is in the strong memories that clerical workers have of their sister workers, in the frettings of office managers over how to cope with 'office gossip,' in the photographs and personal effects that office workers pin to their bulletin boards and put on their desk tops—a statement that they are people with personal lives that invites comment and interaction. But what is not at all clear is the role that the typewriter in particular played in the establishment or discouragement of such patterns of communication.

For it is conceivable that, had office work expanded in the absence of the typewriter or other business machines, the clerical labor force would have grown as well; only instead of an army of typists there would have been an army of copyists. Probably the most sensible argument is that the typewriter, like other technological inventions, was one part of complex structural developments in the United States that changed the face of the office and the sex of the office worker. To pluck the typewriter out of that context and to try to isolate its particular role in the development of communication among men and among women is not only a thankless but also an ill-conceived task. Although the typewriter did play a role in helping to determine the organization of office work, it seems important to remember that technology in no way operates in a vacuum. A successful technological innovation owes its very life to a specific historical situation, and while it in turn may have a great or a small effect on that social context and its development, it is the socio-historical situation that must be understood first and foremost.[1]

THE IMPACT OF THE TYPEWRITER

It was capitalist expansion, not the typewriter, that drew women into the office workforce. As I have written in *Woman's Place Is at the Typewriter* (1982), it was the rapid expansion of capitalist firms and government agencies, accompanied by the growth of correspondence and record keeping, which led to a mounting demand for clerical labor. That demand was met, in part, by the availability of literate female labor. The economic instability of small farm and small business families and the decline of productive work in the home released women to the paid labor force and made the income they could earn more important. They found clerical work more desirable than other working–class jobs because of the higher wages it offered and the comparatively high status it enjoyed; few other jobs specifically requiring literacy were open to women. Meanwhile, literate males were being employed not only for the growing clerical field, but also for management and professional positions, which rapidly increased in number with late-nineteenth-century capitalist expansion. The first women known to work in offices in the United States were employed at the US Treasury in Washington to sort and trim bank notes during the Civil War, when male labor was siphoned off to the military.[2] Women also have been mentioned as copyists, stenographers and bookkeepers in the 1860s. They worked for substantially lower wages than men, another factor which no doubt encouraged some employers to hire them.[3] And when women started working in offices in large numbers, they did much more than type. By 1880, there were more than 4200 women working as bookkeepers, cashiers, and accountants and 2000 employed as stenographers and typists; the figures for 1890 are 27,772 and 21,270 respectively (Edwards 1943; Davies 1982, 178-9).

It is, then, important to understand that fundamental structural change (rather than the technological invention of the typewriter that was itself a product of that structural change) caused the employment of women in office work. Crediting the typewriter leads to a superficial explanation of the changes in women's labor force participation. Worse yet, crediting the typewriter can encourage the conclusion that a technological invention causes women's employment because said invention is particularly appropriate for women, a conclusion that is dangerously close to thinking that women are naturally suited to particular occupations. To argue that 'women's' work or 'men's' work are in some way ordained by nature is to confine women and men to a limited range of human activity. It is crucial to understand the historical specificity of gender-defined work, and to understand the root causes of that gender definition operating in each particular circumstance. Throwing all the typewriters out the window, not to mention the myriad other office machines that have followed closely in their wake, would not in and of itself change women's subordinate position in the office.

Nonetheless, it is easy to understand the sentiments of my friend who purposely refused to learn to type in high school because she didn't want to be pushed by circumstances into office work; or of the young women cited in a 1977 *US News and World Report* who are 'firmly convinced that if they learn to type they will be put behind a typewriter the rest of their lives (Frank talk ... 75).[4] From the earliest days of its commercial production in the United States, the typewriter was seen in association with women as well as with men. A photograph of one of Sholes's early machines shows his daughter at the keyboard and is annotated, 'Miss Sholes 1872. The first typist.'[5] Remington advertised its machine in *The Nation* of 15 December 1875, as an ideal 'Christmas present for a boy or girl. And the benevolent can, by the gift of a "Type-Writer" to a poor, deserving young woman, put her at once in the way of earning a good living as a copyist or corresponding clerk' (Current 1954, 86). The early typewriter stores had people demonstrating the machine for prospective customers; Mark Twain was influenced in his purchase by the 'type girl' who had typed fifty-seven words per minutes (Bliven 1954, 61).

There were plenty of men finding jobs as typists too; in fact, well into the twentieth century most of the people who won the speed typing contests were men. But 'stenographers and typists' was the clerical job category which was feminized the most quickly. Women were already 40 per cent of stenographers and typists in 1880 and over 63 per cent in 1890. After 1910 the absolute number of men in the category began to decline; by 1930 women constituted more than 95 per cent (Davies 1982, 178-9).

It is not really clear to me why the typewriter was operated by women (as well as by men) from its earliest days of commercial production. Possibly it was because the typewriter had not built up a history of being operated by men, and hence women who sought jobs as typists did not face the obstacle that they were trying to do 'men's work.' Possibly it was because female labor was cheaper than male. In any event, the tremendous surge in demand for clerical labor that was well underway by the end of the nineteenth century and continued on into the twentieth century brought hundreds of thousands of women into the labor force as office workers in general and as typists in particular.

The uses made of typewriters also had an impact on the reorganization of office work. The rapidly multiplying paperwork that accompanied capitalist expansion in the late nineteenth century prompted some firms to reorganize their offices. The small office where an owner or manager supervised a handful of clerks was superseded by the large office, which was divided up into a variety of functionally defined departments. This division of labor on a gross scale was accompanied by another division of labor on a finer scale within each department (Davies 1985, 8). Many clerical jobs were broken down into their composite units—there were billing clerks, receiving clerks, payroll clerks, file clerks, typists and so on. The existence of business machines, the first and most ubiquitous of which was the typewriter, helped to justify and entrench this finely tuned division of labor. For once a clerical worker had become proficient at operating a particular machine, it could be and was argued that the clerical worker should do nothing else. If a typist could consistently turn out sixty words per minute, why waste her time on filing or answering the phone? A skilled typist was likely to be kept in her job for as long as her employer could keep her there. As I have argued in *Woman's Place Is at the Typewriter*, this restriction of many clerical workers to one narrow job meant that they lost the capacity to understand how their own work fit into the overall work of their firm or institution, and hence the capacity to exercise much judgment or informed control over their work.

It should be emphasized that there was nothing inherent to the typewriter which compelled such an organization of clerical work. The typewriter, in fact, can be quite useful for people who operate it sporadically: the private secretary who spends a couple of hours a day typing correspondence or reports; the writer who alternates stretches of pounding the keyboard with long periods of staring into space. The organization of work is largely determined by the efforts of businessmen and scientific office managers to organize their clerical labor as profitably as possible, and not to make the 'inefficient' error of having a typist do work that a lower-paid file clerk could just as easily do.

The typewriter was thus a contributing factor in the entrance of women into the clerical labor force and in the mechanization of clerical work. These developments in turn affected communication among women. Grouped together in the workplace, women had a basis for communication that is different from their connections within the family and community. Women in the office talked to each other. Some of their conversation focused on their work— which letters had to be gotten out immediately, what to do about a mistake on a bill, etcetera. But much of their conversation was also personal (Feldberg and Glenn 1983). The writings of scientific managers of the office are full of descriptions of the amount of time wasted in office gossip and prescriptions for what to do about it. Clerical workers' own accounts of their work in popular magazines such as the *Ladies' Home Journal* contain countless references to wedding showers, return visits from former workers to show off their new babies, and so forth. And there are also complaints, particularly during the past twenty years, about the management not granting female office workers promotions when they merited them or about a man moving up the office hierarchy much more quickly than the women who trained him. Women clearly had a lot to say to each other, both about their home and personal lives and also about their work.

That women were gathered together as office workers and that there was much communication among them did not necessarily lead, however, to organization. There have been attempts to organize office workers into unions since early in the twentieth century, beginning with the efforts of the Women's Trade Union League (Feldberg 1980; Strom 1983). In 1939 *Business Week* started to issue annual warnings that clerical workers were ripe for organizing, warnings that had their obverse in the glowing predictions issued in the *American Federationist* by the presidents of the AFL clerical unions. But neither the warnings nor the predictions were the harbingers of widespread unionization among clerical workers.

Although the number of clerical workers has been mushrooming since the 1880s, these office workers have not always worked in large units such as giant typing pools. The extensive division of labor within firms and other bureaucratic organizations meant the actual work unit could be quite small. Furthermore, many office workers did not work for large organizations, but for a real estate office, small insurance agency, or the office of a relatively small manufacturing firm. Separated as they were from each other, it was often hard for large groups of clerical workers to see their common interest. The situation was only exacerbated by employers' efforts to get office workers to identify their interests with those of their bosses, efforts which worked particularly well with personal secretaries. (See Anne Machung this volume.) The low pay and absence of substantial promotional opportunities for many clerical workers contributed to high turnover. When women left clerical jobs to return to the home it was in part because, in the absence of socialized child care, their family labor was crucial to the care of young children, and in part because the loss of dead-end office jobs did not seem like such a terrible thing. The ideology that woman's proper place was in the home with her family only served to strengthen the notion that women's work in the labor force was secondary. No matter that many single women, not to mention the widowed or divorced, remained in the labor force for all their 'working' lives. Many people, notably union leaders who did not put their greatest efforts into organizing clericals, seemed to believe that office workers' jobs weren't important to them and that consequently they were difficult to organize. This is not to belittle the efforts of those, such as the activists in the CIO United Office and Professional Workers of America, who did try to unionize office workers. But overall, clerical organizing was no match whatsoever to the successes among industrial workers.

Since the early 1970s there has been a new surge in clerical organizing, fueled in part by the principles and values of feminism. The rapid success of organizations such as 9 to 5: The National Association of Working Women, District 65 of the United Auto Workers, and District 925 of the Service Employees International Union attests to the growing ability of unions to attract clerical workers. It seems plausible that we are in the beginning years of a significant increase in unionization among clerical workers. As a group of office workers writes in *They Can't Run the Office Without Us: 60 Years of Clerical Work*:

New issues have been raised that will not disappear, and the consciousness of women office workers has changed over the past few decades. Moreover, some of the obstacles to organizing office workers have receded or disappeared. The superior attitude of secretaries who thought they were better or more skilled or more middle class than factory workers is not nearly so common among clerical workers today .... As the Harvard University clerical workers said in one of their union drives: 'You can't eat prestige.' Indeed, given today's wages and working conditions, it is hard to understand the prestige or status once attached to white-collar work. (Massachusetts History Workshop 1985, 74)

Just as the typewriter was one facilitating factor in the entrance of women into the clerical labor force, so was it part of the mechanization of clerical work. Some have argued that the more clerical work is mechanized, the more sympathetic the clerical worker will be to unionism. As a writer in *The New Republic* (1938) described it:

Tillie the Toiler, that independent pardon-my-gum stenog, is beginning to wonder. The changes in the old office during the past ten years have bewildered her and they are beginning to get on her nerves. It began when the company took over another factory, piling so much work on the office that an addition had to be built. Then the office was divided up into filing, transcription and accounting departments, where the company installed telephone filing systems, dictaphones, calculators, billing machines and many other devices. Tillie was put on an assembly line where she does one small job in the business of producing a letter. And worse, Tillie's salary was stopped and she began to be paid by piece rate. As the company buys new machinery and learns to use the machinery already installed in her office more efficiently, the value of a union is growing on Tillie. Her friends are being laid off. Her work is being speeded up. Tillie is now, after ten years of preparation, beginning to join a union. (Stuart 1938, 70)

But the minute division of labor described here was not caused by mechanization; at most it was enabled by it. The decision to assign clerical workers to the repetitious execution of the same narrow task was made by management, not by machines. As Anne Machung (this volume) also argues, it is people who decide how to organize work. The machines only make it possible for the owners and managers to hide their decisions behind the so-called 'technological imperatives' of certain office equipment.

The only direct way in which the typewriter could be said to affect communication among women is that many typewriters operated at the same time in the same room make a lot of noise. A typist for an insurance company told Jean Tepperman (1976):

'One thing we were just talking about at work is noise pollution. It's very loud. And the machines are not easy to type on. It's like—especially for a machine that was designed to be typed on all day long—driving a big truck with standard, without automatic steering. It's very hard and it's very noisy. I can't hear anything when people talk to me. Everybody thinks their hearing is impaired.' (23)

Certainly women in large typing pools would have a hard time talking to each other while working at their machines. But even here the amount of communication is not dictated solely by the machine.

Under the control of the people supervising the work are the decisions about how many scheduled breaks to allow, whether or not to stop typists from taking informal breaks, or whether or not to monitor trips to the bathroom (a well-known site for communication among office workers).

In analyzing the impact the typewriter has had on women clerical workers and communication among them, it is crucial always to bear in mind the historical situation which surrounds the typewriter at any given moment. For the very development of a commercially successful mechanical writing machine was dependent on changes in the political economy, just as it was those changes, and not the typewriter, that brought women into the clerical labor force. It is a mistake to isolate any particular technological invention from the social circumstances which produced it, for in doing so one generally misses the root causes of changes associated with technological innovation.

NOTES

1 *The Writing Machine* by Michael Adler (1973) is the best-documented and most thoroughly researched history of the different machines that he considers can be proved to have been invented. He arbitrarily limits his book to 'unconventional' typewriters, thus eliminating coverage of the ones with which we are most familiar, the 'front-stroke, type bar machines with four-row keyboards' (18). This is actually quite instructive for our purposes, since it provides examples of inventions that were devised at times or in places that were not favorable to the mass production—and hence the successful 'invention'—of the machine. He makes the very apt point that the nationality of the author has a strong influence on the claim of who invented the first typewriter: a French writer credits a Frenchman, an Italian claims the honor for a Giuseppe Ravizza, and US writers generally name Christopher Latham Sholes from Milwaukee, Wisconsin. Certainly both Bruce Bliven, Jr. (1954) and Richard N. Current (1954) name Sholes as the 'father' of the typewriter. Adler does such a thorough and careful job of demonstrating the large number of writing machines that were devised before and after the Sholes machine that it seems ridiculous to call Christopher Latham Sholes the 'father of the typewriter,' even though that label is still common. Adler's book does not appear to be very well-known. Even a careful writer such as Terry Abraham (1980) refers to Bliven's and Current's books as 'the two major works on the typewriter's history' (430). I had never seen this book referred to in writing about the office or business machines in the United States,

and stumbled across it by chance in the stacks of Harvard's Widener Library. Other useful research sources are William G. LeDuc (1916); Frederic Heath (1944); and Richard Current (1947; 1954).

2   For more on these early Washington office workers, see the excellent article by Cindy Aron (1981).

3   See Davies (1982, 51-2). The US Treasury clerks were said to work for $900 a year, half the male wage; a New York merchant hired a woman for $500 a year to replace his $1800 a year male bookkeeper.

4   This *US News and World Report* article also mentions the growing status of male secretaries:

> Some of the most sought-after secretaries, in fact, are men. In some circles, they are status symbols once associated with secretaries who spoke with British or French accents. Frank Arnold, a 42-year-old Chicago secretary, reports: 'My employers always would offer me a job at a higher salary than they were paying female secretaries, and ask me not to mention my pay—something they could never get away with now.' (76)

5   It is unclear when this annotation was written, although it was probably later than in 1872. At that time the people who operated writing machines were called 'typewriters.'

REFERENCES

Abraham, Terry. 1980. 'Charles Thurber: typewriter inventor.' *Technology and Culture* 21:3 (July), 430-4.

Adler, Michael H. 1973. *The Writing Machine*. London: Allen & Unwin.

Aron, Cindy S. 1981. ' "To barter their souls for gold": female clerks in federal government offices, 1862-1890.' *Journal of American History* 67:4 (March), 835-53.

Bliven, Jr., Bruce. 1954. *The Wonderful Writing Machine*. New York: Random House.

Current, Richard N. 1947. 'The first newspaperman in Oshkosh.' *Wisconsin Magazine of History* 32:4 (June), 391-407.

Current, Richard N. 1954. *The Typewriter and the Men Who Made It*. Urbana: University of Illinois Press.

Davies, Margery W. 1982. *Woman's Place Is at the Typewriter: Office Work and Office Workers, 1870-1930*. Philadelphia: Temple University Press.

Davies, Margery W. 1985. 'Women and the office: a historical perspective.' *ILR Report* 23:1 (Fall), 7–10. Published by the New York State School of Industrial and Labor Relations.

Edwards, Alba M. 1943. *Comparative Occupation Statistics for the United States, 1870-1940*. Part of the Sixteenth Census of the United States: 1940. Washington: Government Printing Office.

Feldberg, Roslyn L. 1980. ' "Union fever": organizing among clerical workers, 1900–1930.' *Radical America* 14:3. Reprinted in James R. Green, ed. 1983. *Workers' Struggles, Past and Present: A 'Radical America' Reader*. Philadelphia: Temple University Press, 151-67.

Feldberg, Roslyn L. and Evelyn Nakano Glenn. 1983. 'Incipient workplace democracy among United States clerical workers.' *Economic and Industrial Democracy* 4:1, 47–67.

'Frank talk from secretaries about their jobs and pay.' 1977. *US News and World Report* 82:25 (27 June), 75–6.

Heath, Frederic. 1944. 'The typewriter in Wisconsin.' *Wisconsin Magazine of History* 27:3 (March), 263–75.

Kearney, Paul M. 1951. 'Woman's great emancipator—the typewriter.' *Independent Woman* 30 (July), 192–3.

LeDuc, William G. 1916. 'The genesis of the typewriter.' *The Magazine of History* 22:3 (March), 83–7.

Massachusetts History Workshop. 1985. *They Can't Run the Office Without Us: 60 Years of Clerical Work*. Massachusetts History Workshop, 238 Pearl Street, Cambridge, MA 02139.

Smith, Ellen Ada. 1898. 'The typewriting clerk.' *Longman's Magazine* 31:185 (March), 431–46.

Strom, Sharon Hartman. 1983. 'Challenging "woman's place": feminism, the left and industrial unionism in the 1930s.' *Feminist Studies* 9:2, 359–86.

Stuart, Mal J. 1938. 'Robots in the office.' *The New Republic* (25 May), 70–2.

Tepperman, Jean. 1976. *Not Servants, Not Machines: Office Workers Speak Out!* Boston: Beacon Press.

SHERRY TURKLE

COMPUTATIONAL RETICENCE: WHY WOMEN FEAR THE INTIMATE MACHINE

'I wanted to work in worlds where languages had moods and connected you with people.'
(A young woman talking about mathematics and computers)

The computer has no inherent gender bias. But the computer culture is not equally neutral. This essay looks at the social construction
of the computer as a male domain through the eyes of women who
have come to see something important about themselves in terms of
what computers are not.

There is much talk about women and 'computerphobia.' My
research suggests that women's phobic reactions to the machine are
a transitional phenomenon. There is the legacy of women's traditional socialization into relationships with technical objects, for
many of them best summed up by the admonishment, 'Don't touch
it, you'll get a shock.' There is the legacy of a computer culture that
has traditionally been dominated by images of competition, sports
and violence. There are still computer operating systems that communicate to their users in terms of 'killing' and 'aborting' programs.
These are things that have kept women fearful and far away from
the machine. But these are things that are subject to change. More
persistent are reactions that touch another and deeper set of issues. I
believe that the issue for the future is not computerphobia, needing
to stay away because of fear and panic, but rather computer reticence, wanting to stay away because the computer becomes a personal and cultural symbol of what a woman is not.

Since 1976 I have been involved in studies of computers and people using a methodology both ethnographic and clinical. My concern has been with the detail of people's relationships with computers and with the social worlds that grow up around them. In order
to best make the distinction between phobia and reticence I will take

41

my examples from interviews with women who are involved with computers, women who do not fear them but who take their distance in a way that inhibits their creativity, and that ultimately will impoverish the computer culture as well. In particular, I draw my examples from a study of twenty-five Harvard and MIT women taking and succeeding in computer programming courses. And I focus on one woman, who here I call Lisa, who speaks in a particularly clear voice to a set of widely shared concerns. The central issue for these competent and talented women is not phobia or lack of ability, but a reticence to become more deeply involved with an object experienced as threatening.

REJECTING THE INTIMATE MACHINE

Lisa is 18, a first-year student at Harvard, and surprised to find herself an excellent computer programmer. Not only is it surprising, but 'kind of scary.' Most 'scary' is protecting her involvement with computers from the idea of seeing herself 'as a computer science type.'

> 'You know, the typical stereotype; I had a home room in high school that just happened to be the math lab and there were these little kids who walked around with pants that were too short and they had little calculators with all these fancy functions and they wore them on their belt and they played chess incessantly and talked about their gambits and the things they were doing in their advanced calculus courses and all the great hacks they were doing on the computer; and they were always working with their machines. I was contemptuous of them. They stayed away from other people. They took the computers and made a world apart.'

Women look at computers and see more than machines. They see the culture that has grown up around them and they ask themselves if they belong. And when, in high school and college, they look at the social world of the computer expert, they see something that seems alien. At the extreme, they see the social world of the 'hacker,' a culture of computer virtuosos. It is a world, predominantly male, that takes the machine as a partner in an intimate relationship.

The computer is a medium that supports a powerful sense of mastery. As people develop their mastery of things and their relational skills with people, most strike a balance. They balance the need for mastery of skills and concrete materials with the desire to do things with people where the results are never as clear. For some people, striking this balance becomes a difficult struggle. Relationships with people are always characterized by ambiguity, sexual tension, the possibilities for closeness and dependency. If these are felt as too threatening, the world of things and the world of formal systems becomes increasingly seductive. They turn to formal systems in engineering, in chess, in mathematics, in science. They turn to them for their reassurance, for the pleasures of working in a microworld where things are certain and 'things never change unless you want them to.' In other words, part of the reason formal systems are appealing is because they provide protective worlds.

Pride in mastery is a positive thing. But if the sense of self becomes defined in terms of those things over which one can exert perfect control, the world of safe things becomes severely limited—because those things tend to be things, not people. Mastery of technology and formal systems can become a way of masking fears about the self and the complexities of the world beyond.

This pattern of using formal microworlds as protective worlds existed long before computers were dreamed of. But the computer offers some new possibilities. The computer offers its users a formal system, but it is also active and interactive. It is easily anthropomorphized. Its experts do not think that it is 'alive.' But it is a medium onto which lifelike properties can be easily projected. It supports the fantasy 'that there is somebody home.' It is, of course, only a machine, but because of its psychological properties it supports an experience with it as an 'intimate machine.'

When people fear intimacy, they are drawn to materials that offer some promise, if not for a resolution of their conflict between loneliness and fear of intimacy, then at least for some compromise. The computer offers this promise. It offers the promise of perfect mastery. And in its activity and interactivity, it offers the illusion of companionship without the demands of friendship (Turkle 1984).

Computers become particularly seductive at a certain moment in psychological development: the moment of adolescence. There are new sexual pressures and new social demands. The safe microworlds the child has built—the microworlds of sports, chess, cars, literature, music, dance, or mathematical expertise—can become places of escape. Most children use these havens as safe platforms from which to test the difficult waters of adolescence. They

43

move but at their own pace. But for some, the issues that arise during adolescence are so threatening that the safe place seems like the only place. They come to define themselves in terms of competence, skill, in terms of the things they can control. It is during adolescence that the 'hacker culture' becomes born in elementary schools and junior high schools as predominantly male—because, in our society, men are more likely than women to master anxieties about people by turning to the world of things and formal systems.

In high school, Lisa saw young men around her turning to mathematics as a way to avoid people and describes herself as 'turning off' her natural abilities in mathematics. 'I didn't care if I was good at it. I wanted to work in worlds where languages had moods and connected you with people.' And she saw some of these young men turning to computers as 'imaginary friends.' She decided to avoid them as well. 'I didn't want an imaginary friend in a machine. If I was going to be alone, if I needed to withdraw, well, then I wanted to read, to learn about human psychology by reading about it, if I didn't always have the courage to learn about other people by being with them.'

The computer is rejected as a partner in a 'close encounter.' When women are introduced to it in cultural contexts where the most successful users seem to 'love the machine for itself,' they define themselves as relational women in terms of what the 'serious' computer users are not. Although hackers are a small part of the general population, the culture of young male programming virtuosos tends to dominate the computer cultures of educational institutions from elementary schools to universities. Hackers are not great in their numbers, but they are visible, dedicated and expert (Kiesler *et al.* 1984; 1985; Turkle 1984).

THE NEGATIVE IMAGE OF THE HACKER

The hacker's relationship with computers is often characterized by a violent form of risk taking. This violence is not physical, rather it is psychological: there is intensity, turbulence, aggression. There are the pleasures of flirting with destruction. The hacker at his computer constantly walks a narrow line between 'winning' and 'losing.' Hackers talk about complex computer systems as places where you can let things get more and more complicated, until you are on the edge of being out of control, but where the pleasure is in the challenge of being able to pull them back.

Joe is 23. He has dropped out of a computer science degree pro-

44

gram in order to devote himself more fully to MIT computers. He contrasts his love for the violin ('it can only do so much and your fingers can only do so much') with the limitless possibilities of the computer.

'With programming, whatever you think of—and you are always thinking of something—it can be immediately translated into a challenge. That same night. You can set yourself up to do it some really esoteric, unusual way. And you can make a deal with yourself that you won't be satisfied, that you won't eat or go out or do anything until you get it right. And then you can just do it. It's like a fix. I couldn't get that kind of fix with the violin. I could be obsessed, but I couldn't get the high.'

With the computer as your medium there is no limit to how much you can flirt with losing in your pursuit of winning. There is no limit to the violence of the test. The computer becomes a medium for playing with the issue of control by living on the narrow line between having it and losing it. MIT hackers call this 'sport death'—pushing mind and body beyond their limits, punishing the body until it can barely support mind and then demanding more of the mind than you believe it could possibly deliver.

Anthony, 20 years old, an MIT senior, is a computer hacker who is very aware of the pleasures of sport death and its lack of appeal for women.

'Computer hacking is kind of masochistic. You see how far you can push your mind and body …. Women tend to be less self-destructive—hackers are somewhat self-destructive. They don't take care of their bodies and are in general, flunking out. Burnout is common. Women are not so into sport death; they are more balanced in their priorities. The essence of sport death is to see how far you can push things, to see how much you can get away with. I generally wait until I have to put in my maximum effort and then just totally burn out.'

There are very few women hackers. Though hackers would deny that theirs is a macho culture, their preoccupation with 'winning' and with subjecting oneself to increasingly violent tests makes their world peculiarly male in spirit. There is, too, a flight from relationship with people to relationship to the machine—a defensive maneuver more common to men than to women.

The hacker's relationship with the computer is filled with technical risks, but it gets much of its emotional charge because it offers respite from personal ones. Hackers talk a lot about 'getting burned.' Because if you are primarily motivated by a need to feel in control, 'getting burned' is one of the worst things that can happen to you.

Anthony has 'tried out' having girlfriends:

'I used to get into relationships that usually led to me getting burned in some way .... With computers you have confidence in yourself and that is enough. With social interactions you have to have confidence that the rest of the world will be nice to you. You can't control how the rest of the world is going to react to you. But with computers you are in complete control.'

Sex and romance are desirable, but they are risky. 'Sport death' is risky too, but it is a special kind of risk where you assume all the risk yourself and are the only one responsible for saving the day. It is safe risk. Anthony sees sex and romance as another, more disturbing kind: 'Hacking is safe in that you are in complete control of your computer world, and sex and relationships are risky in that the rest of the world has control.'

Anthony compares human relationships to the sense of accomplishment and control that he can get from a machine. This does not mean that he sees machines as a 'substitute' for women. But he is not sure that he can function in the worlds where you can get burned.

The men in the hacker culture see it as incompatible with a life with women. 'Computer hacking is almost pure pleasure with very little risk. But it is not as fulfilling as romance because in the end you have just made a few lights blink. But you only have so much energy. You can either spend it on computers or you can spend it on people.' The women who watch these men observe their obsessions, observe their antisensuality, observe the ways in which they have put things rather than people at the center of their lives and count themselves out. This does not mean that these women are not computer-competent. But along with their competence comes a fear of the machine as a potentially destructive force.

Robin is a sophomore at Harvard, a musician who has gone through much of her life practicing the piano eight hours a day. But she rebels against the idea of a relationship with the computer. She doesn't want to belong to a world where things are more important than people.

'I saw people being really compulsive but really enjoying it. I saw that these guys sort of related to their terminals the way I relate to the piano and I thought, maybe I can do that too. I saw all these people running around with the same intensity as I have with the piano and they tell me that I'll probably be good at computers. These are the guys who are helping me do this course. And they keep telling me, yes, you're going to be real good at it. Don't worry about it, but you're going about it in the wrong way. They tell me I'm "not establishing a relationship with the computer." And to me that sounds gross. It is gross to me, the way these guys are. I don't like establishing relationships with machines. I don't like putting it that way. Relationships are for people.'

I ask Robin to talk to me about her relationship with her piano, a machine, but she insists that it was a completely different thing. The piano took her away from people, but then it brought her closer to them. The involvements of her male peers with the computer only shut people out. 'These guys are incredibly drained. You can't talk to them. I don't want to be part of their world.'

'I know this guy, this computer person. He never had a friendship at Harvard. He'd come to breakfast saying that he'd stayed up all night with his terminal and he got frustrated and burned out but he seemed to enjoy it somehow. It was better for him, I guess, than staying up all night talking to a friend. That seems really sad. There's a lot of communication going on around here. People stay up all night talking to friends. But, Mike would not do that. He managed with his terminal.'

How does the hacker look to non-hacker men? Many men are critical of the hacker's single-minded devotion to computers, critical of his lack of social skills. Men's reactions to the computer are similar to those of women, but there is a difference in men's reaction to the hacker's style of exploring the machine in a manner close to abandon and which celebrates risk. Men identify with it. They recognize it as a learning strategy which they find admirable and of which they are capable. Women tend to be more defensive.

Risk taking has a gender valence. Boys are taught to react to risks positively, to view them as an opportunity to expand their knowledge and skill. In our culture, when a boy shies away from risk, he runs what may be a greater risk: the accusation of being called a sissy, 'girlish' in his ways. The female child is more often directed away from situations that might cause trouble. The tree may be too tall to climb; the rock may be too slippery to clamber over. Being a 'good girl' is defined as a virtue where good may mean passive enough to not get into trouble. Good may also mean passive enough to accept knowledge only in a safe, directed, 'cookbook' form.

Risk taking opens up powerful learning strategies. Jessie, a computer science graduate student at MIT, recognizes it as something that hackers have and she doesn't.[1]

'It seems to me that the essence of being a hacker is being willing to muck around with things that you don't fully understand. Playing around with things you don't understand requires a certain amount of self-confidence. Every so often things do get broken. If you break something, you have to believe that this is not necessarily because you are incompetent, but because every so often that happens. Every so often somebody fries a board or trashes an important file or what have you. Part of the essence of being a hacker is accepting the fact that some time you may be the one responsible for some such lossage.

When faced with a situation that they do not have the facts to understand, people vary as to how much they are willing to just "try things." A hacker will typically try things if he or she knows enough about the domain to think up any plausible things to do. A non-hacker will tend not to try to make changes until he or she understands what is going on.... Hacking requires that one feel good about solving problems by means other than the "right procedure." '

Jessie has experimented with the 'risky' learning strategy, but does so with inhibition. She sees it, somewhat wistfully, as male.

'I am still teaching myself not to be afraid of "screwing things up." I think that being a "hacker-type" correlates with things like having played with explosives or taken apart things or climbed dangerously up trees and that type of thing as a child. It seems as though women are less willing to take things apart and risk breaking them, to try things when they don't know what they are doing and risk getting into trouble.'

To use risk taking as a learning strategy you have to be able to fail without taking it 'personally.' This is something which many women find difficult. They want to be 'good students.' This can leave them so preoccupied with possible failure that they shy away from the chance of success. In fact, the women in my study have taken risks in learning. Even taking a programming course confronted Lisa, a 'language person,' and Robin, a 'music person,' with serious challenges. But they, like other women I interviewed, made it clear that they saw such challenges not as risks but as hurdles— hurdles that have been imposed from the 'outside.' The risks they are willing to accept responsibility for are risks in relationships. 'There it is worth it; there I can do it.'

Risk taking as a learning strategy demands that you sacrifice a certain understanding of what is going on. It demands that you plunge in first and try to understand later. To take an analogy from the world of the computer's second cousins, the video games: it is almost impossible to learn to play a video game if you try to understand first and play second. Girls are often perceived as preferring the 'easier' video games. When I have looked more closely at what they really prefer, it is games where they can understand 'the rules' before play begins. Both Lisa and Robin crave transparent understanding of the computer. For example, although both apologize for their behavior as 'silly,' both like to program the computer to do everything they need to build their larger programs, even when these smaller, 'building-block' procedures are in program libraries at their disposal. It makes their job harder, but both say that it gives them a more satisfying understanding. They don't like taking risks at the machine. What they most want to avoid is error messages.

When women look at the programming virtuosos around them, they, unlike men, see themselves as cut off from a valued learning style. Male risk taking is equated with computational 'intuition.' In educational and professional environments where hackers present an image of 'the best,' women often see themselves as lesser. They see themselves as 'just users,' as competent but not really creative.

FIGHTING AGAINST COMPUTER HOLDING POWER

The computer is a 'psychological machine.' On the border between mind and not mind, it invites its anthropomorphization, its psychologization. It does this almost universally, for children and grownups, men and women, novices and experts. This does not mean that people see it as 'alive,' but rather, there is a pull to psychologize the machine, to give it an intellectual and aesthetic personality. The computer facilitates a relational encounter with a formal system.

I have found that many women are drawn towards a style of programming that is best characterized as such a relational encounter (Turkle 1984; in press). It is marked by an artistic, almost tactile style of identification with computational objects, a desire to 'play with them' as though they were physical objects in a collage. A fluent use of this programming style can be a source of creativity. But many women fight against something that needs to be distinguished from programming style. They fight against the computer as psychologically gripping. They experience anthropomorphization as seductive and dangerous. Paradoxically, in rebellion against feeling 'too much' they develop an attitude towards the computer that insists it is 'just a tool.'

The 'just a tool' response is widespread in our culture. It is certainly not associated primarily with women. But I believe that when women use it, it is with a special force; particularly strong feelings stand behind their insistence on the 'neutrality' of the technology.

First, insisting that the computer is just a tool is a defense against the experience of the computer as the opposite, as an intimate machine. It is a way to say that it is not appropriate to have a close relationship with a machine. Computers with their plasticity and malleability are compelling media. They have a psychological 'holding power.' Women use their rejection of computer holding power to assert something about themselves as women. Being a woman is opposed to a compelling relationship with a thing that shuts people out.

Contemporary writing about women's psychological development stresses the importance of connection in the way women forge their identities. Women are raised by women. Unlike men, they do not need to undergo a radical break to define their sexual identity. Unlike men, they are allowed, even encouraged to maintain a close relationship with the woman, the mother with whom they had an early experience of the closest bonding. Girls grow up defining their identity through social interaction; boys, through separation

(Chodorow 1978; Gilligan 1982; Keller 1983; 1985).

The boy's experience of early separation and loss is traumatic. It leads to a strong desire to control his environment. Male separation from others is about differentiation but also about autonomy, 'the wish to gain control over the sources and object of pleasure in order to shore up the possibilities for happiness against the risk of disappointment and loss' (Gilligan 1982, 46). Women grow up differently. Men 'shore up possibilities for happiness' by autonomy, rules and hierarchy; women look to affection, relationships, responsibility and caring for a community of others. In *In A Different Voice*, Carol Gilligan talks about 'the hierarchy and the web' as metaphors to describe the different ways in which men and women see their worlds. Men see a hierarchy of autonomous positions. Women see a web of interconnections between people. Men want to be alone at the top; they fear others getting too close. Women want to be at the center of connection; they fear being too far out on the edge. Men can be with the computer and still be alone, separate and autonomous. When women perceive this technology as demanding separation, it is experienced as alien and dangerous.[2]

Lisa began her work with computers by thinking in terms of communicating with them, 'because that's the way I see the world.' But her communication metaphor began to distress her: 'The computer isn't a living being and when I think about communicating with it, well that's wrong. There's a certain amount of feeling involved in the idea of communication and I was looking for that from the computer.' She looked for it, and she frightened herself: 'It was horrible. I was becoming involved with a thing. I identified with how the computer was going through things.'

> 'Wait a minute, a machine doesn't go through things; going through things is a very emotional way of talking. But it is hard to keep it straight. It seems to you that they are experiencing something that you once experienced. That they are learning something and you lose sight of the fact that this whole ability … I don't even want to say the computer's ability. I don't like anthropomorphizing; I fight very hard against attributing emotions to that machine.'

For Lisa, success with the computer has meant a process of alienation from it. Her efforts go towards depersonalization, towards developing a strategy towards computers that is 'not me.' 'I need to become a different kind of person with the machine.' This is a person who commands rather than communicates.

When Lisa psychologized the machine and thought of programming in terms of communication, she was responding to the computer as many people do. The computer responds, reacts, 'learns.' And the machine allows you to externalize your own thought. As one 13-year-old told me: 'When you program a computer you put a little piece of your mind into the computer's mind and you come to see it differently.' The experience is heady and encourages anthropomorphization.[3] But if Lisa's impulses to psychologize the computer were commonplace, her reaction to them was more typical of women than men—to rebel against the feeling of mind speaking to mind, almost to punish herself for it: 'You are working with the computer and you can almost identify with what a computer is going through. But then, that is awful. It's just a machine. It was horrible. I was becoming involved with a thing.'

Lisa's 'identification with what a computer is going through' is an identification with the computer as a mind. The computer is an 'evocative object' (Turkle 1984). It upsets simple distinctions between things and people; there can no longer be simply the physical as opposed to the psychological. The computer, too, seems to have a psychology—it is a thing that is not quite a thing, a mind that is not quite a mind. By presenting itself as an object 'betwixt and between,' the computer provokes reflection on the question of minds and machines. Very soon after meeting a computer, even the novice programmer learns to write programs that he or she perceives as more complex than the rules used to create them. Once people build these kinds of rule-driven systems, questions about the relevance of the idea of program to the working of one's own mind acquires a new sense of urgency.

ROMANTIC REACTIONS

The position toward which children tend as they develop their thinking about people in relation to computers is to split 'psychology' into the cognitive and affective, into the psychology of thought and of feeling (Turkle 1984). And then they can grant that the machine has intelligence and is thus 'sort of alive,' but distinguish it from people because of its lack of feelings. Thus, the Aristotelian definition of man as a 'rational animal' (powerful even for children when it defined people in contrast to their nearest neighbors, the animals) gives way to a different distinction. Today's children 'appropriate' computers through identification with them as psychological entities and come to see them as their new 'nearest neighbors.' And they are neighbors which seem to share in or (from the child's point of view) even excel in our rationality. People are still defined in contrast to their neighbors. But now, people are special because they feel. Children will grant the computer a 'sort of life,' but what makes people unique is the kind of life that computers don't have—an emotional life.

Many adults follow the same path as do children when they talk about human beings in relation to the new psychological machines. This path leads to allowing the possibility of unlimited rationality to computers while maintaining a sharp line between computers and people by taking the essence of human nature to be what computers can't do. This is precisely what Lisa does when she confronts the machine that seems to have a mind:

> 'I suppose if you look at the physical machinery of the computer mind, it is analogous to the human mind. We were looking at a bare machine and how all the little wires could be compared to neurons. So, in that sense, yes, the hardware is the brain and I can see how the software could be the mind. But, the saving grace, the difference is emotion. Now I haven't heard anybody yet reduce emotion to a series of electrical impulses. I hope I never do. And I think that's the line you can draw. That's where you say, "We can emote, this thing may be able to do something like thinking, but it can't love anybody." '

Although she makes them herself, Lisa objects to all comparisons between computers and people. A question in our interview about minds and machines causes her to cut me off sharply and then to reflect on her own inconsistency.

> 'I get really edgy when people start comparing computers to human beings or asking questions about how they might be alike or not alike. And it is a strange thing. I go and attribute all of these qualities to the computer and condescend to get mad at the computer and give it the dignity of my emotion wasted on its stupid metal framework, but at the same time, if somebody starts saying, "Don't you think that there might be similarity between a machine process and a human process or don't you think that there might be a program so that people could come

in and talk to the machine when they are lonely," I go mad. I say, "No. The computer's just a machine." At that point, I'm very able to make the distinction. But at the same time, I can't control my reactions to it as if it were... well, like a person. It's a contradiction. It's totally illogical and I can't explain it. It's like how I feel about abortion. I think it's a bad thing. And then, people show me my inconsistencies, and finally I just have to tell them I can't talk about it. It's just absolute, illogical, but that's how I feel.'

Lisa's experience with the computer leaves her with a sense of danger. The machine seduces you into psychologizing and anthropomorphizing it. 'People have to realize that this is only a machine. It is not going to provide love or compassion or understanding. You can't start attributing human qualities to it. But it's very hard not to.' And since even she was vulnerable, she worries about the dangers for children.

'What if children had them and started to have the idea that it was a being? Because they might start looking to that being for things that only a human can give, like support and comfort or love. Can you imagine a little person coming to love a computer? What if the computer became a mother substitute or a father figure? I think it would be disastrous. And all the more so if this thing that you had conceived of as a living, hearing, laughing, feeling being all your young life, that had been your best friend, and suddenly you realize that it's nothing but a machine. I can imagine a little person coming to that awareness and feeling so lost in not knowing what to do.

My sister loves animals more than people. It makes her a somewhat solitary sort of girl because she doesn't want to get involved with all the things that 13-year-olds do, she would rather go off and ride, but I think her emotional life is not limited really. When you're spending a lot of your time with animals, there's a lot of real love and real warmth and an animal can love you back.... And then there is the definite physical appeal. It's nice to hold a kitten in your lap.... But to even give a name to a computer, to me that has a kind of sinister quality. You can invest thought and get rewards. Perhaps you would get better rewards in terms of intelligence, but you're not ever going to get any emotional feedback from that thing. And so if you start lavishing your own guts on that computer, your own emotional entrails, well, you are going to be horribly disappointed. The longer you do it, the longer you are allowed to do it, the worse it's going to be.'

The Freudian experience has taught us that resistance to a theory is part of its cultural impact. Resistance to psychoanalysis, with its emphasis on the unconscious and the irrational, leads to an emphasis on the rational aspect of human nature, to an emphasis on people as ultimately logical beings. Resistance to computers and the ideal of program as mind leads to a view that what is essential in people is what is ineffable, uncapturable by any language or formalism. For Robin, people have 'great flashes of abstract thought without any logical sequence before it. If you tried to do that with a computer it would tell you it's a system error or illegal! People have two ways of thinking—one of them without logical steps. The computer only has one.' Lisa boils down what computers can't do to a starker form. Most simply stated, it is love.

There is a 'romantic reaction' to the computer presence. As people take computers seriously as simulated mind, they resist the image of the human mind that comes back to them in the mirror of the machine. Simulated thinking may be thinking, but simulated love is never love. Women express this sentiment with particular urgency. It is more than philosophical opinion. A conflict stands behind their conviction. The more they anthropomorphize the machine, the more they express anxiety about its dangers. The more it provokes them to reflect on mind, the more they assert that the computer is just a neutral tool for getting from A to B. In sum, the more they experience the subjective computer, the more they insist that it doesn't exist and that there is only the instrumental machine.

RETICENCE ABOUT FORMAL SYSTEMS

Lisa reacted with irritation when her high school teachers tried to get her interested in mathematics by calling it a language. 'People were always yakking at me about how math is a language—it's got punctuation marks and all that stuff. I thought they were fools and I told them so. I told them that if only it were a language, if only it had some nuance, then perhaps I could relate to it.' As a senior, she wrote a poem that expressed her sentiments.

If you could say with numbers what I say now in words,
if theorems could, like sentences, describe the flight of birds,
if PPL had meter and parabolas had rhyme,
perhaps I'd understand you then,
perhaps I'd change my mind.

If two convergent sequences produced some assonance,
or vectors made a particle of literary sense,
if triangles were iambs and equations anapests,
then maybe I'd acquire a bit of numerical interest.

If Cicero's orations were set down in polar form
and the headaches numbers give me weren't, excuse my
                                            French, enorme,
if a graph could say 'I love you,' it could sing a child to sleep,
then from this struggle I might find some benefit to reap.

But all this wishful thinking only serves to make things worse,
when I compare my dearest love with your numeric verse.
For if mathematics were a language, I'd succeed, I'd scale the
                                                          hill,
I know I'd understand, but since it's not, I never will.

Lisa's poem expresses her profound reticence about formal systems. Despite her talent, she preferred to stay away from them. 'I didn't see that proving a theorem was anything like writing a poem. I never thought of mathematics as creative or human; and the people who studied them, well, when I thought of "people who studied mathematics," I thought of these dry, emotionless little people who ran around and talked to computers all day.'

Lisa's reticence has many facets, but she keeps coming back to two themes. First, formal systems don't bring people together, they rupture what Gilligan called the 'web of connectedness' that dominates women's way of seeing the world. Second, formal systems allow for 'only one way' of doing things.

'When they used to talk to me about mathematics as a language I would say, "Well, look, if I were speaking Spanish, I could say that thirty million different ways." Here, it's either right or it's wrong and that's it. And I don't like the regimentation.'

Lisa dislikes anything where there is 'only one way.' She loves language for its 'shades of meaning.' Ambiguity and nuance make her feel at home. Erik Erikson, writing from within the psychoanalytic tradition, has suggested how women's experience of their bodies as an 'inner space' that is hidden, diffuse and ambiguous affects their experience of the world (Erikson 1963). The 'nailed down' quality of formal systems feels unfamiliar and threatening.

Clearly, women's feelings about formal systems go deep. Erikson's work on body image suggests a terror of the non-ambiguous; Evelyn Fox Keller's work on women and science suggests that women's early and (relative to men) unruptured experiences with closely bonded relationships alienates them from the traditional 'male' stance toward formal systems, a stance characterized by the separation of subject from object (Keller 1985).

The issues that are raised by looking at gender and formal systems are complex, but something about the computer's contribution is becoming increasingly clear. When people are put in computer-rich environments, supported by flexible and powerful programming languages, and encouraged to use the computer as an expressive material, they respond in a diversity of styles. In such environments, the computer, like other powerful media including paints, pencils and words, becomes a screen for the projection of differences. Unlike stereotypes of a machine with which there is only one way of relating, the computer can be a partner in a great diversity of relationships.

People make the computer their own in their own way. For example, some take to the computer in a way that emphasizes planning and structure. Others naturally move toward a different style. They prefer to 'grow' their programs from small elements, often changing their goals as they go along. The programs that result from using these two styles can be equally effective, clear and easy to use. The difference is not in the product but in the process of creation. With the computer, there is not 'one way.' On the contrary, the range of styles of appropriation suggests the metaphor 'computer as Rorschach' (Turkle 1980). Like the Rorschach inkblot test, the computer presents an ambiguous material that encourages the projection of significant inner differences.

In relatively unconstrained settings, the computer facilitates a new basis for engagement in technical and mathematical thinking, one that allows for their appropriation through a 'close encounter' with an interactive, reactive 'psychological machine' and with computational objects that can be experienced as tactile and physical. It is a style that emphasizes negotiation rather than command of computational objects, a style that suggests a conversation rather than a monologue. This is a port of entry into the world of formal systems for many people who have always kept at a distance from them. It is a port of entry with particular significance for women. The computer offers a new cultural opportunity to expand the social base of mathematical and scientific fluency.

But people are not always introduced to computers in a way that exploits this opportunity. In fact, it happens all too rarely. Lisa and Robin are taking an excellent and imaginative introductory programming course, but even there, both of them are experiencing it as a place where they are being told the 'one right way' to do things. This 'one right way' emphasizes 'structured programming' with its aesthetic of control through structure, specification and planning. There is much virtue in this computational aesthetic, but both Lisa and Robin say their learning styles are at war with it. Robin wanted to play with the smallest computational elements and build things from the 'bottom up.' Lisa was frustrated by the strategy of 'black boxing' that helps the structured programmer plan something large without knowing in advance how the details will be managed. Both rebelled against the regimentation of there being 'one right way' to do things.

In the course that Robin and Lisa are taking, those whose intellectual style favors the highly analytical, the structured and the specifiable, will be drawn to the computer, while others, and many women among them, will continue to see what it takes to 'think right' in the computer culture as alien. And even when they succeed in the course, they keep their psychological distance. I believe that a symptom of this distance is their 'neutralization' of the computer when they describe it as 'just a tool.'

We know that pencils, oil paints and brushes are 'just tools.' And yet, we appreciate that the artist's encounter with his or her tools is close and relational. It may shut people out, temporarily, but the work itself can bring one closer to oneself, and ultimately to others. In the right settings, people develop relationships with computers that feel artistic and personal. And yet, for most people, and certainly for the women I studied, this was rare. When they began to approach the computer in their own style, they got their wrists slapped, and were told that they were not doing things 'right.'

When this happens, many people drop out. They see themselves as deviant, as not 'good at the computer.' Or, and this is what one sees most often with talented women such as Lisa and Robin, they 'fake it.' They try to do it the 'right way.' Lisa talks about turning herself into a 'different kind of person.' Robin talks about giving up on her desire to 'build from little pieces on up' and to have a fully transparent relationship with the computer. 'I told my teaching fellow I wanted to take it all apart and he laughed at me. He said it was a waste of time, that you should just "black box," that you shouldn't confuse yourself with what was going on at that low level.'

We cannot know what Lisa and Robin would be feeling if they had been encouraged toward a more personal appropriation of this technology. As I have said, the roots of reticence seem to go deep. But we do know that given the introduction they did have, they, like most of the women I interviewed, ended up denying the computer any role as an expressive medium. This is not surprising: given the way they have been using it, it isn't one. Frustrated in a personal style of use, they become vehement about the computer's status as a neutral 'tool' because they have been denied any other relationship with it. To put it more sharply, they have been denied an authentic relationship with it.

Lisa sums up her computer experience with the word 'regimentation.' She is afraid of children learning to program because she wouldn't want them equally regimented. She wouldn't want children 'tied down to being very careful and very regimented and very concise and syntactically correct.' Lisa says that her best moment in her programming course was when she saw, through the computer, something she might have missed in mathematics. 'In mathematics I could never see that it didn't have to be just one way. But I can see that a little with the computer. And I am starting to get very excited about that.' And then she came back to the question of children with a more optimistic tone: 'I think maybe kids could bring, well, they could open up new frontiers for computers, because they have such wild ideas that they could do great things if people just let them.'

The children may indeed lead us.[4] The computer that could support 'wild ideas' is the computer as an expressive medium. We must ask if the vehemence behind women's insistence that the computer is 'just a tool' will be as great when they have greater opportunities to experience it as material which allows highly differentiated styles of mastery and personalizes the world of formal systems for men and women alike.

NOTES

1 The quotation from Jessie is taken from an interview done by MIT graduate student Ronnie Rosenberg, 'Female Hackers,' unpublished paper, December 1983. In this paper, Rosenberg makes the very interesting point that when women look at male risk-taking style with computers they equate that style with 'intuition.'

2 From this perspective, computers become much more attractive when they are used to support communications through networks. The question here will be whether particular computer networks bring people together—who would not normally have been together or whether they 'deteriorate' communication—that is, people who would have spoken face to face now speak screen to screen.

3 The holding power of a mind-to-mind connection is there even for the non-programmer. When you use someone else's program, software someone else has written, there is still the fantasy of a mind-to-mind communication between you and the software writer.

4 A leading computer visionary who has long stood for the 'personal appropriation' of programming has done much of his work with children. See Seymour Papert, *Mindstorms: Children, Computers and Powerful Ideas*, New York: Basic Books, 1980.

REFERENCES

Chodorow, Nancy. 1978. *The Reproduction of Mothering*. Berkeley: University of California Press.

Erikson, Erik. 1963. *Childhood and Society*. New York : W.W. Norton.

Gilligan, Carol. 1982. *In a Different Voice: Psychological Theory and Women's Development*. Cambridge, Mass.: Harvard University Press.

Keller, Evelyn Fox. 1983. *A Feeling for the Organism: The Life and Work of Barbara McClintock*. San Francisco: W.H. Freeman.

Keller, Evelyn Fox. 1985. *Reflections on Gender and Science*. New Haven, Conn.: Yale University Press.

Kiesler, Sara, Lee Sproull and David Zubrow. 1984. 'Encountering an alien culture.' *Journal of Social Research*.

Kiesler, Sara, Lee Sproull and Jacqueline S. Eccles. 1985. 'Poolhalls, chips and war games: women in the culture of computing.' *Psychology of Women Quarterly* 9:4, 451–62.

Turkle, Sherry. 1980. 'Computer as Rorschach.' *Society* 17.

Turkle, Sherry. 1984. *The Second Self: Computers and the Human Spirit*. New York: Simon & Schuster.

Turkle, Sherry. (In press.) 'Gender and programming: styles and voices in the computer culture.' *Signs*.

ANNE MACHUNG

'WHO NEEDS A PERSONALITY TO TALK TO A MACHINE?': COMMUNICATION IN THE AUTOMATED OFFICE[1]

'Who needs a personality to talk to a machine? You can get very mechanical here. You can just get lost doing that. Wake up five years later—what happened to my life?'

(Paula Pieper[2])

In the spring of 1985 I was a temporary clerical worker. Days I worked at a law firm in downtown San Francisco, using an electronic typewriter and experiencing first-hand the changes that have come about with the electronic office. Nights I was a data entry clerk at a large, cavernous VDT center, also run by a San Francisco law firm, but blocks away from its downtown office. My job as a word processing secretary involved the traditional variety of tasks that legal secretaries do, typing, filing, answering phones, photocopying and mailing forms. My job as a data entry clerk involved nothing more, however, than routine keyboarding; for six hours a night I, and six other operators, processed thousands of forms, first by calling the forms up electronically by number, then by entering dates and numeric codes onto appropriate lines. While we talked occasionally, what struck me most about the VDT center was how quiet work had become and how people kept at their work despite the monotony and seemingly lax supervision.

Between seven and ten million clericals in the US today work in front of video display terminals (or VDTs) like the Wang I operated. Eighty percent of the 17.3 million clerical workers in the US are women; 74 percent of four million clericals in Great Britain are women.[3] Many of the jobs slated for automation at the clerical level in both the US and Great Britain are held primarily by women. It is they—secretaries, bookkeepers, typists and bank tellers—who first acutely felt the impact of the new technology upon their jobs and lives at work.

Underpaid, socially devalued and highly routinized, clerical work historically has not offered women much satisfaction outside of friendships with others in the office. Secretaries especially have valued the opportunity their jobs gave them to interact with a diversity of people at work, everybody from the boss at the top to the file clerk on the bottom. Automation, however, threatens such sources of meaning and satisfaction. The VDT center, in which much routine clerical computer work is centralized, often becomes its own small microcosm, a world set apart from the rest of the corporation. Within such centers, VDT operators interact primarily with each other; most of the contact between the center and the rest of the firm is mediated for operators by their supervisor. It is she who interacts with principals, schedules work, assigns priorities, and handles operators' complaints. Operators primarily type, or 'key in,' as it is often called.

Moreover, VDT work, unlike non-automated clerical jobs, requires constant attention. 'The center of gravity in the workplace,' argues Zuboff (1982), 'has shifted from jobs that require bodily involvement to those that require cerebral involvement' (54). Clericals who once could type, fold, staple and talk on the phone simultaneously now find themselves at the terminal needing to concentrate both visually and mentally as they input and edit. Talking and working at the same time become more difficult.

With automation social interaction is no longer as central to clerical work as it once was. Indeed, socializing can actually become counterproductive in the automated office. Productivity pressures—the requirement that VDT operators maintain a certain quota each day—limit the amount of time available for talking and chatting. Interactions with others come to be experienced as distractions and interruptions rather than as intrinsic to the process of work itself. Communication in the automated office, then, flows not from person to person, but from person to terminal. By shifting operators' attention onto a VDT screen, reducing job-related needs for interacting with others, and constricting the time available for talking, computerization threatens clerical workers with a loss of fundamental job satisfaction—the satisfaction that comes from interacting with others at work. 'Who needs a personality,' grumbled one of the VDT operators I interviewed, 'to talk to a machine?'

Installed at nearly every level of the business enterprise, from the work-station of the lowliest clerical to the desk of the top executive, the computer terminal has transformed office work. Whole new job categories, such as systems analyst, computer programmer and data entry operator, have been created, and other once very common jobs, such as typist and stenographer, are being eliminated. Ironically, new processes of social interaction are also being created in the electronic office. Computer conferencing and monitoring of the productivity of individual workers or units much out of sight are allowing both top and middle-level managers to extend their range of social interaction and control. But clericals, working all day long at VDT terminals, increasingly find themselves feeling controlled by the terminal and isolated in a room full of people.

While business journals optimistically envision the 'end of the social office,' most of the recent critical literature on office automation focuses on how this technology affects employment levels, skill gain or loss, job redesign or worker control, and health and safety issues (Burgess 1985; Howard 1985; US Congress 1985; US Dept of Labor 1985; Cohen 1984; Machung 1984; Murphree 1984; Wernecke 1984; Feldberg and Glenn 1983; Harvard Medical School 1983; Stellman and Henifin 1984; Arnold *et al.* 1982; Gregory and Nussbaum 1982; Menzies 1981; Barker and Downing 1980). Very little of it, however, has examined how automation is transforming patterns of communication and sociability within the office, and how those transformations feel to workers most affected by them.

Between 1979 and 1981 I interviewed fifty secretaries and word processing operators and supervisors in depth about their jobs. (See Machung 1983, for a detailed description of sample and methods.) At that time in San Francisco, computers had just been installed into the back offices of large banks, law firms and insurance companies, and old-fashioned typing pools were being transformed into word processing or document production centers. Sometimes these were even called 'communication centers.' All of the VDT operators I interviewed worked full-time in such centralized word processing centers. Their jobs consisted in repetitiously typing letters, reports and memos of various kinds into the Wang, the Vydeck or the MBI. The secretaries I interviewed, on the other hand, worked in classic, one-on-one relationships with their bosses, usually middle- or senior-level executives, and did a variety of tasks ('everything from light hauling to psychotherapy'). All of them, moreover, worked in front offices, visible to bosses and clients alike, and not one of them used a computer.

Since the middle 1970s, however, the price of computers has

64

dropped dramatically, making them affordable for the front office as well as the back office. Many secretaries today now have their own personal computer or memory typewriter. Used intermittently for typing letters and reports, word processing machines at the secretarial desk function more like conventional typewriters. Bosses may produce more rough drafts and expect cleaner copy, but secretaries still answer phones, open mail and schedule appointments, in addition to typing. I use the term 'secretary' in this paper to refer to those clericals who work in front offices in one-on-one relationships with their bosses. The term 'word processing technician' refers to VDT operators who work in back offices, in large, factory-like centers endlessly typing all day—and sometimes all night—long.

The significant comparison, however, lies not only between these front-office jobs, whether partially automated or not, and the fully automated jobs of the back office, but between jobs held primarily by white women and jobs held disproportionately by minority women. While only 11 percent of all secretaries in the US today, for example, are Black or Hispanic, 19 percent of all computer operators and 22 percent of all typists—those whose jobs are most fully automated—are minority.[4] My sample drawn from San Francisco banks, insurance companies and law firms reflects this distribution; while virtually all of the secretaries I interviewed and quote are white, 40 percent of the VDT operators I interviewed are either Black, Hispanic, or Asian-American. A comparison of front-office and back-office jobs thus reveals both how rapidly computerization has transformed patterns of sociability within the office and how these changes within the clerical sector affect minority women disproportionately more than white women.

THE CRAFT OF LOVE

'To think of a secretary as typing and taking shorthand all the time, I don't. There's days that go by and I don't even see the typewriter. A lot [of my job] is interacting with people.'

Molly Davis

Taught in high schools and business colleges across the country for most of the twentieth century, typing is considered the essence of secretarial work and the great 'fall back' skill for women. But while employers define secretarial jobs in terms of typing skills and write job descriptions up that way, they consistently hire women not on the basis of typing speed but on the basis of personality. Indeed, the essence of most secretarial work is not typing speed and accuracy, but the ability to interact with a diverse range of people and problems. 'I do lots of typing and filing and so forth,' one woman, secretary to a senior bank manager, told me,

> 'But that's not the major part of the job, certainly. Any good typist or stenographer, I am sure, could do that. There's nothing complex about that. [My job is] mostly meeting with lots of different people and customers, being able to work with customers, and having some idea of what to do with them when they turn up with a problem.'
>
> Susan Pinto

For too long, the social interaction skills that secretaries have acquired and used on their jobs have been seen as somehow natural to the feminine personality. Yet these skills develop over time, sometimes consciously, sometimes unconsciously. They give meaning to the secretarial craft in a dual sense: not only is it intrinsically satisfying to create warm and friendly relationships at work, but the creation of such relationships allows for the growth and development of a social self as well. 'I have to admit,' as Susan Pinto told me,

> '... that I learn something new every day. I may not even realize it, and I may not always remember it, but I'm sure that not a day goes by that there isn't something I learn—more about human relationships, I guess, than about banking itself.... Though our cast is standard, we do have our customers, you see, so you have different little dramas played out all the time.'

Here, in the construction of social relationships, lies the real craft of secretarial work—a craft which involves creating, actively and intelligently, relationships between people of similar or divergent status. Needless to say, the construction of these interpersonal relationships involves enormous social and diplomatic skills—skills that are learned, that develop over time, and that are deeply valued.

Interacting with the boss

Ask a secretary about her job and she tells you about her boss. Detailed interviews with secretaries are filled with stories about their bosses—warm feelings, funny anecdotes, distressing complaints. Bosses are compared to each other—present bosses to past bosses, good bosses to bad bosses, female bosses to male bosses. Underneath the stories, the anecdotes, the comparisons and the complaints are detailed characterizations of their bosses' personalities. Except for those just starting out, most secretaries have worked at a number of different jobs and for a number of different bosses. And secretaries know their bosses and can describe in minute detail nuances about their personalities, their moods, quirks, hopes and anxieties. Rosabeth Moss Kanter (1977) has argued that secretaries learn the boss and not the job. But knowing the boss *is* their job and interpreting his personality to others in the organization is a major interpersonal skill their work demands. Betty Weigand is secretary to a man who runs a major community agency in downtown San Francisco. Most people, she says, think Alex, her boss, is 'a very enigmatic and incredible figure.' She ponders that perception of him:

> 'He's got a certain kind of charisma and mystery. It's a very strange thing. And people want to talk to him. And they figure I know him better than anybody. And they say, a lot of people say, "How can you work for him? How can you stand it?," and stuff like that.... Whenever I'm in a conversation with almost anybody, it always comes round to Alex and his personality and his whims and what he's thinking and what he's doing. Which people think I'm the expert on.'

But secretaries not only are the experts on their bosses' personalities and moods of the day, but they translate that to others in the organization as well. In doing so, they shape his image. Bosses reveal parts of themselves to their secretaries that they sometimes do not so freely reveal to others; in secretaries' eyes fearsome bosses can become 'teddy bears' and gruff bosses 'compassionate.' By disclosing this underside to her boss's personality, a secretary can soften his image.

But this knowledge takes time to develop. Especially at the executive level (and perhaps below as well) it takes secretaries a year to learn the job—not so much because of organizational intricacies they must master but because of personalities they must get to know. Becoming a private secretary was quite a step up for Patricia Jiminez. Young, relatively inexperienced and Hispanic, she moved with grace between the corporate culture of San Francisco's financial district and the ethnic culture of the Mission District, the Hispanic neighborhood where she lived. New to her job, she was just getting to know her boss as I interviewed her:

'It's like establishing—anywhere you go and start living with someone—it's like establishing a friendship. You can't jump into it. It has to be a little bit at a time.... It has to be gradual. I'm sure that within a year, I'll know him a lot better than I do now.'

But these relationships, once established, are deeply valued. The closer the working relationship, the more smoothly work gets done. Secretaries who have developed, or cultivated, a good working relationship with their boss often talk about 'anticipating' his orders, 'intuiting' his needs, or 'developing ESP' in order to get the work done. Single and unattached, Liz Morgan had worked for her boss Jack for the past fifteen years, and he had clearly come to depend upon her:

'As a matter of fact, Jack was very embarrassed the other day because—and I think it is just intuition or just judging, knowing approximately when he is going to be needing something or when to bring something in for him to work on. A lot of times he'll call me, and I am already part way into his office. He'll say, "God, you are psychic!" '

Psychic or not, most secretaries conceive of their jobs not just as knowing their bosses, but as pleasing their bosses. The basic skills of the job—typing, filing and shorthand—are usually acquired before the secretary ever enters the job market and are highly transferrable. Still companies are set up differently—correspondence is typed one way here, another way there; bookkeeping and accounting procedures are organized variously; and filing is always individualized. But even within companies, each secretarial job is different, 'as different as the man is different, as his expectations are different.' To succeed at her job, a secretary must therefore adapt herself to these differences—differences not so much in the typing and filing but in her boss's personality and in his expectations. She adapts in any number of ways: calming him down when angry, cheering him up when sad, taking the initiative when he is away, curtailing it when he is present. She learns how to answer the phone, how to greet visitors, how to type correspondence. But it all is done the way he likes it, in his style, using his language. As Mary Leaman told me,

> 'A secretary is much more than what could ever be on a piece of paper. She's what the boss she's working for wants her to be. And if she can't please him, and she's not willing to adapt to do the things that's necessary to please that particular person, then she's got to get out of the profession because that's it.'

If the secretary is not able or willing to do the things necesssary to please her boss, tensions develop. They face each other off, either in cold stares or angry outbursts. When this happens, the blame for the failed relationship falls, almost squarely, on the secretary. 'You're not going to change the boss,' one warned me, 'and you shouldn't even try.'

This process of adaptation is enormously eased, however, by personality congruency between the secretary and her boss. In the best working relationships secretaries and bosses resemble each other. He picks someone he likes, usually someone like himself. Top executives are noted for being outgoing; but not all are, and neither are their secretaries. Still, they often complement each other:

> 'The thing about him and me is that our personalities are very similar. We're both very shy. And we don't reach out with warmth to each other.... I'm afraid to extend that and he doesn't extend it to me. So that we're sort of at a stand-off in this sort of chilly atmosphere. And at this point I'm just too intimidated and shy to do anything about it. But he likes it that way. And in a way I like it that way, too.'
>
> Betty Wienganch

Given that emotional understanding and emotional expressivity are so central to secretarial jobs, finding a boss with whom one can be oneself becomes a central facet to creating a good working relationship. In this search personality is the great 'unstated variable.'

69

Interacting for the boss

Not all bosses, male or female, are tactful, gracious or diplomatic; many are abrupt and abrasive and do not want to spend the time and energy to deal pleasantly with others in the organizational hierarchy, especially those below them. These especially rely upon their secretary to smooth the way for them interpersonally:

'I know in my job I do a lot of buffering and ambassadoring for my boss. My boss may come to me and say "rrr, ggg," and say, "You go to so-and-so and get that done."

And I'll go to so-and-so and tell the latest dirty joke, and "Ho, ho, ho, would you get this for me please? She really is riding my case." '

Sally Laud

When I interviewed her, Sally Laud had spent the past several years working for a woman manager. While the other secretaries I interviewed all preferred male to female bosses and all worked for men, Sally herself found no difference between the two. Most bosses are, in fact, male; but whether one's boss is male or female, the basic interpersonal skills called for are similar: to translate the boss's orders into softer, friendlier language and to foster cooperation for them, rather than resistance. To do this well requires the ability to turn a situation that could get uncomfortable into one that will go smoothly and pleasantly. Humor is one skill that secretaries accordingly cultivate. 'I know with me,' said Liz,

'when there is a lot of tenseness in the air, you have to be serious. But if there is a lot of tension, sometimes just a little relief, a laugh, will be so, and I'll actually go looking for little anecdotes when I find a lot of tension building up in the air.'

Liz Morgan

But fostering friendliness, relieving tension and deflecting hostility requires a sense of tact and diplomacy, even more than a sense of humor. Virtually all secretaries mention tact and diplomacy as a central job skill. 'You can pay for a typist or stenographer,' Meg O'Brien (who had been a secretary all her adult life) told me, 'but you can't always get someone who has those basic technical skills and all these other assets (tact, diplomacy, dependability) to their nature.'

A major part of the job of the secretary, then, requires her to develop special emotional sensitivity to those around her and the social skills to understand and translate personalities. The ability to conceptualize and discriminate among different personalities, to attend to subtle variations in moods, to read into requests, to anticipate needs in advance, and to translate orders in a non-threatening fashion are all part of the interpersonal skills of the secretary, as are a sense of humor, a sense of timing and, above all, a sense of tact and diplomacy.

THE INVERSION OF SKILL

'If your mechanical skills are super, super, and you're lacking in personality, you'll get by because, as I said, in the end production and making money for the firm are the most important. And making hearts sing and people happy would come second because money always talks.'

Cindy Perkins

Secretaries work *with* people, but VDT operators work *alongside* people. VDT operators therefore talk not about the social skills they use and develop on their jobs, but primarily about their mechanical skills. Interacting with a computer all day long, what they mostly need to know is *not* how to get along with bosses, clients and co-workers, but how to type. 'A lot of it,' one operator told me, 'is just typing skills and having good skills to begin with.' 'Typing,' said another, 'is very important. You're not only working with the keys here, but you have a side set of keys also. And you have to know the feel of those too, the placement, so you can do it without looking.'

So while secretaries and VDT operators both talk about 'interacting' at work—one with bosses, the other with computer terminals—the nature of such interactions is vastly different. Computer terminals, unlike bosses or coworkers, do not concern you with personal problems—a child who is sick, a husband who is unemployed; they do not invite you to a party you would rather skip, or bore you with a story you have already heard. Moreover, while the terminal greets an operator each logon session with a friendly 'Good morning, Alice,' it never barks back. In short, word processing machines spell order and predictability. While users sometimes feel strongly about their terminal, terminals never feel anything toward their user. One can pound on the keys, type into

71

the terminal the most loving or abusive language, and receive back only the most mild-mannered response ('unknown command').

Terminals thus not only eliminate 'extraneous' social conversation from the office, but the 'extraneous' emotions that often accompany that conversation. The knowledge required to operate one is linear and logical; the process is intellectualized, not social or emotional. Unlike people, there are no feelings to understand, no emotional nuances to grasp, no 'surprises' to expect. Unlike secretarial jobs, then, social skills are extrinsic to the task at hand, not intrinsic. As a young woman who had just graduated with a BA in Dramatic Arts told me,

'The only social skills I would need are enough so I could get along with everybody in the center. For the job itself, theoretically, I could still come in at midnight when nobody else was around and just transcribe. It would be exactly the same.'

Maureen Woo

While secretaries thus emphasize the importance of social and interpersonal skills, VDT operators emphasize the importance of typing skills and machine knowledge. They talk not about cultivating openness toward other people, but about 'openness' to the machine. 'If your mind isn't open,' proclaimed one operator, 'you can't learn the principle of the machine.'

So just as secretaries learn the boss, word processing operators learn the machine. Unlike secretaries, then, VDT operators never talk about developing ESP, anticipating needs, interpreting moods, translating personalities. Instead they talk about 'sticking it out' and 'adjusting' themselves to typing all day long. Indeed, the new personality skill demanded of the VDT operator is not the willingness to adapt oneself to the personality and needs of another person, but the willingness to sit and type all day long:

'You have to be willing to do the work. Some people aren't. They get tired of sitting there and typing and getting somebody's work to do. We have one operator who quit. She got tired of working by the midafternoon, and she's rest her head on one elbow and type with one hand and not get the work out.'

Lois Flandermeyer

What is happening, then, as high-speed word and data processing is introduced into large corporations and small ones alike, is an inversion of the skills historically required in clerical work. Secretaries are hired (and fired) on the basis of their personality and social skills. But word processing technicians, and VDT operators in general, are hired and fired on the basis of their ability to get the work out—to maintain, that is, high-speed document production over sustained periods of time. The ability to interact socially with a diverse number of people and personalities is not required in these new jobs; in fact, the desire to do so can sometimes be counterproductive. It is productivity that really counts, not sociability.

THE RECONSTRUCTION OF SOCIABILITY

Though social and emotional skills never loom as large for VDT operators as they do for secretaries, word and data processing centers do develop their own personalities. Isolated from the rest of the corporation, such centers become microcosms of personal gossip, petty rivalries, intense loves and strong animosities. Working closely together under tight production pressures, supervisors and operators come to know each other, sometimes quite well.

Almost universally, operators describe their relationships with each other as 'friendly,' 'sociable' and 'congenial'. Needing each other for camaraderie, they come to depend upon each other for moral support. But talk centers not so much on the job (for what is there to say about it?) but on food, sex and weekend plans, the conventional topics of office gossip. Unlike managers and supervisors, operators' talk is not embedded in language about routines and procedures, decision algorithms and microprocessor capabilities, but rather in talk about each other—whom they get along with, whom they are friends with, whom they find difficult to interact with. Ironically, the more fragmented a task, the more minute and routine it is, the more difficult it is to describe and the less one needs or wants to describe it. The task-oriented language of the computer specialist often contrasts, then, with the friendly jabber that goes on among VDT operators themselves.

Interacting primarily with each other, VDT operators also come to identify with each other. And while they may complain about each other—this one comes in late each day; that one does not do her share of the work—it is each other they know best and like best. Still the work is intensely monotonous. Joking, teasing and gossiping then become ways to ease that tension and monotony. But most job talk is small talk. While it breaks the routine, it is not essential to getting the work done:

> 'Like the job I'm working in—I can relate to all the people around me and get along with them pretty well. But the thing you're working most with all day and most intimately is this machine. It doesn't give you any problems at all. It's just a machine. So actually there's a lot less personality problems when you're working with a machine.'
>
> Lois Flandermeyer

Working at the terminal can thus easily become a way to escape social interactions. Relationships operators establish at work are, in fact, secondary to their main task of typing. Moreover, these relationships, unlike the kinds of relationships that secretaries *must* establish on their jobs, can be avoided by turning and facing the machine. As another operator, a woman who had grown up in East Oakland, told me,

> 'What I do now is work on the machines all day. If I feel in a bad mood or something, I just get to sit at my machine, and I don't have to talk to anybody.... It's like I don't have to deal with anybody unless I want to.'
>
> Cecilia Herald

Unlike secretaries, then, VDT operators are freer to select the terms upon which to interact with others. But while this frees some operators from facing difficult social interactions, it leaves other operators frustrated. Those who have developed social skills, who know how to get along with different kinds of people and who like working with others, have little chance in VDT work of doing this.

VDT work also is highly isolating. Operators often sit at terminals located right next to each other, yet they feel alone. Doing the job demands constant attention—in part because the eyes must constantly shift from text to screen; in part because the work has little internal coherence; in part because the flickering dots on the screen capture attention much the same way moving images on a television screen do. The jobs also are arranged in such a way as to leave operators independent and autonomous; they do not need each other in order to accomplish their tasks. While interdependence very much characterizes secretarial work, independence and isolation characterize the work of the VDT operator.

Working at a terminal all day long does not, lastly, simply minimize the amount of social contact operators have with others, it also changes the nature of interactions that occur. Contact with a few people doing the same job is intensified, but contact with many people doing different jobs is reduced, if not eliminated completely. Spatially and socially disconnected from the rest of the firm, VDT operators know little about the users of the center—the 'clients,' 'liaisons,' or 'dictators' as they are sometimes called. Most interactions with staff outside the center are, in fact, mediated for them by a supervisor. Unlike secretaries who are visible throughout the organization, VDT operators are virtually invisible. Bosses frequently do not know the names of anybody within the VDT center, and operators seldom know the faces of those outside the center. Friendships across the boundaries are almost non-existent; contacts are at best cordial and cautious.

Interactions with people outside the center are also limited by the machine character of the work. Corporations purchase computers that can print out sixty or more characters per second. Forgetting that work must be keyed into the terminal first, bosses come to expect their work to be printed out just as fast. I once worked for a lawyer who at 11 a.m. was frustrated because I had not yet mastered a memory typewriter. He wanted his corrections made electronically, not whited out. I explained that I had only started the job at 8 that morning, that the typewriter came equipped with a 130-page instruction bulletin, and that I had not yet figured out how to enter, store and retrieve letters from its memory. 'What's the matter?' he said, 'it's *so* easy,' discounting completely the time it takes to learn how to use an electronic typewriter, the time it takes to key in a text, and the time it takes to print out the revisions. Would the same lawyer, I wondered to myself, put his 16-year-old son behind the car wheel and say so impatiently, 'Come on. Drive the car. It's *so* easy.' In the electronic office, however, bosses forget that 'easy' does not mean 'instantaneous.'

Users thus tend to transpose qualities attached to the computer to the operator. While secretaries sometimes complain about feeling like an extension of their boss, VDT operators complain about feeling like an extension of their terminal. This, of course, is not a function of the computer *per se*, but of business and management decisions that lock operator and keyboard together so that they come to be perceived as a single operating unit. 'When you talk to different

75

people,' one VDT operator asked me, 'has anybody ever said that they feel that whoever uses them or their services thinks that they're a robot? Know what I mean?'

In part, this sense of feeling 'like a robot' is exacerbated by productivity pressures that many VDT operators work under. Automation has enabled managers to keep accurate counts of how much each individual typist is producing by instantaneously recording when she is working and how fast she is typing. In some centers, these 'productivity counts' are turned into 'productivity quotas,' and operators are expected to maintain minimum levels to keep their jobs or receive a raise. Vivian Valentine is highly skilled, well educated, but visually handicapped. She has moved from VDT job to VDT job, hoping to move into management but never quite able to make the leap out. 'When I was a medical transcriber,' she says, reporting on a past job,

'it was just a sweatshop. We had production levels that we had to meet every day—1200 to 1400 lines a day. And that doesn't give you much time for relaxation, or even saying "hi" to your coworkers, or anything. And that's an unhealthy situation.'

Though Vivian is white, a 1984 survey by 9 to 5, the National Association of Working Women, found that Black women are twice as likely to face these kinds of productivity quotas as white women; 57 per cent of Black electronic data processing clerks who responded to the 9 to 5 survey worked under productivity quotas compared to only 30 percent of white clerks in similar jobs (US Dept of Labor 1985, 21). Not only, it seems, are Black, minority or handicapped women more likely to be tracked into back-office environments, but once there, they confront more stringent controls on their social and interpersonal behavior.

By institutionalizing such VDT centers, then, social mechanisms have been designed which both break down social relationships between the clerical and managerial strata as well as eroding ties of dependency, friendliness and mutual support between them. Moreover, computerization in the back office threatens VDT operators with loss of sociability and hence with loss of a fundamental source of job satisfaction. Instead of hiring a friendly secretary, one now can purchase a user-friendly terminal. Indeed, if secretarial-managerial relationships represent the ultimate of non-bureaucratic relationships in large organizations ('pockets of the personal inside the bureaucratic' as Kanter [1977] has described them), the creation of VDT centers represents its antithesis—the extension of vast amounts of electronic control into the clerical sector, with greater constraints placed on social interaction and socializing in general.

THE LOSS OF LOVE

Some people say that word processing technicians 'fall in love' with their machine. 'Once they overcome their initial resistance,' says *Woman's Day* (quoted by Professional Secretaries International 1981:3),

> 'many women speak of "falling in love" with computers.... The equipment has met with such rapid acceptance that any secretary or typist who does not learn word processing is "impeding herself." '

But while supervisors, vendors and magazine editors talk about how much operators love their terminals, none of the operators I interviewed spoke of them with love. There are those who like to type and those who enjoy mastering the intricacies of word processing, but even those who are fascinated by the technology do not love it. While it admittedly makes their lives as typists easier, the satisfaction one can find in word and data processing is limited.

The challenge comes in the beginning, in learning how to use the terminal. But operators learn the basics within a day or so, and master the terminal within a few months. Having learned all there is to know, they become bored and disinterested. Interest peaks after about six months, then declines. As interest declines, page counts drop and error counts rise. Supervisors literally cannot afford to keep the same operator for more than two or three years unless they have changed equipment. Corporations try to reduce time spent training new operators by purchasing terminals that are easy to learn, further standardizing the job and reducing any challenge. Unlike secretaries who sometimes feel completely irreplaceable because their boss needs and depends upon them so much, VDT operators feel highly expendable, replaceable and interchangeable. 'That's the feeling I get over and over,' Maureen Woo told me:

> 'The company seems to be saying to you that you're expendable. So why bother making it really more challenging or humane. Because you are expendable. You can leave, but if

you leave, there are five more who could take your place.'

Secretaries typically find meaning in their jobs through their interpersonal relationships. Lacking access to a larger salary, a substantial promotion or organizational respect, they justify their work in terms of helping other people, and receive in return (when lucky) respect and appreciation from their bosses, sociability from their co-workers, and the self-satisfaction of knowing they have done a good job. It is around these kinds of emotional gifts that relatively simple technical skills—typing, filing and answering phones—are organized and given meaning. And it is their social and interpersonal skills that employers look for (but do not pay for) when hiring and firing their secretaries. Such constitutes the 'craft of love.'

VDT operators, however, work primarily with a machine, not with other people. Structurally isolated from the tasks, people and purposes that make up an organization, their work often feels 'trivial' and 'pointless', their job just a way to make money. Rather than helping another person (a person they never see), they are simply typing away:

'And now that I've been doing it for eight months, it really does get kind of tedious. It's the same thing every day, every hour. You finish one letter and there's another letter. It's either a letter or memo; the form never varies.'

Maureen Woo

Priding themselves on doing a good job within the constraints open to them, in keeping their productivity up and their error count down, in arriving at work on time, and in 'sticking it out,' VDT operators, like secretaries, learn to find satisfaction at work. But the satisfaction they find is extrinsic to the job. Mostly they like the hours of work ('it's only seven hours and thirteen minutes'), the absence of close personal supervision ('she doesn't watch us like a hawk'), or the 'relaxed, friendly atmosphere' of their center. Yet none of these are sources of intrinsic gratification, and none of them lasts very long. Ahead always looms the possibility of making a little more money, or learning a little different machine, or finding another job. Unlike secretaries who are motivated to do well because their boss needs them, depends upon them, or appreciates what they do, VDT operators are motivated because they need the income, they want the experience, they like the hours. The hand is severed from the heart. But where has love gone?

NOTES

1 Research for this project was funded by a Lena Lake Forrest Dissertation Fellowship from the Business and Professional Women's Foundation. I wish to thank the Foundation for its generous support; the views expressed in this paper are the author's and do not necessarily reflect those of the Foundation.

2 Names of all respondents and their bosses have been changed to protect confidentiality.

3 Statistical data on the size and racial composition of the US clerical labor force come from the US Bureau of Labor Statistics, *Employment and Earnings*, 33:1 (January 1986), Table 22 (Employed civilians by detailed occupation, sex, race and Hispanic origin, 1985), 175–9. British data is from the Office of Population Censuses and Surveys, Registrar General for Scotland, *Census 1981: Economic Activity: Great Britain*. London: Her Majesty's Stationery Office, 1984, Table 8 (Usually resident population economically active: occupation orders and groups by sex), 176–8.

4 *Employment and Earnings*, op.cit.

REFERENCES

Arnold, Erik, Charlotte Huggett, Peter Senker, Nuala Swords-Isherwood and Christine Zmroczek Shannon. 1982. *Microelectronics and Women's Employment in Britain*. SPRU Occasional Paper Series no. 17. Social Science Policy Research Unit : University of Sussex.

Barker, Jane and Hazel Downing. 1980. 'Word processing and the transformation of the patriarchial relations of control in the office.' *Capital and Class* 10, 64–99.

Burgess, Charles. 1985. 'Skill implications of new technology.' *Employment Gazette* 93:10 (October), 397–403.

Cohen, Barbara G.F. 1984. *Human Aspects in Office Automation*. Elsevier Series in Office Automation, 1. New York and Oxford: 1984.

Feldberg, Rosalyn and Evelyn Glenn. 1983. 'Technology and work degradation: effects of office automation on women clerical workers.' In Joan Rothschild, ed. *Machina Ex Dea: Feminist Perspectives on Technology*. New York: Pergamon Press, 59–78.

Gregory, Judith and Karen Nussbaum. 1982. 'Race against time.

Automation of the office.' *Office: Technology and People* 1:2&3 (September), 197-236.

Harvard Medical School. 1983. 'VDTs—a new social disease.' *Harvard Medical School Health Letter* 8:5, 1-2, 5.

Howard, Robert. 1985. *Brave New Workplace*. New York : Viking.

Kanter, Rosabeth Moss. 1977. *Men and Women of the Corporation*. New York: Basic Books.

Machung, Anne. 1983. 'From psyche to technic: The politics of office work.' PhD diss. Dept of Political Science: University of Wisconsin-Madison.

Machung, Anne. 1984. 'Word processing: forward for business, backward for women.' In Karen Sacks and Dorothy Remy, eds. *My Troubles Are Going to Have Trouble With Me*. New Brunswick, New Jersey: Rutgers University Press, 124-39.

Menzies, Heather. 1981. *Women and the Chip: Case Studies on the Effects of Informatics on Employment in Canada*. Montreal: Institute for Research on Public Policy.

Murphree, Mary. 1984. 'Brave new office: the changing world of the legal secretary.' In Karen Sacks and Dorothy Remy, eds. *My Troubles Are Going To Have Trouble With Me*. New Brunswick, New Jersey: Rutgers University Press, 140-59.

Office of Population Censuses and Surveys, Registrar General Scotland. 1984. *Census 1981. Economic Activity, Great Britain*. London: Her Majesty's Stationery Office.

Professional Secretaries International. 1981. *The Nugget: Newsletter for the Golden Gate Chapter*, San Francisco (April).

Stellman, Jeanne and Mary Sue Henifin. 1984. *Office Work Can Be Dangerous To Your Health*. New York: Pantheon Books.

US Congress, Office of Technology Assessment. 1985. *Automation of America's Offices*. Washington, DC: US Government Printing Office (OTA-CIT-287).

US Dept of Labor. 1985. *Women and Office Automation: Issues for the Decade Ahead*. Washington, DC: Women's Bureau.

US Dept of Labor. 1986. *Employment and Earnings* 33:1 (January), 175-9.

Wernecke, Diane. 1984. *Microelectronics and Office Jobs: The Impact of the Chip on Women's Employment*. Geneva: International

Labor Office.

Working Women. 1981. *Warning: Health Hazards for Office Workers*. Cleveland, Ohio: Working Women.

Zuboff, Shoshannah. 1982. 'Problems of symbolic toil: how people fare with computer-mediated work.' *Dissent* 29:1 (Winter), 51–61.

JUDY SMITH and ELLEN BALKA

CHATTING ON A FEMINIST COMPUTER NETWORK

'I never thought about computers this way before.'
(A Women's Studies student, 1984)

Women have been creative in finding ways to send messages to each other. Whatever it is called, network building among women has been around for a long time, with the use of many types of transmission, from information exchanges at the well to washroom mirror notices, to the operation of international communication systems for women during the 1985 Women's Forum in Nairobi. Now, often the messages exchanged are *about* how messages are or can be exchanged, including discussions about communication technology. The well-attended Technology and Tools event at the Nairobi conference, and the special editions on women and technology by the international ISIS Collective, and *Connections: An International Women's Quarterly* are evidence that these discussions are not limited to any country or hemisphere.[1]

In many countries literacy rates for women are very low, posing special problems for communication among isolated rural women, and for poor women. Even in countries with high literacy rates women have very limited access to mass media and have to use a multitude of conventional and non-conventional methods to exchange information. We read predictions in men's periodicals that the new communication technology will have a democratizing effect, eventually allowing everyone near equal access to information. But while men are perfecting telecommunication systems for their own uses, many women worry that they will be left using typewriters and the slow postal system. By 1983, the US Department of Defense had spent $25 million just to institute a common computer language for all their computers.[2] Meanwhile women's community service groups are making do with manual filing systems and very limited telephone and mailing budgets.

However, some women's groups, increasingly aware of the pos-

sibilities and necessities of using new technology in order to organize and share experiences and resources, are planning interest and
political action networks. In this paper we discuss a Canadian-US
effort to establish a feminist computer network to share information
on women and technology. First Judy describes her strategies for feminist assessment of technology and for the uses of computers to
help individuals and social change groups save time and mobilize
resources. Then Ellen describes her work designing a feminist computer network. Both Judy and Ellen address the question: can there
be sisterhood in computer talk?

JUDY: FEMINIST ASSESSMENT OF TECHNOLOGY

I don't think of my computer as a person, it's a machine. I'm not a
hacker. I don't choose to spend time with my computer rather than
with people. On my off time I'd rather be outside hiking around on
a sunny day or inside reading a book when the sun's not around.
But I like my computer. When I do think about it, positive images
and feelings come to mind. It has its room and when I'm in that
room I'm working. The computer makes my work easier and helps
keep me in touch with people. That's my work: educating and organizing people.

For more than nine years I have been educating and organizing
about technology and its impacts on women. Several of us in the US
Northwest have been working to develop a feminist assessment of
technology (Bush 1983; Smith 1983). Decisions about science and
technology affect our lives and we must be involved if we are ever to
have our interests represented in those decisions. We can't afford to
ignore or refuse to participate in this decision making because of
technophobia, math anxiety, or political purity. Not that we have
to become producers of science and technology—the scientists and
engineers—although some of us may. We must become techno-
literate, educated consumers, able to understand, advocate and participate in public decision making about science and technology.

It's no longer news that technology affects women differently
from men. In this culture, as in most, women have different experiences from men, different roles, needs and interests. Therefore technological processes, from cars to contraceptives, have specific impacts on women. As this volume attests, there's a growing body of
literature identifying and examining these differential impacts. (See
also Zimmerman 1983.)

Methodologies for assessing the impact of technologies on so-

83

ciety have been developed and technology assessment has become a professional field of study. People who do technology assessments rarely, if ever, have asked what impact a particular technological development would have on women and on the home and family, the institutions of society that have been traditionally seen as women's (Balka 1985).

I've suggested the development of a *Sex Role Impact Statement* (SRIS) that would be used just like the Environmental Impact Statement (EIS) which is legally required by many public agencies before development decisions can be made. The environmental movement made the EIS an important public policy tool; the feminist movement could do the same with a SRIS.[3] The central question would be: what effect would this development have on sex roles?

Would it broaden or restrict women's traditional options?
Would it increase or limit women's chances for economic self-
sufficiency?
Would it decrease or increase the time needed for home and
family maintenance?
Would it increase or decrease women's mobility?
Would it reduce or increase women's privatization in the home?
Would this development be dangerous to women's health?
Would it make sex roles more interchangeable so that either
women or men could do what needed to be done or
would it re-enforce traditional sex role stereotyping
and division of labor?

Some technologies have obvious sex role impact, such as contraception and domestic electrification. Others are not so obvious in their effect, like mass transit and diesel tractors, for example.[4] In most cases, there's a balance of costs and benefits that needs to be assessed and alternatives proposed that minimize the negative impacts.

And then there are the ecological concerns about technology. As the implements and systems of technology have gotten bigger, more complex, and more energy- and capital-intensive, our society has faced the realities of resource depletion, pollution and toxic waste. In the past we thought that bigger was better and there were no limits to growth. We relied on a belief in tech fixes—that technology can take care of all our problems. We believed that the experts could come up with solutions for whatever happened.

Now that we are familiar with nuclear power disasters, spreading toxic dumps, destroyed farmland, and acres and acres of cement and high rises, we're beginning to understand that the tech fixes themselves are a large part of the problem, and the experts aren't really the ones who should be making the decisions. More and more of us realize that quality of life isn't measured by the size or number of the technologies we use. We're looking for a sustainable society that won't destroy the environment or use up the available resources, a society where we can feel we have some sort of control over what happens.

The people who are concerned about the negative effects of large-scale technology are proposing a new standard for technological development. They propose that technology be appropriate: that the size and complexity should fit the end use of the technology (e.g. Don't use nuclear power to make electricity to heat a room. Use a solar collector or burn wood instead). They are developing a set of criteria for what would make a technology appropriate: small as possible, non-polluting, reliance on renewable resources, locally controlled, labor–intensive. Unfortunately, these appropriate technology advocates have not yet integrated sex role impact into their criteria for appropriateness (Smith 1978).

To do feminist technology assessment we need to blend sex role impact concerns with appropriate technology criteria. We need to develop a process that assesses particular technological developments, proposes alternatives that minimize negative impacts, and mobilizes women to become involved in the decisions surrounding the implementation of the technology.

The selling of women and computers

Computers are a mix of costs and benefits for women. Depending on whom you talk to, you hear of the marvels of the communication age or the degradation of the workplace and concentration of power in the hands of the power elite. One feminist I visited with recently was of the computerphile school. She was going back to a university to learn computers and told me she didn't accept the analysis that the automated office was a major problem for women. I more often run into the computerphobe feminist who dismisses any liberating potential a computer might have. In fact, much of the feminist focus on computers seems to be on the negative impacts.

85

There doesn't seem to be as much energy going into developing feminist computer applications as I would expect, and I think part of the reason is a general feminist unease about technology.

There is, of course, reason to be uneasy. The selling of the automated office is an excellent example of the traditional lack of concern for technological impact on women. The ads have been pitched to management, of course; we see the before shot of the typing pool of ten to fifteen women and the after shot of the one woman and the computer. Wonderful: displace fourteen women with a computer. Oh well, the computer salesperson says, technology always creates new jobs so those women can just go out and find other employment. And besides, those weren't really great jobs anyway.

No one mentioned that it was specifically women's jobs that were being displaced—the very jobs that women have increasingly filled in the last twenty years. The automated office has the potential to displace a significant percentage of the women who work outside the home (Gregory 1983; Menzies 1981). The new jobs that are created by computers don't require the skills these women have. When employers automate their offices they rarely offer retraining or job placement for those displaced. What are these women to do? Most have taken jobs out of economic necessity; a growing number are single heads of families. They've been making low wages and have very few economic resources. These women are often the least able to find other employment.

And for the women who keep their jobs in the office, the nature of the work itself may be degraded. 'Deskilling' is the term. Instead of doing a variety of tasks as a secretary, the job may become totally routinized, the worker simply entering key strokes (see Machung this volume). Work may be monitored through the computer (the number of key strokes/time measured) so the office job becomes much more like piece work in a factory. In fact, Barbara Garson (1981) in her article 'The electronic sweatshop' concludes that 'the office of the future is the factory of the past.' And there may well be health hazards involved. Sitting in front of a VDT (video display terminal) hour after hour is known to cause eyestrain and some believe can cause birth defects and other serious problems (National Women's Health Network 1984).

The automated office is only one example of the computer displacing women's jobs. Bank tellers, phone operators and airline reservation clerks are all affected. The places in the economy where women have been able to find employment are the very places easi-

86

est to computerize. They're the low-skill, dead-end jobs with re-petitive, routine tasks with little decision making. It's true they're not the jobs that we particularly want, but they're what women have in order to support themselves.

Displacement and deskilling don't have to be the major results of computer applications in the office. Computers could be used as a way to save on labor costs to better use the time of a more skilled workforce. Part of the problem, of course, is that office workers have little to say about how office work is done. Like many women's occupations, office work has little status and is not well paid. Very few office workers are unionized and so it is difficult for them as a group to influence company or agency decision making (see Davies this volume). However, if office workers were able to work with management to decide how computer technology would be applied in their worksites, things could be done differently. Jobs could be structured to ensure that everyone had a variety of tasks to do; in the time saved, new skills could be regularly developed to broaden each employee's occupational options; healthful worksta-tions could be established and policies adopted that minimized any health hazards associated with VDTs, and training and job place-ment services could be offered to employees whose positions were lost.

9 to 5, a leader in organizing and educating office workers about the potential hazards of the automated office, is working overtime to see that US office workers have some say about how computer technology is implemented in their offices. Internationally, women's groups and unions are doing similar organizing. An edi-torial in the new Uruguayan feminist quarterly *La Cacerola* states, 'We emphasize the effects of this changing technology on our lives as women. We are faced by a new technology (micro-electronics) which will deskill, reduce or even completely do away with existing jobs. We reserve the right to be retrained, and not fired' (quoted in 'Retrained, not fired' 1985).

Another potential negative impact on women of certain applica-tions of computer technology is the further concentration of power in the hands of those who already have so much control. A govern-ment, a large corporation, or anyone with enough resources can gather a great deal of information about any of us. Anything that denies access to computers, that makes computers expensive or hard to use, that keeps certain groups from learning the skills to use computers, works to concentrate power for those who can buy the technology and the people to run it.

The socialization of girls to avoid machines and mathematics is one example of how power is concentrated in male hands. As Deborah Brecher, author of *Women's Computer Literacy Handbook* puts it,

> Not all women are afraid of computers but they are often more afraid than men because of the culture in which they've been raised. That culture says to them, starting early in childhood, 'Machines are part of a man's world. Who fixes cars? Men. Who fixes typewriters? Men.' Women become afraid that they will break a complicated, expensive piece of machinery. (Brecher 1985)

Empowerment tools

However, if information is power, it can be used to empower as well as control. Power can flow up and down and around in an information system depending on how it's designed. If everyone gets and manages all the information, power is not concentrated.

Computer technology does increase access to information and what we can do with that information. For the first time, even here in Missoula, Montana, I can be hooked up with feminists throughout the country and around the world. I can share resources; I can know I'm not alone. This is a particularly significant kind of information to share. For those of us who are part of social change movements, who often don't feel a part of much of the culture around us, we need to know there are lots more of us out here. I can live most anywhere, places where feminists are few and far between, and still be part of a feminist reality. Then I don't have to depend on the commercial media which I already know denies me information about feminist projects. Literacy is an empowerment tool for the disenfranchised; that's why so many Third World liberation groups have literacy campaigns. Computer literacy can be the same type of liberating force for women in a technological society.

Computers can give women an opportunity to learn to manage technology: to gain a new competence in an area where many women are reluctant to enter. Learning to make decisions about one technology helps us feel that there are ways to make decisions about and control other technologies.

Computers can help individuals save time. My word processing and mailing list computer programs are invaluable to me. And now with networking capability, I don't have to rely on the copy machine and the mail to share what I know or get the word out quickly. I can have access to a feminist library, I can check on the latest developments on a full range of feminist issues, I can leave a message for other rural feminists to call me and talk. Using a computer network doesn't mean you never actually call or visit people. Studies and personal reports suggest people probably do more personal communicating because of the 'high tech, high touch' phenomenon (Dillman 1985). Computer network members keep in touch with four or five times as many people as they would otherwise. As an organizer, this is particularly important to me. Many new options open up when we can support women who want to make their own choices wherever they live, when we can help them feel part of a movement that is alive and growing even in rural areas.

Computers can also help social change groups save time and mobilize resources. I think of the women I talk to from small towns in Montana and Wyoming who tell me they want to do something on women's issues but the hardest part is not having other feminist women around. Often they just stop talking about what's important to them; they give up the expectation that change is possible. I think of all those resources we have in small towns and rural areas that aren't used because we can't offer the needed support. A feminist computer network and bulletin board could help mobilize those resources for all kinds of educational and political activity.

I dream of a pro–choice bulletin board to use to alert all members of the local pro–choice organization about phone calls and letters needed to be sent to legislators, upcoming marches, and clinic support efforts. I would simply put the message on the bulletin board and update as necessary. (I've read of someone calling out 150 citizens to a community meeting by using one bulletin board message and no phone calls.) When we need to mobilize large numbers of people, computers give us possibilities we didn't have before. Perhaps we can reach some sort of critical mass with the numbers mobilized as we did during the anti-Vietnam War protests, which forced the policy makers to react?

Other social change groups have realized the potentials of computer networks for organizing. For example, an Indigenous People's Computer Network, dedicated to the needs of the Native community, provides a link to the Indigenous Press Network and a

Weekly Report of national and international Indian news items (P.O. Box 71, Highland, MD 20777). A new network designed specifically for the US Peace Movement, PeaceNet, is recruiting members (1644 Emerson, Suite 32, Palo Alto, CA 94301). There's also the Community Memory Project dedicated to providing an alternative communication utility that provides community communication between user groups. According to their newsletter *Community Memory News* (1985), they've installed three public access terminals and 'each month each terminal gets about 600 uses and over 1000 new messages added to the data base.' They are now planning to install two more terminals and simple coin box mechanisms to help make the system self-supporting (2617 San Pablo Avenue, Berkeley, CA 94702).

We've been talking about a feminist network and bulletin board for a number of years. We do have a mailing list and literacy project (National Women's Mailing List and Women's Computer Literacy Project, 1195 Valencia Street, San Francisco, CA 94110). Women's art organizations are trying to establish a national alliance linked by computer. This project, TARTS/Teaching Artists to Reach Technological Savvy, plans to develop a national database on women artists and create a computer bulletin board listing for jobs and exhibition (Women's Studio Workshop, P.O. Box V, Rosendale, New York 12473).

And now a women and technology computer network project is starting up. It's more specialized than a feminist network and bulletin board but it's a beginning. We'll have a chance to see what can evolve and how we can make the network as accessible as possible. This means the necessary hardware and software has to be available and relatively inexpensive and that the system be easy to learn.

I'm not too worried that computer chatting on a feminist computer network will be depersonalizing. Our use of the word 'chatting' is a good example; the women I work with use that term instead of 'messaging' or something more technical. Further, since users will never really see, hear or touch each other, we want to design our system so it allows for personalities to emerge, and emotions to show. We'll have to develop some new non–verbal signals. Or maybe we can design a feminist graphics package that can add in the emotional cues. (This is my favorite feminist computer application at the moment.) We'll also need user–generated categories rather than relying on those provided with most software programs. We have to be able to exchange whatever type of information seems relevant to feminist communication.

I work in a building with a number of feminists. We check in with each other on a regular basis; at least every day we say hello, find out what's happening, talk about the latest news about women, etc. We're a form of community; we offer each other support, and occasionally work together on a political event or cultural project. That's how I view chatting on the feminist computer network: checking in, exchanging ideas, telling a few stories, asking for help on a project, creating community.

It's too early to tell how *our* computer networks and bulletin boards may be different than others. I do know that feminist communication in the forms now available tends to stress interaction, re-definition, and cooperation. We're striving to design these options into our computer communications.

ELLEN: A CASE STUDY OF A 'WOMEN AND TECHNOLOGY NETWORK'

My interest in electronic networks began in 1982, shortly after I began working with computers. I imagined that computers might allow me to stay in touch more easily with other women who were concerned about how women historically and presently were affected by technological change. The best way to do this, it seemed to me, was through a computer network.

However, my general background in technological change and my experiences with other technologies suggested that computer communication networks, to date, were designed without consideration of women.

Feeling a need to provide a network which women would use, I have become involved in designing and planning a computer network. The Women and Technology Computer Network will allow geographically dispersed women with access to computers to communicate about a wide variety of issues related to technological change.

We hope to provide a service which will allow participants to (1) access bibliographies on a variety of topics, (2) access lists of network participants, interests and current activities, (3) have ongoing dialogues with network participants on topics related to women and technological change, (4) collaborate on writing and other projects, and (5) share information about conferences, recent publications, work opportunities and other activities related to women and technological change.

As a starting point in designing a computer communications network, we have prepared a one-page summary of our goals, attached to a brief questionnaire. The questionnaire asks potential users questions about their needs for computers, access to computers and modems, and, most important, questions about what topics they would like included and what services they'd like a computer network to provide. With adequate outreach, this technique should allow potential users to have a great deal of input into the design process.

One nice thing about computer networking is that it lends itself well to being participant-controlled. For example, rather than considering ourselves 'in charge' of a service, we can view ourselves as facilitators of a process. Participants could determine what topics they'd like to discuss, as well as what topics for which they'd like to build bibliographies. They could also decide which topics a book or article should be catalogued under. Users could elect to receive mail only from people they designated, or from anyone. They could elect only to read mail directed to them, or only general announcements, and they could elect to make their messages and comments public or private.

In a system that isn't user-controlled, users have to go through a petition process or lobby to have a portion of the computer and financial resources set aside for their group's interest. A person or persons are then designated to manage whatever goes on. From my use of commercial services it isn't at all clear how these people are selected, or what they do besides restrict people with foul language and disorderly conduct from using the network.

But will computer networks result in dehumanized communication?

While it is often assumed that something inherent to computers prohibits all forms of personal communication, from my experience and Judy's, this hasn't been so. 'Signing on' to my university's computer system to check my mail and send messages has become a part of my everyday life. My day-to-day use of computers for communication falls into three categories. First, I chat with people on the computer when I need a technical question answered about the computer. In this case messages usually aren't personal, though they may be humorous. Second, I send messages which fall loosely into a category I call maintenance of daily life—changing meeting times, arranging carpooling to school, and so on. And lastly, I use

92

the computer for maintaining personal contact with friends who are hard to reach. These messages contain everything from the dream a friend had last night to her latest frustration with the women's movement.

It is often assumed that using a computer will render communications less personal than writing letters or phoning. I have found that computer messages (especially the equivalent to memos and other forms of communication which contain content which normally isn't very personal) tend to be less formal than their typed or handwritten counterparts. I suspect two factors may lead to this. First, unlike a memo or a letter which exists on a piece of paper which is sent to someone who is expected to file it somewhere, computer messages are often sent with the assumption that they will be either read and destroyed, or else saved on a individual's computer, where the message will not be widely accessible. In this sense computer messages become more private, which accommodates a more informal approach. Second, computers don't always do what we want them to; this being the case, there seems to be a general tolerance of occasional sloppiness. As with other technologies, the impacts are mixed; I find the informality of computer messages refreshing, while I worry a little about the long-term effects of tolerated sloppiness.

What are the advantages of computer communications for women?

I am frequently asked why I communicate by computer rather than by phone or by mail. Telephones, while offering the users the potential for very personal interaction, are also potentially disruptive. When I call Judy in Missoula, I may reach her when she's in the middle of a meeting but has forgotten to unplug her phone or turn on her answering machine. Or, I may call her and not reach her, which means I have to keep trying. If I send a message by computer, I avoid having to call back if the person I'm trying to reach isn't in. I don't have to worry about calling at a bad time, and I don't have to worry about what time it is on the other end.

In addition, computers can be a less expensive way to reach someone. (This depends on whether or not the communications network being used is a profit-making enterprise.) If I phone Judy in Missoula from Vancouver after 6 p.m. and talk for six minutes, it costs $2.57. If I call the university computer after 6 p.m. and spend six minutes writing her a message, it costs me 12c to send, and less for her to read. In Canada it costs 39c to mail a letter to the US, and usually takes a minimum of ten days to be delivered. So, if it is a short message, it is less expensive and much more timely than the mail. If I were sending a long message, I would compose it on my computer, and then upload it and 'post' it, which would minimize the time I'd spend connected to a host system I'm paying to send messages through.

Computer communications offer other advantages. If I want to send the same letter to several people, without the use of a computer I would either have to write to each one and then mail them all, or I'd have to send a form letter to each one. In order to send a letter to several people on the computer (using the message system I currently use), I type 'Send.' The computer responds with the prompt 'To?' At that point I can specify a single name, several names, the name of a group which is listed elsewhere on the message system, or *all*, for all the people who use the message system. I then compose the message, edit it if necessary, and then type 'post.' The computer then replies that my message has been posted. This would be a very appropriate way to notify people about a conference, or to ask for help locating a copy of a hard-to-find article.

Another positive use of computer communications is conferencing. I may be interested in finding out about others' experiences in teaching women how to assess technological change. To do this, I would call up the host computer, and select the option which allows me to begin a forum. Next, I would briefly describe the topics of the forum, and then I would leave a message or some comments. I could set up the forum so that anyone could access it, or only some people could. If someone else was interested in the topic, they would call up the host computer, access the forum program, and either respond to my comment or simply leave a comment related to the topic. In this way, geographically dispersed women can have ongoing dialogues.

How can computer networks be improved for women's needs?
One of the services I would like us to provide is information to potential users explaining the features of modems and communications software. My assumption here is that demystifying the service will increase its use. In addition, I'd like to provide information about communications software which should be avoided (because it is either difficult to use, or is obscure and cannot be used with a variety of host computers), and software which is free, and compa-

tible with our host computer. Typically, these issues are not addressed and consequently the availability of networks is reduced.

Another thing which limits access to computer networks is costs. Virtually all commercially available services charge a one-time hook-up fee. The average is Canadian $50, and one news network charges $75 to sign up. Occasionally, these fees can be avoided—I recently bought an inexpensive cable which allowed me an hour free on each of two services, and waived the hook-up fee if I kept my accounts open. Most of the services offer only two methods of payment—by credit card, or by 'check-free,' a service which allows the computer network to directly bill your checking account. In Canada, one can only pay by credit card, which eliminates a substantial number of potential users.

Once an account is established with a commercial network, the user is charged per minute. One might assume it would be wise to have a fast modem, since it would mean fewer minutes would be spent using the service. In fact, the commercial networks charge a higher per minute rate for faster modems. In addition, a higher rate is charged for daytime use. Some services charge a minimum monthly fee ($10 to $15) and all of the services charge you more if you call from a place, such as a rural area, that doesn't have a special phone line sponsored by that network.

We hope to avoid high costs by operating on a non-profit basis. Ideally, we will provide our service for free. This can be accomplished by securing sponsorship which comes in the form of donated computer time. For example, a group of high school teachers concerned about computers and education has such an arrangement with the University of British Columbia, which donates computer time to groups for educational purposes.

In addition to computer time, other costs include writing documentation about how to use the system, initially entering information (such as bibliographies) onto the computer, and possibly salary for someone to answer queries. With the exception of the salary for a trouble shooter, the costs are one-time costs. Paying off these bills will no doubt require some creativity. For example, we may be able to take advantage of a summer job creation program. Or, we might be able to make an arrangement with a local women's group which has a library on women and technological change.

It is essential that we keep in mind that technology in general, and computer technology in particular, affects the organization of work. A computer network which encourages its users to do tasks previously done by a clerical worker or a postal worker or an airline clerk (many of whom are women) could contradict women's efforts to ensure adequate employment for women. While a network can be designed to meet women's needs, if in using it these concerns are not taken seriously, it will cease to be an appropriate use of the technology. We can avoid this situation by using Judy's Sex Role Impact Statement, by discussing the feminist network project with workers who might be affected by the network, and by working to make the network accessible to women. We want computer networks that are compatible with feminism.

NOTES

1   ISIS International. 1982. 'Women and new technology.' *ISIS Women's International Bulletin (no.24)*. (ISIS International, Via Santa Maria dell'Anima, 30, 00186 Rome, Italy). People's Translation Service. 1985. 'Changing technology.' *Connexions: An International Women's Quarterly* 2 (Winter). (Connexions, 4228 Telegraph Avenue, Oakland, CA 94609).

2   Reported by Sharon Begley in *Newsweek*, 10 January 1983, 71.

3   There is much discussion about the term *sex role*, because it has been used by some writers to imply built-in behavior linked to biological sex. In my work with the SRIS concept, I use the term *sex role* to describe the experiences and interests women have as a result of the role this society has traditionally assigned to women.

4   Women, who as a group have fewer financial resources than men and often don't own reliable cars, are more dependent on mass transit for their mobility. Transportation costs and accessibility for themselves and their children are significant factors for many women when deciding where they can afford to look for employment. (See the essay by the Women and Transport Forum this volume.) Women's role in farm production is restricted with the advent of large-scale farm machinery which is not considered suitable for women to operate.

REFERENCES

Balka, Ellen. 1985. 'Technology assessment in the United States: a feminist perspective.' Unpublished paper. Vancouver: Simon Fraser University.

Brecher, Deborah. 1985. *Women's Computer Literacy Handbook*. New York: Plume.

Bush, Corlann Gee. 1983. 'Women and the assessment of technology: to think, to be, to unthink, to free.' In Joan Rothschild, ed. *Machina Ex Dea: Feminist Perspectives on Technology*. New York: Pergamon, 151–70.

Community Memory Project. 1985. 'New community network gets good response.' *Community Memory News* (no. 2).

Dillman, Don. 1985. 'The social impacts of information technologies in rural North America.' *Rural Sociology* 50:1, 27–37.

Garson, Barbara. 1981. 'The electronic sweatshop.' *The Best of Mother Jones*. San Francisco: Foundation for National Progress, 28–39.

Gregory, Judith. 1983. 'The next move: organizing women in the office.' In Jan Zimmerman, ed. *The Technological Woman: Interfacing With Tomorrow*. New York: Praeger, 260–72.

ISIS International. 1984. 'Women in action.' *Women's Journal Supplement* (no. 1), 36.

Menzies, Heather. 1981. 'Women and the chip: case studies of the effects of informatics on employment in Canada.' Montreal: Institute on Public Policy Research.

National Women's Health Network. 1984. 'New video display terminal data.' *Network News* (January/February), 14.

'Retrained, not fired.' 1985. *Connexions* 7 (Winter).

Smith, Judy. 1978. *Something Old, Something New, Something Borrowed, Something Due: Women and Appropriate Technology*. Missoula, Montana Women and Technology Project.

Smith, Judy. 1983. 'Women and appropriate technology: A feminist assessment.' In Jan Zimmerman, ed. *The Technological Woman: Interfacing With Tomorrow*. New York: Praeger, 65–70.

Zimmerman, Jan, ed. 1983. *The Technological Woman: Interfacing With Tomorrow*. New York: Praeger.

MARK SCHULMAN

GENDER AND TYPOGRAPHIC CULTURE: BEGINNING TO UNRAVEL THE 500-YEAR MYSTERY

For us to create a feminist space where women in the print trades can share and increase power, make new connections and revive spirits to survive Reaganismo, there is one deadly problem. MONEY.... If we don't have the down payment by May 7, thus endeth one of the greatest feminist fantasies ever conceived—when, just think, it would be a part of everyone's memoirs. So send in your money for a historic conference in the home of the Free Speech Movement, this time of women's voice.

(Mailing for the Third National Women in Print Conference, 1985)

AN ACT OF IMAGINATION

Imagine, if you can, that this book does not exist. Imagine that there are no other books either, no pamphlets, no magazines, no newspapers.

There are no cutely worded greeting cards, no colorfully packaged products, no risk-no-money matchbook covers, no strikingly designed posters, no buy-me-to-be-beautiful advertisements.

No calendars, horoscopes, almanacs, dictionaries, encyclopedias, scientific or mathematical tables, maps.

Bookstores and newsstands, libraries and archives, schools and universities do not exist.

Alphabets have not been invented.

If we could imagine this world, we would know what it was like to live in a culture of orality/aurality.

After suitable contemplation of that world, we might repopulate our imaginary cosmos with some but not many of the things we had dissolved shortly before. We would reinvent the alphabet, hand-written books for a tiny elite of men (not a generic term here, of course) who also had all the maps, libraries and universities for themselves. In our new brave world, we sense what came after oral-

98

ity, a culture of scribal chirography (or 'handwritten words').

But the worlds of oral and scribal culture are basically unimaginable to us. Five hundred years of living with the technology of print have irrevocably removed us from a consciousness of a lifestyle in which printed materials and their distribution systems are non-existent. As Marshall McLuhan put it, in one of the few of his unending strings of aphorisms with which even his most vehement critics can agree, 'Nobody knows who discovered water, but we are sure it wasn't a fish.'

My task in these brief pages is to introduce the subject of how print affected us. The *specific* effects I am attempting to uncover— one of the major secrets of five centuries of typographic technology—involve issues of gender and communication, of women and print. As with many other aspects of women's relationships to technologies, much of the material which will reveal this information for our analysis is lost or elusive or not yet written. Thus I reach quickly limits on what can be known on the subject.

There is another limit, beyond the depressingly familiar one of the silences in history surrounding women. Our *overall* understanding of print culture's impact on human beings, on other communications technologies, and in the development of social institutions, is sadly inadequate at this moment. On the one fin, this is a limit of fishes explicating water. For us humans, on the other hand, it is a result of the chronic confusion about technology and causality.

Technological causes and effects

What, exactly, does technology *do* to us?

The question, both in general and for communications, remains unresolved. In a sense, it is an epistemological question for which there can be no one, discrete, commonly accepted answer. What we need, therefore, is not an absolute definition but rather a range of possibilities, or a sensitizing concept, for our use.

We can agree that the crucial communications technologies of speech, writing and print transformed relationships in every sphere of human existence (see Leed 1980). We can also agree that the transformations continue with the media of the twentieth century, particularly the electronic configurations of radio, television and other devices of telecommunications, as well as the computer.

The problem comes with the attempt to cite *causes*. Calling a culture 'oral,' because of rhetors, or 'chirographic,' because of scribes, or 'typographic,' because of printers, tends to brand the culture as an *effect* of the technological cause. We cannot solve the question of causality, but we can come to terms with it. Jennifer Slack (1984) has written extensively on the issue:

> I begin by suggesting that we reject the notion of technology as a thing ... we must begin to rearticulate a discourse on technology that does not, while purporting to be treating something other than things, in fact treat things.... I do not want to trade the tyranny of autonomous technology for the tyranny of structures. This means, then, that our discourse on communication technologies must be constructed such that it can acknowledge, where they occur, both correspondences and non-correspondences in the social formation as well as in the relationship between the social formation and the technological. (9)

Much of what has been written by communication scholars on print technology and its impact, particularly in relation to women, tyrannizes with a discourse of thingness. Given these circumstances, the best strategy is to leap in and to do what we can, realizing that, when we reach the end today, large gaps will remain. We can, however, give those who take over tomorrow—among whom may be some of the readers of this book—a leg up. And we can fruitfully begin the detective work by delineating what we now understand about the effect of the technology of printing on women.

UNRAVELLING THE MYSTERY

The dimensions of how print technology contributed to changes in women's communication, and how women have used print to interact in new ways with others, can be considered in the relationships of gender to the creation, production, distribution and consumption of typographic culture. What we know so far on the subject can be categorized in terms of women's roles within those four areas. Working from the point of consumption back to the point of creation, we can start with reading and end with writing. Also requiring attention are a few alternatives to the mainstream pattern. In a sense, we seek clues toward the mystery's solution.

Women as consumers of print
Reading is not the one-dimensional activity it might seem to be at first glance. The 'reading public' is actually a diverse group, and

people read many different things: prices on products, textbooks, billboards, periodicals, newspapers, brand name descriptions, paperbacks, labels, instruction manuals, recipes, video display terminals ... the list goes on and on.

For the first two centuries of print culture, women were excluded from many reading, writing and interpreting activities which were available to men. In this sense, much of the influence of print on women came from the ways that men—husbands, clergy, business proprietors, fathers—used books and other material to construct their own role definitions and the concomitant role definitions for *their* women. Marilyn French in *Beyond Power* assigns motherhood to the centuries of book dissemination: Because women were now confined to the home and to domestic tasks as they had not been since the days of Athens, they were forced to gain their identity solely from their domestic roles. With guidance from a literature of domesticity, they created a new profession—motherhood. In the process childhood was discovered, at least for boys.

This is certainly a significant part of women's interaction, and if it is true it demonstrates arguably the *most* important way print has transformed gender. By the seventeenth and eighteenth centuries, when literacy was spreading among both sexes, women became a large part of the reading public, a concept which needs separate examination for its cultural importance.

In trying to understand the uses of reading, we need to find out more about the time, means and reasons to read that women and men carved out, separately, for themselves. This leads to the private sphere/public sphere dichotomy which divides women in the home and men in the outside world—certainly a factor in the consolidation period of print culture. One of the problems in assessing this aspect is the unreliability of literacy statistics for the period 1600–1800. Protestant leaders believed that girls should learn to read and write, so they could study the Bible and later read it to their children (French 1985, 174). The Reformation and its aftermath was a boon for women's literacy; this affected mainly women of means, however, who sometimes attended schools and often learned from their educated fathers and brothers at home. Of course, what women read, and were taught, was not necessarily a liberating inspiration. In 1675, for example, the London publisher George Sawbridge issued a book by Gervase Markham whose lengthy title says it all:

The English House-Wife, containing the inward and outward Vertues

101

which ought to be in a Compleat Woman: As her Skill in Physick, Chirurgery, Cookery, Extraction of Oyls, Banquetting stuff, Ordering of great Feasts, Preserving all sorts of Wines, conceited Secrets, Distillations, Perfumes, Ordering of Wool, Hemp, Flax; Making Cloth and Dying; the knowledge of Dayries; Office of Malting; of Oats, their excellent uses in Families; of Brewing, Baking and all other things belonging to the Household. A Work generally approved, and now the Eighth Time much Augmented, Purged, and made the most profitable and necessary for all men, and the general good of this Nation. (Ong 1982, 190)

The construction of the masculine and the feminine, symbolized by scientific knowledge/publicness for men and etiquette/ household management for women, accelerated along these lines throughout the 200 years. But there was a contradictory aspect too.

On the one hand, women learned to read and dutifully studied devotional literature and self-improvement works. On the other hand, in a phenomenon that grew as more girls attended school in the eighteenth century, women—particularly in the new middle class—began to read for entertainment. French (1985) cites this time as the birth of the sentimental romance tradition, the roots of which she traces to the twelfth-century literature of 'courtly love' (177–87).

As literacy spread, new kinds of readers and new kinds of literature appeared. This is a complex and not fully understood issue which bears extensive examination. Shirley Brice Heath points out, for example, in 'The functions and uses of literacy' (1980), that print in seventeenth-century France both diffused elements of control but also 'made possible new kinds of control over the people,' based in people's measurement of 'themselves against a widespread norm and ... doubt [of] their own worth' (124). The worth of women in their own self-image as a consequence of norms spread by literacy seems an area to pursue diligently.

The meaning of print for women *consumers* over the last 200 years is a vast topic which I can only outline here. By the 1800s, women in most countries of Europe and in the US were the majority of the reading public, though the variance by class was tremendous: poor women were usually illiterate. But with the spread of universal education (which is a primary book-place in Western culture) and the growth of mass circulation magazines and newspapers (related directly to the transformations of print technology), women readers were the first market which publishers eyed.

Today women in the US are more likely than men to be literate, and more likely than men to read books as well as periodicals. Women are also, more often than not, the target audience of print advertising, not only in women's magazines but also in general circulation publications.

Women are consumers of massive amounts of print. We are only beginning to understand the ways that consumption has changed their consciousness and their interactions with others over the last five centuries of print culture.

Women as distributors of print

Without the printing press, three modern institutions (among others) would not exist: the bookstore, the library and the school.

Within the histories of those institutions, women's communication needs to become a developed theme. For bookstores, women today represent the main clientele as the major consumers of books, as well as the labor force for the low-paid positions as clerks in most of the chains which dominate the trade. The history of the transition from coffee houses (which were the bookish places of England several centuries ago, and were a male domain) to the modern bookstore (which serves a suburban population in the US in shopping malls, which are a female domain) will be a part of the print distribution/gender story.

Librarians in the popular image are women: it is true that the occupational category is dominated by women, but, like most industries, the higher levels of the public and university library are male enclaves. Important for an understanding of women's communication, however, is an analysis of how the female librarian as book distributor developed over the centuries, and the consequences for women as workers. Also important is the study of women as patrons, particularly mothers who bring their children to libraries for story hours and to check out books to read to them at home. There are sure to be class and ethnic differences in both the occupational and clientele categories which will need clarification, too.

As elementary school teachers, women are on the front line of educating girls (and boys, too, of course). Print technology is the overwhelming pedagogical mode in education, as it has been for centuries, despite the media's portrayal of an infatuation with computers and audio-visual technology in the schools. Textbooks are part of the water that we human fishes tend to overlook: one estimate found 250,000,000 textbooks for the 50,000,000 US elementary and high school students in the late 1960s (Olson 1980, 189). The same study found books occupied 75 percent of school time and 90 percent of homework time; a study of high school science classes in the 1970s revealed that 90 percent of the teachers used a textbook approach despite the educational rhetoric about 'discovery learning' (Olson 1980, 190). Occupationally and as pupils, women and girls communicate around and through print technology in every school at every level on every day. That is a profound influence which we need to understand, as it developed historically, and as it exists today.

One other distribution role needs to be mentioned: women as censors. The history of censorship of print materials will reveal, I think, disproportionate impacts on and participation by women. There is also the self-censorship of women writers who believed they were 'not good enough' to create, because they bought patriarchal lies. And any treatment of censorship will have to consider the current difficult controversy over pornography in which some women have provided leadership in the movement to legalize governmental repression of certain printed (and electronic) materials.

Women as producers of print

We know that throughout the five centuries of print we can discover women who were producers. What impact on their attitudes and interactions did this production capability induce? Was a print shop supervised or owned by a woman different than that of a man? Did women printers and publishers produce dissimilar materials to men's? Though we have clues to the answers, we need to piece the puzzle together for an historical view.

Only in the last two centuries, in fact, were there clear and separate roles for publishing and printing. Women in publishing is a subcategory that requires full and discrete treatment. A chapter in *Books: The Culture and Commerce of Publishing* (Coser et al. 1982), 'Women in book publishing: a qualified success story,' provides an excellent sketch of the parameters of that occupational story.

In this category, too, gender issues need to be played out against the labor stratification that has occurred throughout history, with women clumped at the bottom and (in publishing, at least) the middle of the employment pyramid. Also to be explained is the relationship of transformations of printing technology to women as producers and consumers. The effect of print culture was not just with the invention of movable types; changes of the last 200 years have also contributed to massive realignments. Radical books and magazines, for example, as part of the working-class movement arose with both political and technological conditions, as did the mass newspaper of the last century. Offset technology and gravure, which have replaced letterpress as the print technology of choice in most advanced capitalist countries, demand different labor forces and produce more and divergent (typographically and visually) materials. For instance, women engaged in the new electronic typesetting occupations—which have emerged over the last decade as a female-dominated craft—are replacing the male linotypists and compositors throughout the industry.

Women as creators of print

Of all the categories I have mentioned, women as writers is the one about which feminist scholarship has provided the most detail in the last two decades.

Rediscovery of women writers throughout print's history, and of the relationship of women to forms of fiction (the novel in particular and romances within that genre), has been a happy result of such scholarship. Gender as an appropriate category for literary criticism, and the revalorization of the subjects deemed relevant and the approaches recognized as appropriate, are evolving, exciting outcomes of this emphasis. The very act of creation for typographic distribution has been reinvented in some women's writing. The male notion that writing is the epitomal private act, never to be shared until it has been reified in The Book or The Essay, has been challenged by women who work collectively on their creations, and often publish as a group as well.

Women writers and journalists create for the print culture: this is the clearest example of how print technology affected women's communication in its creative aspect. The more we know about how 500 years of women creating for print publication has transformed gender relationships, the fewer secrets remain, not only about women but also about men, within typographic culture.

Women outside the mainstream

Outside the male-dominated production and distribution processes of typographic culture, women have been molding their own alternative print culture for at least a century.

Perhaps the most important aspect of this countercultural movement has been the initiation and development of women's production and distribution mechanisms. In 1985, according to *Ms.*, there were more than three dozen feminist presses in the US—not counting 'presses that publish the work of only one author, and gay men's and university presses, some of which are seriously committed to women's issues' (Clardy 1985, 65). The women's bookstore movement includes a network of about eighty-eight stores throughout the US. British women's publishing groups number at least five and women-only presses the same number. There are two women's bookstores in London. Figures from 1981 indicate a dozen in France, and twenty to thirty in West Germany (Cadman *et al.* 1981).

The Third National Women in Print Conference in Berkeley, California, in 1985 attracted a large group of women who met to discuss issues of periodical and book publishing, printing, freelancing, bookstores, libraries and computer skills. The extent of this activity, which has also precipitated an interest in feminist issues by mainstream publishers, indicates that the mysteries of women as print producers are coming unravelled in the feminist alternatives of this century.

A word on what we need to know in areas that are also 'outside' in terms of the Eurocentric bias of scholarship: we can mention but not detail the effects of print on women in countries other than the capitalist world, on women of color, and on working-class women. This applies to the differentiation of communicational outlooks among those women in the present and past. We know, for example, that movable type was used for the ancient equivalent of modern Wall Posters in China several centuries before Gutenberg. What did this mean for gender and typography in China? What was that relationship in other Asian countries, or in Latin America, or Africa?

And how do these questions relate to Third World women today, in their countries and within the US? How have poor and working women, who were the last to become literate, and in many countries today remain the largest illiterate group, fitted into this picture? What do the transformations of the future portend for them, for women in industrializing nations, for girls not yet born who will go to schools not yet invented? Finding clues here also aids in the solution of the larger mystery.

SORTING THE CLUES: CONSTITUENTS OF A GRAND THEORY

The parts of the story of women and print, viewed as clues to a mystery yet unsolved, fit partially into overarching theoretical perspectives on technology and communication. From feminism, from Marxism, and from a neo–McLuhanist perspective come important constituents to begin transforming clues into patterns. Here we shall attempt to see where those three patterns take us in our search.

Feminism and women in print

A feminist perspective brings to the issue of women and print an affirmation of a continuity rather than a discontinuity. With print technology as the variable and patriarchy as the constant, feminism is willing to grant an impact to typographic culture which transcends everyday events. But there is also an insistence that it is in those events of daily life that we find a continuous reinforcement, rather than a discontinuous rupture, of male-dominated culture. In other words, the printing press, a man-made and 'masculine' machine, *was* seminal, an etymologically appropriate usage.

There is no comprehensive feminist treatment of print technology yet, though there are the contours of that treatment in the recent work of feminist scholars and activists. Lana Rakow (1985) makes the point that, 'In particular, little is known about how communications technology per se has affected men and women differently because that technology restructures social relationships through time and space.' Rakow identifies the feminist critiques of the last two decades which look at both mass communication and language as important steps toward enhanced knowledge of technology. To her list of materials which touch on aspects of the print technology question—Janice Radway's *Reading the Romance: Women, Patriarchy, and Popular Literature* (1984), Alison Adburgham's *Women in Print: Writing Women and Women's Magazines from the Restoration to the Accession of Victoria* (1972), Marion Marzholf's *Up From the Footnote: A History of Women Journalists* (1977), Anne Mather's 'A history of feminist periodicals' (1974–5)—could be added, for example, *Women in Print II* (1982), Joanna Russ's *How to Suppress Women's Writing* (1983), Dale Spender's *Women of Ideas and What Men Have Done to Them* (1982), and Ellen Cadman, Gail Chester and Agnes Pivot's *Rolling Our Own: Women as Printers, Publishers and Distributors* (1981).

As feminist scholarship reveals more about women as readers, writers and workers in the industry, the overall picture regarding women's communication and print will clarify. From another direction, too, can come further clarity. Within a theoretical macro-critique of patriarchy, of necessity the analysis zooms in on print culture. Marilyn French's wide-ranging analysis of, and attack on, patriarchy in *Beyond Power: On Women, Men, and Morals* (1985) is a good example. Though her scope is far greater than just print and its effects, her historical treatment of women and girls, as their new socialization patterns emerged from typographic culture, is a short but provocative section of the book (170–88).

Marxism: print and class

Marxism has seen history as feminism has: an overall continuity disrupted by certain significant breaks with the past. In the Marxist view, and in the view of those who do not call themselves Marxists but acknowledge their debt to its insights, the historical continuity of classes in struggle is ruptured by revolutionary political and economic changes. The communications technologies concomitant with those changes serve the ruling class's needs, except in the instances when dominated classes seize control of them or invent their own alternatives. Marxism certainly goes for the Grand Theory but has neglected communications to the extent that it has been called 'the blind spot of Western Marxism.'

The relevance of Marxist interpretations of the relationship of print technology to women is severely limited by frequent inattention to both subjects. There is, however, a growing body of material that links feminist and Marxist concerns (see Matterlart 1982); there has been considerable concern among a few Marxist scholars with the communications technologies (see Williams 1966). And both trends are growing through significant new work of the past decade.

The value in studies of women and communication within the Marxist problematic is in its insistence on the interplay of technology, history and culture which allows the posing of more useful questions in that relationship's dialectics. In addition, a Marxist feminism, with its focus on women's role as reproducers of capitalist relations within the private sphere, can situate the study of print products, from advertising to romance novels to popular magazines, in a helpful way for further work. Probably the clearest contribution perspectives from Marxism can offer to such studies is in the class analysis of women in the print industry. Marxists are not very concerned with print technology as a change agent, seeing it instead as a tool among many other tools. Instead their focus is the industrial structure which molds workers to that tool under capitalism.

Thus, a study as Alan Marshall's *Changing the Word: The Printing Industry in Transition* (1983) provides insights into not only the general questions of capital in a redefined print industry and worker-management relations, but also the circumstances of 'the invisible membership,' women who 'have been working in various parts of the trade throughout its 500-year history' (103). Working women, in print, as in any other industry, have developed new relationships with their families, friends and coworkers; the study of these changed circumstances is particularly interesting since it can juxtapose the role of printed materials in both creating and transforming the socialization of women, and their movement from home to workplace (and too often back again to home) at moments in history.

Neo-McLuhanism: where are the women?

The last two and a half decades have seen the publication of many significant works on print and its effects. While there have been, of course, important efforts to define the impact of typographic technology before 1960, we can use the early years of that decade as a pertinent starting point to identify what I call the neo-McLuhanite perspective. It was about that time that Marshall McLuhan burst onto the cultural scene.

With the hardback publications in the early 1960s of McLuhan's *The Gutenberg Galaxy* (1969) and *Understanding Media* (1965), we have an impassable theoretic on the effects of print. It is also impossible. There is no way to briefly delineate the scope and tenets of McLuhan's concepts. The form and the content of his work resist classification, and he has gleefully told his supporters and critics alike that there is no way to determine whether what he has written is true or even his own opinion: he creates mosaic investigations, not linear and logical statements, he says. But the fundamental principle of McLuhan's work is technological determinism—the effect of revolutionary transformations of human sensibilities with media technology.

Others have carried forward McLuhan's work, which itself originated in the theories of Harold Innis. Walter J. Ong has been more careful and less flamboyant in his development of these themes over the years, and most recently with *Orality and Literacy: The Technologizing of the Word* (1982). But Ong, like McLuhan, views the technological thing as the determinant thrust—if my image seems phallocentric it is not coincidental. Both men—Father Ong a Jesuit and McLuhan a devout Thomist Catholic—reflect a nostalgic bias toward oral culture (though they have been known to deny it), and a resistance to the mind-messing print culture: the irony that they express this in the form of books has been noted before.

For these technological determinists, what does women's communication have to do with it? The answer is 'Not much.'

McLuhan is uncharacteristically cogent on the question of women and print, for he tells us the reason for silence on the subject in *The Gutenberg Galaxy* (1969). After quoting a nineteenth-century saying, 'Woman is the last thing to be civilized by man,' he pontificates on the Female Principle According to McLuhan: 'Mere print had not been intense enough to reduce her to uniformity and repeatability and specialism.... Pictorial advertisements and movies finally did for women what print technology had done for men centuries before' (254-5).

The main reason to study McLuhan today, however, is to prepare for the crucial aspect of neo-McLuhanism in our search. Perhaps it is too facile, but it still may be fair to say that the best thing McLuhan did for women's understanding of communications technology was to inspire a woman, Elizabeth L. Eisenstein, to write her invaluable history *The Printing Press as an Agent of Change* (1979).

Eisenstein is not a technological determinist, but she presents a neo-McLuhanist perspective in viewing the change in culture brought about by print (and speech and script) as a discontinuity beyond the explanation of any evolutionary transformation. The thoroughness and depth of her presentation—800 pages of meticulously documented historical detail which she suggests only reveals the iceberg's tip—contrasts with McLuhan and Ong's sweeping, overdetermined, masculinist forms.

Eisenstein argues that print caused an 'unacknowledged revolution,' characterized by unanticipated and yet irreversible 'shifts' in the dissemination, standardization, reorganization, collection, preservation, amplification and reinforcement of human knowledge. The first two centuries of print culture reshaped all human endeavor, thoroughly overwhelming the previous scribal culture (she rejects Ong's [1982] chirographic/typographic designations), abruptly redirecting the trajectory of the Italian Renaissance, and precipitating the Reformation and what became the modern scientific way of knowing.

I cannot do justice to the breadth of her approach and richness of her insights here. Along with Steinberg's *Five Hundred Years of Printing* (1955), *The Printing Press as an Agent of Change* is the essential work to comprehend the argument for the rupturing, totalistic impact of print on humanity. Eisenstein mentions, though only mentions, some of the themes which need full treatment for our eventual understanding of gender and typography.

There are, for example, two footnotes about women as printers during this era (24, 87). A brief but pointed paragraph isolates the private sphere/public sphere duality which relates to femininity/masculinity, what and how women read, and 'the age-old battle between the sexes that has yet to be fully explored' (134). There are references to novel reading, household and etiquette books, female authorship, and other aspects of women's communication sprinkled here and there in the text. But there is no coherent and developed argument in *The Printing Press as an Agent of Change* which leads to as rich an understanding of women as Eisenstein provides us for men. It is true, as she points out, that the period which she considers was not crucial to the developments mentioned above. Her concern is the early modern fifteenth and sixteenth centuries, not modernism itself. Nevertheless, while we can thank Eisenstein for illuminating the male/public sphere, we need to continue our search elsewhere for the female and private lives transformed by print into the future.

ENDINGS AND BEGINNINGS

What we *do* know about 500 years of printing can be summarized as follows.

Print abetted (some say caused) massive transformations in the culture of Western Europe and the United States. Those changes can be described, but their description does not allow us to determine the causality which operates, and we need more information from further research to make some of those determinations. The research we do have focuses on 'the public sphere,' and therefore on men, ignoring women.

In broad terms, the first two centuries after Gutenberg invented movable types, 1450 to 1650, were years of dissemination of the new technology and its products in the male-oriented intellectual and cultural arenas. In the rest of the seventeenth century and the eighteenth century, print culture consolidated its hold on modern nations: this is not to say it caused nationalism or capitalism, but it surely aided their formation. And, as Eisenstein notes, it defined what science would mean by standardizing mathematical tables as well as drawings of nature. Nation running and science, however, were not for women. Gender *was* affected by the role definitions of typographic culture. Since everybody could read about and view drawings of expected roles in the same forms and constructions, 'conforming' became a social possibility. Print did not, contrary to McLuhan, *cause* conformity, but it did clarify what was expected of people and what would be considered atypical.

The nineteenth and twentieth centuries brought continual refinements of print as a technology and the spread of literacy to many women. It is important to keep in mind that the methods of printing which have developed over the last century, and those which are developing now and will develop, demonstrate that, first, there have been *continuing* transformations—not just an end of scribal culture and beginning of print culture. Second, the notions of the reading public, and of women's place within it, of printers/publishers, of literacy and illiteracy—all need evaluation and reevaluation diachronically.

At the end of our current search, then, where can we look to find the next clues which will lead us closer to the solutions tomorrow—of revealing the gender-typography connection?

One important piece of evidence-to-come involves men and women: the myth that print is a dying industry will be exploded in the next few years. Transformations will continue, but the print culture will survive with as much importance as ever. The motor of change will be the continuing technological advances and how the owners use them in the industry. In the last quarter–century, for example, the availability of inexpensive printing processes with web-offset presses and computerized typesetting made alternative movements such as feminist periodical publishing economically feasible. Xerography, digital technology and printing–on–demand are new forms of typographic reproduction that depend on new machines such as the computer. But they do not replace print—if anything, as offset has in the past, they may expand the amount of printed material available in the future. Some say that the newest forms of 'print' are the bulletin board systems set up with microcomputers (see Smith and Balka this volume), and the magazines and books instantaneously distributed and collectively amendable—a new technology of electronic periodicals and books.

Computers in the print industry are changing every phase of the production process. As jobs change and more women enter the industry, particularly through the operation of electronic typesetting and related aspects, we need to chart the transformations of women's consciousness and communication.

It is not just the technology, but its uses by the structure that controls it that need attention. The political and economic nature of the print industry is changing dramatically, through consolidation of book publishers, mergers and growth of chains among periodical publishers, conglomerate formation (where many communications companies become one) sometimes owned by a corporation (like Gulf & Western) that has had no prior interests in print or other media.

As new technologies and structures continue the two centuries of transformation in the four phases of print cultural movement (creation, production, distribution and consumption), the questions of gender and typography of the past will themselves transform to address the future. But scholars of those questions will by no means write the obituary of print culture; if anything, they will be called upon to write the birth announcement of its next generation, and the one after that, and the one after that....

REFERENCES

Adburgham, Alison. 1972. *Women in Print: Writing Women and Women's Magazines from the Restoration to the Accession of Victoria.* London: Allen & Unwin.

Cadman, Eileen, Gail Chester and Agnes Pivot. 1981. *Rolling Our Own: Women as Printers, Publishers and Distributors.* London: Minority Press Group.

Clardy, Andrea Flack. 1985. 'Best-sellers from Crone's Own, Light Cleaning, Down There, and dozens of other feminist presses.' *Ms.* (August), 65-8.

Coser, Lewis A., Charles Kadushin and Walter W. Powell. 1982. *Books: The Culture and Commerce of Publishing.* Chicago: University of Chicago Press.

Eisenstein, Elizabeth L. 1979. *The Printing Press as an Agent of Change.* Vols I and II. Cambridge: Cambridge University Press.

French, Marilyn. 1985. *Beyond Power: On Women, Men, and Morals.* New York: Summit.

Heath, Shirley Brice. 1980. 'The functions and uses of literacy.'

Journal of Communication 30:1 (Winter), 123–33.

Leed, Eric. 1980. "Voice" and "print": master symbols in the history of communication.' In Kathleen Woodward, ed. *The Myths of Information: Technology and Postindustrial Culture*. Madison, Wisconsin: Coda Press, 41–61.

McLuhan, Marshall. 1965. *Understanding Media: The Extensions of Man*. New York: McGraw-Hill.

McLuhan, Marshall. 1969. *The Gutenberg Galaxy: The Making of Typographic Man*. New York: New American Library.

Marshall, Alan. 1983. *Changing the Word: The Printing Industry in Transition*. London: Comedia Publishing Group.

Marzolf, Marion. 1977. *Up From the Footnote: A History of Women Journalists*. New York: Hastings House.

Mather, Anne. 1974–5. 'A history of feminist periodicals.' *Journalism History* 1 (Autumn 1974), 82–5; 2 (Winter 1974–5), 108–11; 3 (Spring 1975), 19–23 and 31.

Mattelart, Michelle. 1982. 'Women and the cultural industries.' *Media, Culture and Society* 4, 133–51.

Olson, David R. 1980. 'On the language and authority of textbooks.' *Journal of Communication* 30:1 (Winter), 186–96.

Ong, Walter J. 1982. *Orality and Literacy: The Technologizing of the Word*. London: Methuen.

Radway, Janice. 1984. *Reading the Romance: Women, Patriarchy, and Popular Literature*. Chapel Hill: University of North Carolina Press.

Rakow, Lana F. 1985. 'A paradigm of one's own: feminist ferment in the field.' Paper given at the International Communication Association Conference, Honolulu, Hawaii, May.

Russ, Joanna. 1983. *How to Suppress Women's Writing*. Austin, Texas: University of Texas Press.

Slack, Jennifer Daryl. 1984. 'The development and use of communication technologies: critical issues.' Paper given at the International Communication Association Conference, San Francisco, California, May.

Spender, Dale. 1982. *Women of Ideas and What Men Have Done To Them: From Aphra Behn to Adrienne Rich*. London: Routledge & Kegan Paul.

Steinberg, S.H. 1955. *Five Hundred Years of Printing*. Harmondsworth, Middlesex: Penguin.

Williams, Raymond. 1966. *The Long Revolution*. New York: Harper & Row.

Women in Print II: Opportunities for Women's Studies Research in Language and Literature. 1982. New York: Modern Language Association of America.

WOMEN ON THE MOVE: HOW PUBLIC IS PUBLIC TRANSPORT?

'Oh, we've been taken for a ride, that's for sure.'
(Woman talking about the lack of public transportation in a
Black neighbourhood)

Before the era of telegraphic and electronic communications, 'communications' meant to move around physically. For women, physical mobility is still of paramount importance. They have less daily access to the means of electronic communications, such as telexes, electronic mail through computers, and company-paid telephones. Yet, most women still have to go to the shops, they still have to collect the children from school, and they still have to get to work. For women in the UK, public transport is a decisive factor in determining whether their meetings with friends and family are a pleasure or an expensive effort.

Public transport includes aircraft, ships, buses, trains and taxis. After our own two feet, buses and trains are women in the UK's most common form of transport. Our dependence upon buses and trains is demonstrated by the fact that in the UK only one-third of women have a driving licence, and only a quarter have access to a car when *they* need it. (See Scharff, this volume, for information on women's access to cars in the US.)

In this essay, we outline the history of women's invisibility in government policy and transport planning, and we present the discrimination exercised by those with the power to make policy decisions regarding the development and deployment of new technology in transport. We examine the impact that this has upon women's ability and safety to move around and we present the economic justification for enhancing women's communications. To end on an optimistic note, we describe the ways in which women are challenging the *status quo*, adopting a new concept of industrial democracy, putting to good use innovations in transport, and increasing their own mobility.

Figure 1   Bus shelter and seats at a London bus stop. In the UK only one-third of women have driving licences, and only one-fourth have access to a car when they need it. Because women are more dependent upon public transport, a commitment to public transport is also a commitment to women's rights (photo by Eddie Tulasiewicz)

This paper has been written by the Women and Transport Forum, a group of professional women working for the Greater London Council (GLC). Beyond our own experience as urban women, some of us with children, we have tried to develop our sensitivity towards the problems faced by unwaged women, Black and ethnic minority women, women with disabilities, lesbians, women who live in rural areas, young and older women, all of whom have different experiences of and needs for public transport. For example, in the past we felt we had achieved much by persuading the planners to collect and break down data by gender. Now we know that this still conceals as much as it reveals.[1] Black women's travel patterns are often different from those of white women's. Some ethnic minority women have the additional fear and reality of racist attack to deter them from using public transport. For elderly women the distance to the nearest bus stop is crucial. The differences in our requirements need to be examined at every stage of planning and

117

campaigning so that we provide and are provided with transport for all of us. The issues surrounding women's employment are also vital to this discussion. They are mentioned in this paper only in passing owing to space limitations.

Figure 2   Older woman climbing unaided on to a one-person operated bus. For elderly women, the distance to the nearest bus stop is crucial. More women than men travel with grocery bags, baby carriages, and wheelchairs. More women accompany dependants (photo by Sarah Saunders)

MEN'S TRANSPORT: WOMEN'S INVISIBILITY

The importance of walking for women is likely to be a reflection of their lack of access to cars compared to men, and the fact that many of their journeys are fairly short in length (particularly local shopping trips). However, this in itself is a reflection of the unsuitability of public transport to many of their needs. (GLC, WCSU 1985b, 6)

Women's needs

Women have certain basic and as yet largely unmet needs in order to maintain their mobility and liberty. Women need an adequate disposable income, secure employment outside the home if they so choose, easily accessible child care facilities, mobility and security. Laurie Pickup's (1985) work on women's low travel mobility has demonstrated that the greatest constraints on women's lives are related to child care. Other major constraints are the lack of economic independence, and the fear of attack and harassment, 'the ultimate enforcing mechanism by which women are still kept in the home—sexual attack by force' (Matrix 1984, 51).

A transport system which is operated with women's particular needs in mind must be one in which women can be employed and which they can use freely, without being tied to the home either by twenty-four-hour child and other caring, or by the possibility of violent attack. These broad needs must be met by society as a whole, by the political and economic system. The political commitment to the maintenance of public transport is also a commitment to women's right to move around because women are more dependent upon public transport than are men.

The type and level of services is vital to women's independence and economic opportunities for several reasons. First, women tend to have more part-time and shift work jobs; therefore, they tend to travel in off-peak periods when the services are more erratic. Moreover, their journeys to work are increasingly relevant to transport planning. For example, in Hertfordshire, 'the period 1971-1981 saw a 20 per cent increase in female employment in the County compared with less than 1 per cent increase in male employment' (Hertfordshire County Council 1984).

Second, women's journeys to work, because of their triple roles as mothers, unwaged homeworkers and waged workers, tend to be more complex than men's. They may have to deliver the children to school, go on to do the shopping, then go to work. On the way home, they may have to collect children from school and call at the health centre before reaching home.

Third, the complexity of their journeys means that if service frequencies are cut, the time taken to make a number of changes lengthens significantly; and if the service levels in off-peak times are cut, the number of part-time and shift jobs that women hold are restricted.

Fare levels are another issue relevant to the complexity of

Figure 3   Women and children on a London bus. The greatest
constraints on women's lives are related to child care, the lack of
economic independence, and the danger of attack and harassment.
Transport systems are seldom planned or operated with particular
concern about women's mobility (photo by Gina Glover)

women's journeys to work. The more complex their journeys, the
more fares they must pay unless an integrated ticketing system
exists. This is a women's issue because the jobs women do have,
whether or not they are part-time, tend to be lower-paid, their
disposable income is commensurately less and the proportion spent
on transport higher than men's. Low fares and integrated ticketing
are therefore generally of greater advantage to women, who also accompany children more often, than they are to men.

The accessibility of public transport is crucial because more wom-
en than men accompany dependants and travel with shopping trol-
leys, buggies and wheelchairs. Women's perceived and actual security, both as employees and passengers, must be provided for and
should be a major consideration in the design and operation of buses
and trains. As the Greater London Council's survey on women and
transport has shown, 'just under half of the harassments reported in
the survey occurred whilst women were using or waiting for public

transport' (GLC, WCSU 1985c, 7). More women than men are vulnerable to attack and harassment.

In rural areas, women are the large majority of passengers as they travel to work, to the shops, and to health centres. Often services are provided for all these purposes, whereas in urban areas traditionally services have been provided primarily to ferry the workforce. On the other hand, in rural areas the service frequencies are often so low that the mobility of people without cars is severely curtailed.

In the light of these needs we can evaluate how 'public' is public transport and how well it is facilitating women's movement and interaction. Government policy, the managers, the trades unions and the political parties will be examined to see how they plan and operate public transport.

Government transport policy

The parlous state of Britain's public transport should not be blamed simply upon the impact of private transport or of the unprofitability of public transport, but rather on government priorities and inept management.

Transport in the UK has had a low profile as a political issue. Government policy has always been biased towards road building and private transport and, at best, ambivalent towards public transport. This stems from a long-held belief that cars are 'the future' and that everyone has or will soon be getting a car. Two-thirds of all trips made by middle-aged men are by car (Department of Transport 1978-9), and it can be inferred that it is an even higher proportion for white, middle-aged, middle-class men—the decision makers—who base their policy on their own experience. Urban motorways and rural trunk roads cut through women's lives, driving a noisy, polluting, dangerous wedge between their homes and workplaces, schools and health centres, causing them to walk roundabout routes, through hostile subways or over windy bridges, diverting and lengthening bus journeys, and creating unsafe, no-go areas of blank walls and derelict spaces.

The present (1987) Conservative Government in the UK has adopted the view that public transport should be a fully commercial proposition—as it is nowhere else in the Western world. In 1984 the Government took control of London Transport from the GLC and it became London Regional Transport. Margaret Thatcher's Conservative Government has tried to outlaw policies adopted by Labour local authorities to subsidize public transport and to encourage its popular use as part of transport and wealth distribution strategies. Since 1979 the Conservative Government has cut back transport subsidies and privatized many services (Hayes 1985). In rural areas, the combination of centralization of services and increases in public transport fares results in long and expensive journeys. In Cumbria, for example, people have to travel as much as ninety miles, at high expense and for six hours, to reach the nearest hospital in Manchester.

A 1982 House of Commons report on transport in London was produced by a committee on which no women sat and from evidence in eighty-nine memoranda, none of which were from women's organizations. It is no surprise, therefore, that women were not mentioned once, nor that the effects on women of the 1985 Transport Act to regulate the bus industry have not been considered by the Government. The outcome of no direct local political control over bus services and of no cross-subsidization from one route to another is viewed with gloom by transport officers and campaigners.

The political parties and local councils have been slow to adopt women's issues, and women's mobility is far down the list. In a survey of local authorities in the United Kingdom, 91 per cent of the seventy who replied did not consider women's needs, let alone meet them (Oliver 1985). The responses displayed muddled reasoning and misunderstanding of the concepts of discrimination and equal opportunities. One man, obviously rattled, replied, 'No policies refer explicitly to women's needs (or, for that matter, men's needs)'! Others replied that they were not aware of any problems over public transport or lack of facilities which women in particular encountered. The county transport coordinators failed to understand that considering women's needs is not sexist; it redresses a balance now largely in favour of men who own and have more access to cars and other means of transport. Such an attitude condones and leads to discrimination against women in policy and practice. For example, in Somerset safe after-dark public transport is not seen as an issue because no evening services are provided. The implications are clear for women in Somerset without access to a car or who have no driving licence.

Another argument which the local authority respondents in the survey forwarded was that women do not need 'special policy' because they are not a minority. Just because women are not a minority does not mean that they enjoy equal opportunities with men. If they are a majority of public transport users then policy which takes into account their needs should not be 'special', merely obvious and normal.

The impact of women's invisibility: their safety and satisfaction

The absence of safe travelling environments pervades all women's lives, and often dictates their level of mobility and mode of transport. It is the fear they feel for themselves and those they care for that inhibits their movements, limits the places and people they can see, and constrains their standard of living.

The GLC survey on women and transport, the first of its kind, highlighted the issue of security. It discovered that nearly a third of women in London never go out alone after dark, and for Asian women the figure is 40 per cent. Of those who do travel at night, Asian and Afro-Caribbean women feel less safe than do white women. All women have cause to fear for their safety: about 10 per cent of the women surveyed had been attacked at some time, and over 10 per cent had been threatened or harassed within the previous year. Black and ethnic minority women fear racist as well as sexual attacks, and lesbians fear attacks by heterosexist people.

Security and the feeling of safety has diminished with the introduction of new technology, such as one-person-operated buses and driver-only trains. Empty platforms and carriages, sexist and violent advertisements, lonely bus stops, blind corners, tunnels, long waits, poor lighting and directions, and no ready access to help are endemic on our public transport systems. British trains have a 'communication' cord which stops the train dead in its tracks. On a train with separate carriages or compartments this is no security at all should the train be in a tunnel at the time. There is a £50 fine for 'improper' use, hardly an encouragement to use it when we are scared and threatened.

Many stations around the country are poorly staffed and surveilled, and with automatic fares collection the number will increase in the next few years. In stations which have not been designed with security in mind, closed-circuit television is more effective at protecting property than people. In Newcastle-upon-Tyne closed-circuit television, at present restricted to central stations, is to be extended to cover all stations, with cameras in the ticket concourses, the upper and lower escalator concourses and the platforms. But in the control room only two stations are viewed at any one time and, because there are no station staff, help is delayed when trains run only every ten minutes. For women, the stations do not feel secure at night.

In London, 15 per cent of the harassment of women occurred in railway stations, and 10 per cent at bus stops (GLC, WCSU, 1985c, 7). There were 752 reported attacks on the underground in 1982; in 1984 there were 1,254. Even while the number of transport police increased by 25 per cent attacks on staff in the first half of 1985 rose by 37 per cent compared with the same period in 1984 (CAPITAL 1985, 1). How much of these huge increases is due to station and train de-staffing can only be conjectured. In the London survey, 80 per cent of women mentioned their preference for the presence of staff. In the words of one woman, 'I think it would be an idea if there were a few more guards around down the tunnels or just on the platforms. I mean it's horrible if you're in a carriage and it's just you and a drunk or someone'. (GLC, WCSU 1985c, 15)

Meanwhile London Regional Transport (LRT) has told Women for Improved Transport that the best solutions to safety and access problems are 'mechanical solutions'. And yet simple technical aids have not been applied to full advantage to help people with different abilities. For example, seats and lighting are not yet provided at all bus stops throughout the country. Steps between the station and the train endanger many passengers and their children, and lifts are not available in all underground stations. As more women than men have a disability and more women use public transport, it is important that accessibility is on the agenda.

Service levels and routes are not designed to enable women, as mothers, waged workers, homeworkers and friends, to attain their destinations when they need to and in the time they have available. Most urban systems are designed with the mostly male commuter in mind, hence orbital services are inadequate—ones from hospital to shops to school to home for example—and off-peak services are infrequent and unreliable. Passengers take four times as long to board the new one-person-operated buses than they do doorless, crew-operated buses where a conductor and not the driver collects the fares. This causes slower journeys and less reliable services, and eliminates help to passengers.

Locational policies are also relevant to women's mobility. Policy to disperse rather than concentrate jobs may end up 'trapping' women in the area close to home unless it is closely related to transport policy (Stevenson 1985, 2). 'Good, cheap and reliable public transport is of key importance if women's choice of job is not to be restricted' (GLC, WCSU 1985b, 7). This issue is particularly pertinent to Black and ethnic minority women who often live in areas of cheap housing which are underresourced by shops and other facilities, and where job opportunities are poor. Inadequate public transport compounds their disadvantages. In London, Afro-Caribbean and Asian people make proportionately more use of public transport than do white people (GLC, Transport Committee 1985, 2j). The current cuts in bus services and routes and the high level of British Rail fares exacerbate their disadvantages and highlight the difficulties suffered when there is no alternative mode of transport.

In many rural areas, some services run only once or twice a week. Those women who depend upon the bus are closed off in their communities for the rest of the week. Even where there are more regular rural services to schools and to urban centres, they are not accessible to many people, they are expensive and time-constraining, and they do not run at all in the evenings or at night.

Comprehensive fares policy which aims to accommodate all groups of people and to assist particular disadvantaged groups does not exist. Currently, short-distance fares are disproportionately high, fares paid by, for example, women travelling locally. Free travel for the elderly and people with disabilities is still a rarity and some transport authorities do not offer them any concessions. There are no transfer tickets for women who make complex journeys, or concessionary passes for people who work part-time and have irregular travel patterns, and no work has been done upon the discriminatory effect of various fares policies. For example, Black women's position in the labour market is currently one of the lowest pay and the longest and most undesirable hours. Transport policy which does not consider their needs compounds their position in a racist society:

> Fares policy is undoubtedly a substantial tool of intervention in the income distribution and standard of living of Londoners and more work is necessary to identify the precise income distribution effects and the way fares policy could be targetted better to assist particular disadvantaged groups. (Miller and Taylor 1985, 4)

In the eighteen–month period (July 1984 to January 1986) after the

Government took control from the GLC, LRT imposed fares increases totalling 16 per cent. This average conceals that both children's and short-distance bus fares increased by 50 per cent, the maximum children's underground fare by a massive 200 per cent, and that there is no longer cheap travel on Sundays. All these costs fall most heavily on women who accompany children and other dependants, and who have an average lower disposable income than men. Season tickets do not benefit women who do not travel every day.

Women on the move: changing the system

Women have been campaigning for better public transport for many years, especially in rural areas, but they have only recently begun to voice their demands as a women's issue. Only in the past five years have women's groups and local authority women's committees achieved concessions and services specifically for women. The GLC survey found that 85 per cent of women's journeys are by foot. Obviously there is scope for public transport to be used for some of these journeys, but currently it is failing to meet the needs of many women.

One way of ensuring that women's needs are met is to incorporate more women into the management of public transport, giving them an opportunity to voice their demands and to plan for them. For example, even though 'the most important mode of motorised transport for women is the bus' (GLC, WCSU 1985b 3), women have never been involved in vehicle and infrastructure design.

Traditionally both bus and rail management have been overwhelmingly male (Dawson 1985). Where women have managed to break into traditionally male-dominated jobs within the transport industry Diana Robbins's (1985) interviews with British Rail's management confirmed that the male managers frequently regarded these women 'as unfit and unnatural'; some were subjected to continual sexual harassment. Within British Rail, out of 22,000 staff in driving grades only one was a woman. The hurdles for women wanting to work in public transport range from getting a job and passing the driving tests to fitting in the antisocial hours, being assaulted on the job and finding child care (Mackay 1985). Nor are the unions much better than management when it comes to women's issues. In the National Union of Railwaymen only 3.5 per cent of members in 1984 were women. Their lack of participation is due to the unions' organization and attitudes (Hayes 1985). Crèches are not provided during meetings, which are often held in the evenings when women have household work to do and children to look after. The union's language and procedure is off-putting and mystifying for those women who are brave enough to attend a first time.

Before the Greater London Council lost control of London Transport it appointed an Equal Opportunities Officer who, had the GLC remained in control, might have carried out far-reaching reforms to employ more women, to promote more women and Black and ethnic minority males into managerial positions, and to examine the effects on groups in the community of the services provided.

In Nottingham the ratio of women to men bus drivers in 1984 was 1:40. The City Council Women's Subcommittee passed a resolution that as a long-term goal 51 per cent of all drivers should be women. The Council no longer considers only those applicants who already have Public Service Vehicle licences. The number of women with such a licence is very low indeed. Now new recruits are given the opportunity to train for the licence as part of the job, and job advertisements referring to female drivers mention the training facility (Wakeley 1985, 1). At the Nottingham Women's Training Scheme where women can do the bus driving training, priority is given to low-income women and a crèche is provided. The training is free and does not affect state benefit payments.

The same Council has encouraged the introduction of 'midibuses' which can go along roads which are unsuitable for the traditional double- or single-decker buses, and which are more easily accessible to people with disabilities. These buses are staffed with a helper as well as a driver (Deakin 1984). However, because they are operated on low frequencies and in off-peak hours only, and because the helpers' job is not perceived as skilled and is therefore less well paid and less secure, women are still campaigning for improvements and extensions to the midi-bus services.

Other local authority initiatives include the role of Equalities, Women's Rights and Race Relations Officers. These officers advise others on how to perceive, among other issues, women's needs as an integral part of their work. The GLC's women and transport survey findings referred to already has had a marked impact: 'in particular, the stark differences in women's experiences of transport have surprised and shocked transport experts' (Stevenson 1985, 1).

The Women's Committee Support Unit (WCSU) of the GLC pushed successfully for women's interests to be integrated into the transport policy advocated in the Greater London Development Plan (GLDP), and to strengthen the arguments for less emphasis on traffic growth and road development. As Beverley Taylor (1985) remarks,

> Getting women's issues incorporated into such weighty tomes as the GLDP and TPP (Transport Policies and Programme) may seem rather remote from the day-to-day transport problems that affect women. But it has proved an important way of changing the rather narrow views of many transport planners who are making major decisions which affect our lives. (31)

The WCSU also organized day seminars for male transport officers at which women's issues were presented directly to men many of whom had been sceptical.

Unfortunately, many of the alternative strategies had to rely for their funding on left-wing metropolitan authorities, the ones which the Conservative Government abolished in April 1986. Campaigns have been directed both at maintaining pressure on the politicians and transport planners and at making the public more aware of the issues.

Those projects which are run by women for women, although usually very small, have had a huge impact both on their immediate locales and clientèles and as models for wider action. Stockwell Women's Lift Service began in 1982 as a voluntary group which was concerned for women's safety on the streets at night. On Friday and Saturday nights they used their own cars to provide a transport service run by women, enabling women who had never been out at night to go out, as well as providing security for those who had already done so. In 1984 they received GLC funding for a vehicle and premises, and two part-time workers to supplement the volunteer drivers and telephone helpers. Similarly, after a succession of rapes in Oxford, the Oxford Polytechnic Student's Union instituted a mini-bus service to take students home at night. Camden Council has given a grant to Black and ethnic minority women to set up a community transport scheme so that they can tailor the service to meet their particular needs.

Women for Improved Transport are campaigning for safe, accessible and cheap public transport that goes where and when women need to travel. They are campaigning for better lighting at stops and stations, more frequent services and more direct services, the better positioning of bus stops and better directions, the safeguarding against all sexist, racist and violent advertising and graffiti, and the design of buses, trains and stations to accommodate women and their various needs. Most important of all, in contrast to LRT management's response to increased violence, which is to employ more transport police, they are pressing for adequate, well-trained staff 'to observe, advise and assist' (Bashall and Torrance 1985).

As there are more women than men with a disability, women benefit most from the services for people with a disability which have been set up in several cities. These mini-buses can carry wheel-chair users and provide trained help for people with all forms of dif-ferent ability. Women are campaigning for these services to be made available to women in the last stages of pregnancy for whom travel-ling by ordinary buses can be extremely uncomfortable.

In one London borough Dial-A-Ride was set up in 1980 to cater for people who are unable to use public transport easily. Now it is London-wide and 75 per cent of the users are women. The services are heavily oversubscribed. Although it has remained after the GLC's abolition, the level of funding is uncertain in the longer term and it is unlikely to have the resources to grow to match its demand. The situation is similar for Taxicard, a scheme to allow all people with a disability to travel in a taxi for £1 up to £6-worth of distance, which has given people who previously had little or no mobility the facility to move around independently.

Thanks to pressure from sympathetic local authorities and women's groups, a few small measures have been taken by the pub-lic transport operators themselves. LRT has produced a bus which caters for up to eight wheelchair users. So far only three of them are running, but it is a step in the right direction. LRT has put in split steps and better handrails on some buses, and it is to experiment with a new alarm/microphone system, one which allows the alarm to be raised without stopping the train. Recently, a woman bus driving instructor has been employed.

In Strathclyde, where 60 per cent of bus users are women, a micro-bus to serve people on estates straddling an urban motorway has been introduced. In Manchester the free carriage of children has been raised from 3 to 5 years old; there is an off-peak 'clipper card' which is an advantage for longer shopping trips; bus stations have been provided with nappy changing areas; and 'Manchester Ring-A-Ride' is being set up for people not able to use public transport easily and safely, for example, women with children in prams.

Like those services to help people with disabilities, although not initiated explicitly to aid women, community transport schemes have been developed which service mother and toddler groups, single parent facilities and community care schemes. All of these initiatives are piecemeal. Many more are needed to add up to adequate mobility for everyone. There are no model examples, but in Lille, in the north of France, the national and local governments have provided an example of an improved urban transport system, one which does not ignore the inhabitants of the surrounding rural areas.

The Greater Lille Council has built a new light railway which national government has subsidized. The line opened in 1984 and passenger usage has exceeded all expectations, with a 50 per cent increase on the buses and trams as well. Unlike in the UK where the Government is not committed to reduce private traffic in city centres, in Lille the line was constructed to do just that. The bus services have been rerouted and enhanced to integrate with the new metro—eleven stations also have bus termini—and the metro was planned to link with the existing tramway to Roubaix. At the ends of the line free car parks entice people out of their cars.

The trains are fully automated, without driver or guard. The platforms are enclosed, with landing doors in the glass wall overlooking the track which open automatically to align with the train doors. Trains run every one minute forty seconds in peak hours and at least every five minutes at all other times between 5 a.m. and 1 a.m. The supply of trains is adapted to meet demand: if platforms are seen to be crowded, another train can be sent down the line and no train is ever empty.

Fares are fully integrated with one-price through tickets (i.e. tickets for buses, trams and trains and for transfers) valid for one hour. Children (up to 4 years) travel free, but from that age upwards there are no half fares.

The stations have natural lighting wherever possible and direct access from street to platform, ruling out the need for corridors. The stairs and escalators overlook the platforms so that people waiting can be seen by and can see people approaching. Interphones, activated by push-button, enable two-way conversations between passengers and control room staff. They are located on all platforms, and in all trains and lifts. Advertising encourages people to use the phones for help and information as well as for protection. For example, one woman accidentally left her baby on the platform.

The control room staff watched the baby on the television while she returned to collect it. Closed-circuit television cameras in all stations watch lift entrances, ticket machines, escalators and platforms, although the twenty-four screens in the control room can watch only four stations at once.

No suicides or accidents have occurred, mostly because of the system of enclosed platform with doors that open only when the train is in the station. Platforms run all along the line through the tunnels in case of emergency evacuation. People in wheelchairs are not left stranded. The metro is not only a means to get to work, but also serves a hospital, a new town and the university.

Such improved security can be achieved only by a completely fresh approach to system design, one which incorporates security right from the start. However, Lille has not taken note of women's preference for staff on stations and trains, and women are not enabled to participate in the system's operation in a democratic way. Employment practices are not advantageous to women or to Black and ethnic minority males. None of the control room staff are women, and there are 'maybe one or two' women out of 140 people on Greater Lille Council.

It must be stressed that unstaffed trains and platforms are not safe in any system which involves corridors, obscure entrances, empty carriages, no intercom system and inadequate electronic surveillance of each carriage, platform, lift, toilet and entrance; and even in model designs women prefer to have staff in attendance. There is much yet to be done before women can feel that they have benefited equally at work and in leisure from transport technology as it is applied to public transport.

CONCLUSION

The gap remains between what women need if they are to be as mobile as men and the provisions made for them, despite laws against sexual and racial discrimination. The private car has made a huge impact on our lives, but for the majority of women, especially in inner cities, this has been a negative impact. Imminent widespread privatization and deregulation of public transport in the UK will diminish women's standards of living and curtail their interactions.

Despite strong economic arguments to support mobility for everyone, many women, particularly low-income, Black and ethnic minority women still remain trapped at home in underresourced residential areas, often without reasonable access to a job or to friends and relatives. By 'reasonable access' we mean access by using transport that enables them to move around comfortably and without financial hardship with children and shopping, that ensures they can journey safely and arrive unscathed within a specified time.

The gap between what the planners think of as 'public' and the pluralistic public which actually exists, between what women want and what they actually receive, will be perpetuated until women are in a position to provide for themselves and each other safe private and public transport.

The segregated environments in which they have to coordinate their lives as workers, mothers and women in their own right with connections to friends and relatives must be reintegrated with the help of improved mobility between the parts of their lives. Only then will they be able to take remunerative work, shop economically, and conduct their relationships without constraint.

Women's poor deal on public transport cannot be seen effectively in isolation from a broader, integrated view of women's oppression and other oppressed groups. Women are making demands right across the spectrum of economic activity, including transport which should provide freedom of movement. We need to educate politicians and officers to understand the situation as we experience it and we need to campaign for a change to the present situation in which 70 per cent of women are unable to travel around with ease and without fear or financial hardship.

NOTE

1   There is little published material on women and transport in the UK. Most of the information included here is from the 'Women and Transport' conference (GLC, Public Transport Campaign Unit 1985) and from a series of booklets called *Women on the Move* (GLC, WCSU 1985a) which publicizes the results of the first survey on women's transport needs conducted in the UK by a public authority.

REFERENCES

Bashall, Ruth and Hilary Torrance. 1985. 'Safe public transport: women's needs.' Paper given at the Women and Transport Conference, Greater London Council, October.

CAPITAL. 1985. *Not LRT News* (London), no. 4.

CILT (Campaign to Improve London's Transport). 1985. 'Privatisation.' *CILT Newsletter* (Autumn), 20-3.

Dawson, Helen. 1985. 'Women and employment.' Paper given at the Women and Transport Conference, Greater London Council, October.

Deakin, D. 1984. Report of the General Manager, City of Nottingham Transport to Nottingham City Council Equal Opportunities: Women's Sub Committee Meeting, 20 May.

Department of Transport. 1978-9. *National Travel Survey*. London: Department of Transport.

Greater London Council, Public Transport Campaign Unit. 1985. Women and Transport Conference, Greater London Council, County Hall, London, October.

Greater London Council, Transport Committee. 1985. GLC/LRT Travel Diary Panel—Monitoring the changing patterns of public transport use. Report T1723, 22 October.

Greater London Council, Women's Committee Support Unit. 1985a. *Women on the Move*. GLC Survey on Women and Transport, no. 1. Initial research preliminary to survey: women's group discussions. London: Greater London Council.

Greater London Council, Women's Committee Support Unit. 1985b. *Women on the Move*. GLC Survey on Women and Transport, no. 2. Survey results: the overall findings. London: Greater London Council.

Greater London Council, Women's Committee Support Unit. 1985c. *Women on the Move*. GLC survey on women and transport, no. 3. Survey results: safety, harassment and violence. London: Greater London Council.

Hayes, Julie. 1985. 'Equal opportunities in transport employment.' Paper given at the Women and Transport Conference, Greater London Council, October.

Hertfordshire County Council, Planning Committee. 1984. Agenda item no. 8, 22 November.

Mackay, Tina. 1985. 'Working on the buses.' *GLC Women's Committee Bulletin* 25, 32-4.

Matrix. 1984. *Making Space: Women and the Man Made Environment*. London: Pluto Press.

Miller, Joan and Beverley Taylor. 1985. 'Racism in public transport.' Paper given at the Women and Transport Conference, Greater London Council, October.

Oliver, Kate. 1985. 'Women's public transport needs: a survey of local authority transport planners outside London.' *GLC Women's Committee Bulletin* 25, 39–41.

Pickup, Laurie. 1985. 'The gender-role and women's low travel mobility.' In G. R. M. Jansen, P. Nijkamp and C. J. Ruijgrok, eds. *Transportation and Mobility in an Era of Transition*. The Hague: Elsevier.

Robbins, Diana. 1985. 'Discrimination in employment.' Paper given at the Women and Transport Conference, Greater London Council, October.

Stevenson, Drew. 1985. 'What can men do to campaign on women's issues?' Paper given at the Women and Transport Conference, Greater London Council, October.

Taylor, Beverley. 1985. 'Women's Committee: spreading the word on transport.' *GLC Women's Committee Bulletin* 25, 29–32.

Wakeley, Marcus. 1985. 'Recruitment policies—Transport Department.' Report of the Acting Chief Executive, Nottingham City Council to the Joint Consultative Group on Equal Opportunities (Trade Unions), 10 July.

VIRGINIA J. SCHARFF

PUTTING WHEELS ON
WOMEN'S SPHERE

I had never driven until I had a lot of cabbage, and I wanted my mother
to help me make sauerkraut. It was the first time I had ever drove ... I
herded that old Model T and I got there. Sometimes I had to stop and
think what I was supposed to do. My dad cranked it for me when I
started to come back home, but I stayed two days and we made sauerkraut.
(Pearl Sollars, age 70, Tippecanoe County, Indiana ([Eleanor Arnold,
1985a, p.43-4])

Ever since the beginning of industrialization, with the separation of
home and workplace, American cityscapes have come more and
more to resemble maps of the ideology of separate spheres for
women and men. Critics of this spatial segregation, feminists included, have pointed to the automobile as a crucial force in per-
petuating women's oppression by increasing the distances from
home to workplace, child care, shopping and community life.
Many writers see car culture suburbia as inimical to women's eman-
cipation. They assert that the low–density North American metropolitan landscape, if in part a product of the continent's vast spaces,
also reflects planning and investments by men, for the convenience
of men, as well as an assumption that private automobiles (driven
primarily by men) will dominate transportation (Cichocki 1980;
Fava 1980; Hayden 1984; Markusen 1981; 1983; Perin 1977; Popenoe 1980; Strasser 1982; Women and Transport Forum this
volume). 'Suburban environments,' writes Sylvia Fava, 'offer a
secondary place to women, a place inhibiting the full expression of
the range of women's roles, activities, and interests' (1980, 129).
And a chief feature of that oppressive place is its sequestration of
women in stifling dollhouses with attached garages.

The automobile did not create a middle–class suburbia, but, as a
number of scholars have said, it catalyzed, expanded and accelerated
a process already facilitated by streetcar lines (Bottles 1984; Fogelson 1967; Foster 1971; 1975; 1983; Wachs 1984; Warner 1962). Cer-

tainly, the decentralization of the city that automobile transportation promoted did tend to exacerbate urban sprawl, and did make cars necessary for much of suburban women's social life and consumption work (Interrante 1983).

Any analysis of the effects of the automobile on women's access to social life must begin by taking into account not only the immensity of the United States and the lack of natural barriers to urban sprawl for many American cities, but also early twentieth-century American conceptions of middle-class womanhood. Gendered conceptions of the Good Life—of home, community, and the proper roles of women and men—shaped metropolitan America and the car culture. More specifically, cultural ideology molded automobile use. Most middle-class Americans in the early years of the popular adoption of the motor car assumed that domesticity would (and should) define most women's days and identities. Some did see housewives' social isolation as a problem of metropolitan life, but only a few visionaries and reformers were willing to sacrifice (single-family) home and (domestic) motherhood to bring women closer to community life (Hayden 1984). In the initial years of its acceptance by the American public, the auto was widely heralded as the key to wider social contacts for women in the countryside as well as the suburbs, a concept at least one historian of the car culture shares (Flink 1975, 87). Further, most people—including Black Americans and other minority group members restricted by legal segregation and income to urban ghettos—assumed that the suburban environment combined the best features of city and country, and offered a beneficial setting for family life (Fogelson 1967, 146). Not until mid-twentieth-century American feminists challenged the ideal of domestic womanhood did the auto begin to seem more a trap than a tool for American women.

As Joseph Interrante (1983, 103) has noted, such factors as class, race and age structured automobile use in complicated ways. A discussion of all these considerations is beyond the scope of this article, though scholars have begun to examine each (see, for example, Berger 1983; Paaswell 1978; and Preston 1979). To understand a narrower issue, the impact of the auto on middle-class housewives' lives, we need to see both women and cars in the context of suburbanization. As early as 1909, some Americans pondered the effects of suburbanization on the nation's housewives. *Good Housekeeping*, a publication which sought to both shape and reflect middle-class women's lives, ran a number of articles debating the costs and benefits of women's lives in the suburbs. In an article titled 'The commuter's wife', writer Grace Duffield Goodwin referred to the archetypal suburb as 'Lonelyville', and admitted that, 'The days are long in these suburban towns ... devoid of interest and companionship' (Goodwin 1909, 363). Yet Goodwin's appraisal of suburban living was on the whole more positive than such sentiments would imply. If life in a low-density neighborhood deprived women of the casual contact with neighbors characteristic of life in close urban quarters, such isolation could also be regarded as blissful privacy:

> First among advantages there is a whole house to one's self, with no evil-eyed janitor ... no unbending neighbor whose half of a piazza or a cellar one is forever innocently intruding. Better the dinner of herbs on the peaceful gas stove, a poor thing, but your own, than the contentious kitchen of a combination flat. (362)

According to homemakers surveyed in a November 1909 *Good Housekeeping* piece called 'Testimony from many places', suburban life afforded more than protection from prying eyes and kitchen competitors. The magazine had solicited women's opinions in suburbs of cities including Boston, New York, St Louis, Chicago, San Francisco, Los Angeles and Baltimore, and in nearly all cases informants said that the benefits of life on the outskirts of town outweighed the costs. A number of women voiced some version of one housewife's statement that, 'We have all of the advantages of a city with none of its disadvantages,' citing especially improvements in housing, family health and children's social life. None mentioned social isolation as a problem; however several discussed the higher cost of living, an understandable concern given their role as managers of family consumption. While many agreed that prices, especially for food, tended to be higher in the suburbs than in the city, the informants offered various schemes for minimizing food costs. Some women said that they made occasional trips to the city (chiefly via commuter railways and trolley cars) for provisions. Since, at that time, many stores delivered free of charge, these women were not always faced with the problem of managing large loads of groceries on public conveyances. Others prevailed upon their husbands to pick up fruit, vegetables and other supplies before returning home in the evening ('Testimony from many places' 1909, 590–3).

Good Housekeeping editors, catering to an audience of homemakers, were apparently as concerned with the suburban/city price discrepancy as they were with the problem of loneliness. The magazine ran a piece in that same issue on 'Suburban prices, New York in and out.' The author admitted that, 'Yes, it costs more to live in the suburbs than in an apartment in the city,' but insisted that 'care and foresight will greatly decrease the difference in cost, and increased health and happiness will amply repay the rest' (590). She suggested that suburban homemakers needed to break 'bad city habits' in order to economize. 'Chief of these,' she wrote, 'is giving orders to the tradesmen who call at the door, instead of going to market yourself.' She also cautioned housewives to beware the suburban bad habit of going to the nearest store, since comparison shopping would yield cheaper goods and better quality (588-9). Access to an automobile (something not very many commuters' wives had in 1909) would obviously make it much easier for the homemaker to accomplish both objectives.

Just as importantly, the automobile had the potential to make Lonelyville less lonely. A humorous short story in the same issue of *Good Housekeeping* told the story of a young wife, new to the suburbs, who overcame her social isolation by breaking up dog fights as she strolled through the neighborhood. As the story ended, the heroine astonished her commuter husband by returning the greeting of a merry group of women in an automobile. While the automobile had not actually put an end to her social dislocation, the readers were left to assume that the formerly lonely protagonist would soon be sharing the pleasures of her neighbors' happy motoring.

During the 1920s, advertisers regularly pictured the automobile as a setting for and tool of women's social life, and auto manufacturers depicted their product as the solution to the problem of women's social isolation. Companies illustrated advertisements for products as varied as electric ranges, crackers and motor oil with pictures of people in groups (sometimes just women, sometimes women and men) in cars, implying that since the auto had made social contact and visiting so easy, women required other goods to keep pace with a society on wheels. An ad in the September 1920 number of *Sunset* featured a picture of two couples alighting from an auto, as seen from a kitchen window, with the caption, 'Company never embarrasses the pantry shelf stocked with National Biscuit Company products.' Often, advertisers contrasted automobility and leisure with domesticity and work. In *Sunset*'s October issue, a Westinghouse electric range ad depicted two smiling women out for a drive, one apparently declaring, 'I go anytime—I've an *Automatic* Cook.' Below, the company asked, 'Wouldn't *you* rather be motoring ... or doing any one of a hundred things than standing over a hot stove in a hot kitchen?' The Standard Oil Company apparently found such approaches a bit strident. Simply taking for granted the motor car's role as a vehicle of women's social life, the company promoted its Zerolene motor oil with a picture of a pair of women obviously at ease in a car, stating, 'Correct lubrication makes a good car better' (*Sunset*, October 1920, 3).

Auto manufacturers, advertising in such publications as *The Ladies' Home Journal* and *Good Housekeeping*, pressed the identification of their products with women's sociability, while trying to refute any idea of conflict between automotive leisure and domestic responsibility. The ads feature smiling groups of well-dressed women enjoying each other's company in Cadillacs and Chevrolets and Overland Sixes, frequently setting the dry comfort of the closed car (which took over the market in the 1920s) against a backdrop of rainy weather outside. Ford Motor Company was especially interested in portraying the Ford as, in the words of a 1925 *Ladies' Home Journal* ad, 'An "open door" to wider contacts', asserting that 'By owning a Ford car a woman can with ease widen her sphere of interests without extra time or effort' (March 1925, 70). Significantly, the ad continued, 'She can accomplish more daily, yet easily keep pace with her usual schedule of *domestic* pursuits' (emphasis mine). Ford ads showed women in a variety of situations— vacationing, going shopping, pursuing social engagements, and even conducting business—but always emphasized the social aspect of the product. No woman need feel lonesome, Ford implied, because 'The car is so easy to drive that it constantly suggests thoughtful services to her friends. She can call for them without effort and share pleasantly their companionship' (*Good Housekeeping*, March 1924, 99). In a rare departure from its usual strategy of depicting the women in its ads as homemakers and social beings, Ford affirmed in a 1924 ad that even the businesswoman, despite 'her habit of measuring time in terms of dollars,' would find that the Ford 'is such a pleasant car to drive that it transforms the business call which might be an interruption into an enjoyable episode of her busy day' (*Good Housekeeping*, April 1924, 100).

Like any prescriptive literature, advertising does not necessarily reflect popular opinion or social action. Neither does advertising speak with one voice; car ads in men's magazines surely reflected a different view of women's relation to cars. At the social level, studies of post-World War II automobile use in the United States and Canada indicate that proportionately more men than women have obtained drivers' licenses, and that men have tended to have greater access to cars than women do (Cichocki 1980, 158; Freeman 1981, 9). Fragmentary evidence suggests that despite auto manufacturers' appeals to women, male drivers far outnumbered their female counterparts. The *Los Angeles Times* reported on 11 April 1920 that, 'California has taken the lead of all states in the number of women drivers. In Los Angeles, San Francisco, and Oakland, 20 percent of all the motorists are women, the new 1920 registration indicate [sic] while the country sisters constitute 15 percent of the motoring population.' An article in *The Literary Digest* that same year estimated that there were 15,000 women motorists in New Jersey, or 5 percent of the total ('Where women motorists excel mere men', 1920). While many states did not issue drivers' licenses, and in any case only a minority of drivers in this period bothered to get licenses (*Statistical Abstract of the United States* 1920, 314–15), there is no reason to assume that proportionately more women than men dispensed with the formality. And without independent access to a car, the housewife in an increasingly sprawling city would certainly have found herself dependent on husband, children or friends to carry on some aspects of her work and social life. Still, a question remains as to the geographic distribution of those early women drivers. Were suburban women (who were presumably among the most affluent in society) more likely to drive, and have regular access to cars, than women in the city center?

For at least one group of women, the motor car appears to have genuinely diminished social isolation. Rural Americans experienced the raw vastness of the landscape more than any other group in the nation. The census of 1920 was the first in United States history in which more people resided in metropolitan areas than in rural areas, and many women who still lived on farms regarded the automobile as a solution to the problem of distance from community life. Michael Berger found that by the beginning of the twentieth century, 'Of all the members of the farm family, the farm wife felt the isolation most acutely' (1979, 57). Automobiles enabled farm women to participate in town life much more frequently than they had in the days of horse and foot transportation. Moreover, according to

Berger, 'The motor car provided rural women with their first opportunity for independent mobility, and there was every indication that they intended to use it' to attend club meetings, visit friends, shop for items formerly produced at home, and generally to relieve the monotony of the household routine (65-6). One farm woman expressed her preference for the auto over other conveniences like bathtubs quite simply, telling an interviewer, 'You can't go to town in a bathtub' (ibid.).

In 1919, US Department of Agriculture home demonstration agents conducted a survey of over 10,000 women in farm homes to determine farm women's attitudes toward their situation. The results of the survey, summarized by Florence E. Ward, appeared under the title 'The farm woman's problems' (1920). Ward asserted that 'The farm woman feels her isolation from neighbors as well as from libraries and other means of keeping in touch with outside life' and cited impressive statistics to back the point. Her findings indicated:

> an average distance [from the farm] of 5.9 miles to the nearest high school, 2.9 miles to the nearest church, and 4.8 miles to the nearest market, show[ing] that country people are far enough from the centers of trade, social, and religious activities to tempt the spirit of individualism and to put their neighborliness and piety to the test.... The automobile contributes materially to community life by reducing the distance factor (445-6).

According to Ward, an average of 62 percent of farms in the USDA study reported owning cars, with the highest percentage in the midwest (73), next highest in the west (62), and lowest in the east (48). Berger has also cited an article in the *Rural New Yorker* based on 1920 Commerce Department records indicating that more than 166,000 farms (or 8 percent of all farms in the country) might have had more than one car (52). Yet just having a car did not guarantee the greater mobility and increased sociability which farm women clearly saw as the chief benefits of access to autos. Mechanical difficulties, lack of driving ability or experience, and wretched roads sometimes barred the door to wider contacts. However, Katherine Jensen's assertion that 'rural women's relation to economic production demands that they gain a higher level of skills and more diverse technological competence than is usually expected of urban women (and most urban men)' (1983, 136) would seem to be borne out by country women's ingenious solutions to their transportation problems. Many rural women found great satisfaction in attending homemakers' extension clubs organizations intended to enhance both social life and domesticity. A Montana woman told an oral history interviewer that, 'We looked forward to the meetings—the information they gave there, and the sociability that was involved. It was really the social life of the community' (Arnold 1985b, 210). While USDA extension agents sometimes visited individual farmhouses, and meetings were sometimes held within walking or horseback riding distance of the farm woman's home, the auto promised to bring more extension activities within the farm woman's compass. In the early days of the car culture, that promise might nevertheless require both creativity and cooperation for its fulfillment. One Posey County, Indiana farm woman recalled a time when extension agents held a meeting to teach club members how to preserve food by the coldpacking method:

> I drove a horse and buggy halfway, and I met up with Carlena Cowan Ramsey. She had a car. I could drive a car straight forward, but I could not back one. So I picked her up and Lena Thompson Holler up and Lena had one of those new-fangled coldpackers, and I drove the car up to Farmersville School, and we worked all day canning.
>
> When we got ready to go home, Carlena couldn't drive that car straight, but she could back it, so she backs it up, and we loaded Lena in with her precious coldpacker, and I drove the car home, and got my horse and buggy and come on home. (Eleanor Arnold 1985a, 43-4)

This delightful anecdote suggests not only that farm women sometimes achieved remarkable feats of technological creativity and cooperation, but also that country women, in any case, did not necessarily regard domesticity and sociability as contradictory, even when the two endeavors were spatially segregated. The notion that women needed to confine themselves to the home to carry out the demands of domestic work persisted as a cultural fiction (indeed, a 1916 article in *Motor Age* accused rural women of gadding about in autos and neglecting their laying hens (Berger 1979, 66)), but not necessarily as universal social practice. In the above story, the auto was only one tool of housewifery, and a finicky and subordinate one at that (the *coldpacker* was the high-tech item here)! In such cir-cumstances, greater geographical mobility, in the form of more reli-able vehicles, better driving skills and better roads, appeared to be the rural homemaker's answer to the problem of isolation.

This glimpse of popular ideology and a few American women's experiences in the early part of the twentieth century suggests that any feminist critique of metropolitanism and its primary tools (in this case, the automobile) must begin with an attempt to understand the values that shaped choices about how, and where, Americans would live. The choice of low–density neighborhoods on the outskirts of cities reflected concepts of ideal family life and com-munity which included domesticity as women's identity and voca-tion. The sources cited here indicate that many women shared such ideas. As the problem of social isolation began to manifest itself, the automobile appeared to provide a way to link home with social life. At the same time, the suggestion that the motor car provided wom-en with 'an open door to wider contacts' implied the possibility that automobility might enable women to transcend the domestic sphere and grasp opportunities for public achievement. That possibility, however, went largely unfulfilled.

This promise of wider public opportunities, embodies not only in the rhetoric of automobility but in concurrent discourses linked with the suffrage crusade, the growth of higher education for wom-en, and the entry of women into the workforce, sometimes comple-mented, but often contradicted the practice of car culture domestici-ty (most painfully embodied in Betty Friedan's image of the house-wife trapped in a station wagon full of screaming children [Friedan 1963]). All too often, the cultural fiction of liberty and equality for American women remained a frustrating, even seemingly impossi-ble dream. No wonder, then, that for many women, feminist reawakening should have begun with the question, 'Is this all?'

REFERENCES

Arnold, Eleanor, ed. 1985a. *Buggies and Bad Times*. Indianapolis: Indiana Extension Homemakers Association.

Arnold, Eleanor, ed. 1985b. *Voices of American Homemakers*. Wash-ington DC: National Extension Homemakers Council.

Berger, Michael L. 1979. *The Devil Wagon in God's Country: The Automobile and Social Change in Rural America, 1893-1929*. Hamden, Conn.: Archon Books.

143

Berger, Michael, 1983. 'The great white hope on wheels.' In David L. Lewis and Laurence Goldstein, eds. *The Automobile and American Culture*. Ann Arbor: University of Michigan Press, 59–70.

Bottles, Scott L. 1984. 'The making of the modern city: Los Angeles and the automobile, 1900–1950.' PhD thesis, University of Southern California.

Cichocki, Mary K. 1980. 'Women's travel patterns in a suburban development.' In Gerda Wekerle, Rebecca Peterson and David Morley, eds. *New Space for Women*. Boulder, Co.: Westview, 151–64.

Fava, Sylvia F. 1980. 'Women's place in the new suburbia.' In Gerda Wekerle, Rebecca Peterson and David Morley, eds. *New Space for Women*. Boulder, Co.: Westview, 129–50.

Flink, James J. 1975. *The Car Culture*. Cambridge, Mass.: MIT Press.

Fogelson, Robert M. 1967. *The Fragmented Metropolis: Los Angeles, 1850-1930*. Cambridge, Mass.: Harvard University Press.

Foster, Mark S. 1971. 'The decentralization of Los Angeles during the 1920s.' PhD thesis, Los Angeles: University of Southern California, Department of History.

Foster, Mark S. 1975. 'The Model T, the hard sell, and Los Angeles' urban growth: the decentralization of Los Angeles during the 1920s.' *Pacific Historical Review* 44:4, 459–84.

Foster, Mark S. 1983. 'The automobile and the city.' In David L. Lewis and Laurence Goldstein, eds. *The Automobile and American Culture*. Ann Arbor: University of Michigan Press, 24–36.

Freeman, Jo. 1981. 'Women and urban policy.' In Catharine R. Stimpson, Elsa Dixler, Martha J. Nelson and Kathryn B. Yatrakis, eds. *Women and the American City*. Chicago and London: University of Chicago Press, 1–19.

Friedan, Betty. 1963. *The Feminine Mystique*. New York: W. W. Norton. *Good Housekeeping*, March and April 1924.

Goodwin, Grace Duffield. 1909. 'The commuter's wife: a sisterly talk by one who knows her problems.' *Good Housekeeping* 49 (October), 362–6.

Hayden, Dolores. 1984. *Redesigning the American Dream: The Future of Housing, Work, and Family Life*. New York: W. W. Norton.

Interrante, Joseph. 1983. 'The road to autopia: the automobile and the spatial transformation of American culture.' In David L. Lewis and Laurence Goldstein, eds. *The Automobile and American culture*. Ann Arbor: University of Michigan Press, 89–104.

Jensen, Katherine. 1983. 'Mother calls herself a housewife, but she buys bulls.' In Jan Zimmerman, ed. *The Technological Woman: Interfacing With Tomorrow*. New York: Praeger, 136–44.

Ladies' Home Journal. March 1925.

Los Angeles Times, 11 April 1920.

Markusen, Ann R. 1981. 'City spatial structure, women's household work, and national urban policy.' In Catharine R. Stimpson, Elsa Dixler, Martha J. Nelson and Kathryn B. Yatrakis, eds. *Women and the American City*. Chicago and London: University of Chicago Press, 20–41.

Markusen, Ann R. 1983. 'The lonely squandering of urban time.' In Jan Zimmerman, ed. *The Technological Woman: Interfacing with Tomorrow*. New York: Praeger, 94–101.

Paaswell, Robert E. 1978. *Problems of the Carless*. New York: Praeger.

Perin, Constance. 1977. *Everything in its Place: Social Order and Land Use in America*. Princeton: Princeton University Press.

Popenoe, David. 1980. 'Women in the suburban environment: a US–Sweden comparison.' In Gerda Wekerle, Rebecca Peterson and David Morley, eds. *New Space for Women*. Boulder, Co.: Westview, 165–74.

Preston, Howard L. 1979. *Automobile Age Atlanta: The Making of a Southern Metropolis, 1900–1935*. Athens, Ca.: University of Georgia Press.

Statistical Abstract of the United States. 1920. Washington, DC: Department of Commerce.

Strasser, Susan. 1982. *Never Done: A History of American Housework*. New York: Pantheon.

'**Suburban prices: New York in and out**. 1909. A comparative record of the cost of living in a New York apartment and in a suburb as kept by a family of two.' *Good Housekeeping* 49 (November), 588–90.

Sunset, September and October 1920.

'**Testimony from many places to show that if the suburbs are more expensive, they are better**.' 1909. *Good Housekeeping* 49 (November), 590–3.

Wachs, Martin. 1984. 'Autos, transit, and the sprawl of Los Angeles: the 1920s.' *Journal of the American Planning Association* 50, no.3 (Summer), 297–310.

Ward, Florence E. 1920. 'The farm woman's problems.' *Journal of Home Economics* 12:10 (October), 437–57.

Warner, Sam Bass, Jr. 1962. *Streetcar Suburbs: The Process of Growth in Boston, 1870-1900*. Cambridge, Mass.: Harvard University Press.

'Where women motorists excel mere men.' 1920. *Literary Digest* 67 (4 December), 75–80.

CHERIS KRAMARAE

TALK OF SEWING CIRCLES AND SWEATSHOPS

'I'd rather talk sewing than just about anything. It's the most friendly talk.'

(Woman talking about fabric shopping and sewing)

In the 1850s, writers in *The Lily*, the first US feminist periodical, welcomed the sewing machine as a new machine which would ease the burden of seamstresses, and give other women more time to enrich their lives and others' because it would free women from excessive sewing time. In 1860, *Godey's*, the popular illustrated journal for women, characterized the sewing machine as 'The queen of inventions,' predicting that it would be a revolutionary device:

> The Sewing Machine will, after a time, effectively banish ragged and unclad humanity from every class.... In all Benevolent Institutions these machines are now in operation, and do, or may do, a hundred times more toward clothing the indigent and feeble than the united fingers of all the charitable and willing ladies collected through the civilized world could possibly perform. (Quoted in Green 1983, 81–2)

The sewing machine, according to these predictions, would revolutionize the lives of all the women who sewed for long hours for themselves and other members of the households, as well as the women who did 'putting out' work. It was also going to provide inexpensive clothing for the indigent. Indeed, use of the sewing machine did change many women's lives. For example, many home sewers were moved to sweatshops where sewing still remained women's lowly paid work. (In Great Britain and in the white North American colonies, tailoring was a male skill—but it was the home work of most women, including slave women, since the sexual division in slave work was as strict as among the whites who determined the slave occupations [Matthaei 1982, 91].)

147

Given the continual sexual division in sewing work in the past hundred years, and given the continual misery of many of the women who did the sewing, I found the recent brief social history of the sewing machine, published in a national news magazine, an astonishingly androcentric and misleading account. The report was of the sale by the Singer company (makers since 1851 of Singer sewing machines) of its sewing operations. (The Singer company will now concentrate on its defense business.) The report begins:

> Mahatma Gandhi called the Singer sewing machine 'one of the few useful things ever invented.' Admiral Richard Byrd carted six Singers with him to the Antarctic. During the late 19th century, Russia's Czar Alexander III ordered workers to use the machines to make 250,000 tents for the Imperial Army. (*Time*, 3 March 1986, 62)

An accompanying illustration of a Singer ad, circa 1880, shows a girl being taught to machine sew by a woman. Yet, in the two-column report, women (who have, of course, run up many more millions of hours on Singers and its competitors than have men) are not mentioned except for a reference to Isaac Singer's 'two wives and at least three mistresses.'

This report prompts me to suggest some of the concerns which would be included if women and their relationships were considered. What follows is not, of course, a full social history of the sewing machine in the West. It is a report which indicates that, while many women have extracted much enjoyment, many others have suffered pain in working with sewing machines—which were, after all and despite the hopes of early feminist advocates, not designed for the domestic convenience or the specific needs of women. Here, too, we note that the uses which the capitalists and the women operators have made of the sewing machine have contributed—along with other social processes—to changes in the ways women interact.

Needlework and friendship

In her historical account of needlework published in 1844, just a few years before the first sales of sewing machines in the US, Mrs. Elizabeth Stone points out that historians typically ignore women's history. She writes of the 'ungallent silence' of the male historian who is only interested in the 'blazoning of manly heroism, of royal disputations, or of trumpet-shirring records' and who consistently overlooks women's activities. She points out that women are 'courted, flattered, caressed, extolled' by 'lords of creation'—who might talk an interest in women but make certain that only their own pursuits are the themes of historians (3,4).

Meanwhile, Mrs. Stone writes, women discharge their domestic duties ('the world forgetting, by the world forgot') adding 'very materially to the comforts of the other half' (4,5). Hers is, she believes, the first Western history of needlework ever published.

At times in her book, Mrs. Stone uses the words *needlework*, *stitchery* and *sewing* without distinction. In most accounts, however, *needlework* has referred to fine, handcrafted and artistic work which is often displayed (on bed, wall, floor, person). As the work of Judy Chicago and artist colleagues both emphasizes and contradicts (in The Dinner Party and The Birth Project), needlework has historically been 'women's work' and not art. Chicago (1985) writes that in the 1960s (before her work on the two major projects which have now won her international recognition and brought increased attention to such traditional women's work as china painting, crocheting and fine needlework) she would have been humiliated if a male artist or dealer had seen her sewing a button on her husband's shirt or working at an embroidery machine or at a loom.[1] Now, after years of creating art works with techniques traditionally used by women,[2] she states:

> It was a great relief to enter, first, the world of the china-painter and, later, that of the needleworker. I enjoyed the warmth of women's conversations, the open sharing of feelings, and, because most women know how to cook, the frequent sharing of food. (5-6)

Needlework, when it is done in the places and conditions chosen by the stitchers, has obviously given women much pleasure. Sometimes it provides time alone, away from family. (The twentieth-century sewing books often mention the desirability of having a small brightly lit sewing room reserved just for sewing.) It has served other important functions over the years. In the eighteenth-century, knowing how to sew well was a way for slave women to work away from fields (Jensen and Davidson 1984, 3). Often it has provided an approved way of talking and relaxing with family or friends while still working. We have thousands of paintings and photographs of Western women sitting in the evening (with other family members who are usually reading) sewing, knitting, crocheting, embroidering or mending.

Many women have justified time spent at women's church groups and friendship groups by doing hand sewing. Nineteenth-century housewives almost always sewed when they gathered, taking their sewing boxes along on their visits. Susan Strasser (1982) writes that 'more than any other household task, sewing filled spare moments and provided social activity' (132). Even fashionable women would regularly sew with other ladies.[3] Those with little leisure time sewed together less frequently, but did get together for quilting bees. Strasser points out that for generations and for women of all classes sewing has been linked to adult companionship (134).[4]

The evidence is clear that for many women sewing has been a pleasurable, companionable activity. However, much sewing has been a task done in addition to many other tasks. Bernice Johnson Reagon (1982), in writing of the revolutionary struggle of Black Americans, writes about 'My mothers':

My mother was born in Worth County
Her mother was a seamstress
Words from my mother about her mother were like
'I never knew when she went to bed'
She was a farmer
When she got home from working the farm
My grandmother would do her work as a seamstress
To my mother she was always a seamstress
Even while she picked cotton or pulled corn or cooked peas and
rice. (83)

Women in slavery returning from the fields often sewed late into the night even after the men had gone to bed. If there was any saving grace to this extra duty domestic work it was that the women had chances to interact with each other. The women looked forward to doing laundry together, and quiltings (called 'frolics' and 'parties' by the women) were times that the women could talk together (White 1985, 122-3).

Nonetheless, sewing was usually not sufficient for a profession. *The Revolution*, edited by Elizabeth Cady Stanton and Susan B. Anthony, reported on starvation deaths of seamstresses. Even those who were reportedly doing well were not well paid. Commenting in 1868 on a newspaper report which stated that 'a lady in Lee, Mass., has earned $900 in five years with a sewing machine,' the editors ask, 'We wonder if a man can be found, who would be contented with earning $900 for five years' work' (17 December, 380).

We also have some information about nineteenth-century women called 'slop workers' who did plain sewing at home (often the making of shirts). They were paid very little by contractors, who could keep wages low because there were so many women who were trying to be self-supporting by sewing. The slavery of the women is described in Thomas Hood's 'The Song of the Shirt' first published in 1843 (in the Christmas issue of *Punch*):

> With fingers weary and worn,
> With eyelids heavy and red,
> A woman sat, in unwomanly rags,
> Plying her needle and thread—
> Stitch! Stitch! Stitch!
> In poverty, hunger, and dirt,
> And still with a voice of dolorous pitch
> She sang *The Song of the Shirt*!
> ...
> Sewing at once, with a double thread,
> A shroud as well as a shirt.
>
> (Neff 1919, 131–2)

Even when it didn't kill, sewing was often a difficult task for nineteenth-century homemakers, although one through which a woman could feel a sense of accomplishment. One woman reminiscing states,

And the sewing we had to do! I think I had more faculty for that sort of thing than most women have, but, goodness knows, it was hard enough for the most skillful of us.... I used to feel very proud of the beautiful gauze-like shirts I'd made for my babies out of the tops of my old white cotton stockings. (Harriet Brown 1929, quoted in Juster 1979, 100)

We can compare this pride with the remembered frustration of two seamstresses who, to earn more money, took a job in a sweatshop:

> We kept our day work and our night work separate. We never
> let anybody at the factory know about the other sewing. Any-
> way, sewing in the two places really was as different as night
> from day. At night we sewed for our patrons. In the day we
> didn't know who we were sewing for. One morning I put a lot
> of sleeves into the bodices backwards, and the supervisor said,
> 'Nobody will know. Go on.' (Fields 1983, 153)

Machine sewing and women's networks

Once sewing machines were on the market, *Godey's* editors suggested that to overcome the high price of the new machinery,
several families pool resources and form a 'sewing machine club';
diary accounts suggest that women who owned machines frequently loaned them to friends (Green 1983, 82). But, ironically enough,
Godey's helped prevent a real revolution in the amount of time
women spent sewing. The clothing and home decoration projects
illustrated and described in *Godey's* became more elaborate after the
availability of the sewing machine, thus encouraging as much or
more sewing time. The sewing machine, like so many other household technologies, did not reduce the amount of time women spent
in household tasks (Cowan 1983; see also Baron and Klepp 1984, 37;
and McGaw 1982). Even women who owned machines continued
to get together with other women to do hand needlework.

But what about the effect of the sewing machine on the toil and
eyestrain, independence and income of women who tried to make a
living through their sewing? While sales techniques involving
monthly installments and trade-ins were devised by the sewing
machine companies to increase home sales, still most sales were to
manufacturers and most sewing machines were used by women
(and some men) working at very low prices for contractors. Many
women did piecemeal work either in their own homes on machines
they could barely afford or, after 1880, increasingly in tenement
houses turned into rooms called sweatshops—with deplorable
working conditions including unsanitary work space, inadequate
ventilation, long hours and low pay (Levine 1924, 18).[5]

The devaluing of women's work was illustrated in other ways in
the sewing industry. Within capitalism, much of women's work is
spent in relations of intimacy and care. (Many theorists make the ar-

gument that, in contrast, male identity is constructed through denial of relationships with others (see, e.g., Ferguson 1984, 158, 159).) Yet, the industrial mechanization of needlework made sewing more tied to one place and more noisy and therefore made talk among sewers more difficult. Many of the workers were recent immigrants and sometimes there was no common language, which made interaction among the women even more difficult. In describing her work in an early sewing factory, Mamie Garvin Fields remembers,

> We had never seen anything like the rows of sewing machines all going at once.... Here, nothing but machines, and everybody busy at a machine. Nobody was sewing anything on her hands. (Fields 1983, 148)

> The first thing our supervisor put me on was sleeves, nothing but sleeves. Sleeves to what, I didn't know, just sleeves to put together all day long.... There were girls, just like us. I sometimes wondered ... were they working for the same reason I was? Were they engaged to a man back home? ... But I couldn't communicate with them well enough to find out all that. The greater part of our talking was done by sign language. (Fields 1983, 149, 150)

There was obviously some interaction (after all, the women managed to organize many strikes [Jensen and Davidson 1984]). But also obviously, the uses which capitalists made of the machines and women operators drastically changed the kind of interaction sewers were accustomed to when sewing in their homes. Today, many poor women in Latin America and Asia sew under similarly terrible conditions for very little money. Many women sew piecemeal at home so they can have flexible hours to care for children and do other family work. While this gives them some 'freedom' this isolation from other sewers means that the women have few opportunities to discuss their working conditions or to organize to improve those conditions.[6]

At times the advertisers for the sewing industry have shown some awareness of the way women have enjoyed doing needlework in the company of others. A 1909 ad in *Harper's Bazaar* for a portable, fold-up, lightweight portfolio containing hand sewing equipment suggests using the Portsewcab on the front porch or at the home of a friend. Automobile travel possibilities and wars, while not organized by women, certainly changed women's work and places of interaction. The ads for early portable sewing machines advised women that the machines could be carried to the neighbor's or, during World War I, to the war relief work rooms. ('Why,' exclaims one woman to the other in the 1918 *Red Cross Magazine* ad, 'it [the sewing machine] will almost go into my knitting bag!') Some ads during the war featured two women wearing Red Cross or nursing caps, seated next to each other at sewing machines. Other ads showed one woman at a machine while another sat nearby knitting or admiring the work produced by the sewer. Others (seemingly modeled on the nineteenth-century pictures of women sewing in the living room bathed in the glow of family love and candles or gas light) place a woman at the sewing machine in the living room with a man in a nearby easy chair. Ads for Singer sewing classes in the first half of the twentieth-century show many women smiling, sewing together and modeling clothes for each other.

Yet, while advertisements suggested the possibilities of companionable group sewing on machines (in imitation of the gatherings of hand sewers), the size, weight and noise of the machines suggested the impracticality of this for many tasks. Many women who own machines have continued to create some items by hand in part because such sewing can be done in close company with other women or family members. The machine serves some valuable mechanical functions, but it does not answer women's emotional and intellectual needs for companionship and exchange of information.

There are, of course, many other things which can be said about the sewing machine, women's work and communication. The pattern books can be studied for their statements about what machine home sewing has been thought to be. Until the twentieth-century, household sewing was considered a built-in housewife job, a necessity like cooking, rather than an option. Many items were not available commercially. Even after men's clothing, first, and women's and children's clothing, later, became available in stores or through the mail, women still had to make towelling, sheets and furniture protectors. Just as women often made such tasks as canning fruits and vegetables more pleasant by doing it together, they often did domestic sewing together.

Even after clothing and most 'necessary' household cloth items were available commercially, many women continued to sew for the pleasures such activity can bring—such as tactile pleasure, creative pleasure, technical artistic pleasure, image control, personal expression and independence from manufacturers. In the US during

COME
Meet with your friends

Learn to Make the Lovely Clothes You Want Through FREE Personal Instruction at the Nearest SINGER Sewing School

Now you can learn in a new delightful way to make all the lovely dresses you want. At the nearest Singer Sewing School you and your friends can meet in a social group. From the very beginning, step-by-step, you are shown just how to plan and completely make the dress of your choice. An instructor helps you select a design and material appropriate for your type—the right fabric, the right lines to be distinctively becoming.

Then you are guided safely, surely, in cutting it out, stitching the seams, fitting and finishing it to the last detail. You learn those little secrets that enable you to give a smart appearance to sleeves, necklines, waistlines, skirt finishes. In a few delightful hours, in a pleasant atmosphere and with the use of the finest equipment, you have completed a really smart dress and are ready to put it on and proudly show it to your family or your friends. Whatever your previous experience in dressmaking, you will learn many new methods that make the creation of a dress simpler and easier for you.

This new service is provided *free* with the new Singer sewing machines. Now when the tempting new fashions prompt you to want more new dresses than ever before, enjoy this opportunity to learn to make them under personal instruction.

Whether or not you attend the nearest Singer Sewing School, you will find that every Singer Shop is prepared to give you, with every Singer sewing machine, a set of the Singer Sewing Library and an invaluable service that includes free expert instruction in modern machine sewing. Ask any Singer Shop or Representative about the instruction service available in your community, and for a free copy of "How to Make Dresses," "How to Make Draperies," or "How to Make Children's Clothes."

SINGER
Sewing Machine Company, Inc.

Figure 4 Sewing machine manufacturers often advertised their product as something which could provide not only happier and more beautiful lives for the members of the family of the woman doing the sewing, but also a better social life for her. This invitation to 'Come Meet With Your Friends' (and take sewing lessons) is from a 1930s advertisement (D'Arcy Collection, University of Illinois, Urbana–Champaign)

the 1960s, home sewing machines were necessary equipment for sewers who worked from the many patterns modeled after the clothing Jackie Kennedy wore, carefully tailored, lined suits and dresses, designed for church and committee meetings. These patterns called for unusual and difficult construction, seaming and welting. Hand work was required for finishing double-faced yokes and hems. Many women did this work listening to radio, watching TV, attending civic meetings, or when visiting with friends.[7]

Some of the interaction created and supported by sewing activities takes place in fabric stores, which are traditionally staffed by women who often talk with shoppers about fabrics and about solutions to sewing problems. (A friend reported that when she walked into a fabric store recently, a male clerk approached her and asked her if he could help. Her first (unspoken) response was 'No, of course not.') Shoppers often talk with each other—asking advice, talking about fabric performance, and sharing delight with interesting designs. Additionally, fabric shopping is often a joint venture as home sewers often sew for other family members who come along to help choose fabric and patterns. Perhaps all the talk among family members facilitates talk to strangers in the fabric stores.

In the past twenty years, as in the preceding years, there have been multiple and related factors affecting women's home sewing. Household sewing is no longer a household necessity for most, although larger women still report difficulties in finding commercial clothing adequate in size, fabric and style. House dresses are no longer featured in pattern catalogues. Commercial standardized sizing S(small), M(medium) and L(large) has changed the types of patterns available; clothing is less fitted. Entire garments can be finished by machine as new techniques have become available and as designers and sewers have revised their notions of what constitutes a finished edge. Many more women are employed outside the home and there are fewer women's church or neighborhood meetings. The number of women in the US who sew has gone down (from forty million in the mid-1970s to twenty-eight million in the mid-1980s) (Forman 1986, 79) and the sewing centres, once highly advertised as places to learn sewing techniques in classes with other sewers, are disappearing. The new sewing machines are less noisy, and some women report listening to radio talk shows as they sew.[8] Linda Turner Jones, the editor of a sewing magazine, agreed that the function of sewing has changed dramatically over the years. Now, the sewer 'works hard [at something else], comes home and locks herself in the sewing room with the radio on. It's a form of therapy' (quoted in Forman 1986, 80). The sewer is isolated from others, but turns on the radio.

It may not seem surprising that most social historians writing about technology have paid little attention to women's discussion of and around sewing machines; most historians have little knowledge of the social aspects of women's sewing work and most historians do not think of the sewing machine as having anything much to do with women's conversations. That's the point, and that's the seamy problem.

NOTES

1   In the 1960s, one of the ways a male hippy made clear his rejection of traditional occupation, clothing and wars was by wearing embroidered clothing. As Rozsika Parker (1984) points out in *The Subversive Stitch*, this behavior seems 'less a subversion of sex roles than a longing for the freedom of an idealized image of childhood—mother-loved, anarchic and untouched by daddy's world' (204).

2   The Dinner Party is an open triangular table, 46 feet, 6 inches on each side, covered with white linen cloths, and 39 place settings with individually sculpted and painted plates and needlework runners representing women in Western civilization. The table rests on a floor of hand-cast porcelain tiles enscribed in gold with names of 999 women. The Birth Project, also a collective work conceived and developed by Chicago, consists of eighty works executed in or embellished with needle or textile techniques (Chicago 1985; Chicago 1980).

3   While many colonial women, for example, sewed much of the utilitarian family clothing, wealthy homemakers spent hours doing fancy and decorative needlework (Matthaei 1982, 46-7). Single, widowed or deserted women sewed to survive. In the nineteenth century, some seamstresses worked in their own homes, while others went from home to home, sometimes fashioning and cutting dresses but leaving some of the sewing to the women of the family (Strasser 1982, 131).

4   In the late nineteenth century and first half of the twentieth, all over the US sewing circle members of city branches of the Needlework Guild met monthly to sew thousands of garments and quilts. An annual report from a junior chapter noted that the girls enjoyed sewing during vacation time, and that they had sold Easter eggs to make money to buy goods to sew. The girls welcomed the left-over

material from adult sewing projects, for, the report stated, every little piece could be used to make a garment for a baby (Report of Needlework Guild, 41st, 1926, 36).

5   The contractors and subcontractors were known as sweaters because in times of intense competition they would bid low, sweating a profit out of the workers.

6   An astonishing, clear account of how women producing export goods in their homes are made invisible in official statistics of workers is available in Maria Mies's (1982) *The Lace Makers of Narsapur*. Because the makers work in their homes, their labor and their product are either denied or considered a natural leisure-time activity, even though lace making is a matter of economic necessity for them. The lace makers are women; the traders and exporters are men. Most of the agents are men—who can collect the lace by travel on bicycle. (Women walk or take a bus; the bicycles belong to men.) While the division of labor in the industry is determined in part by caste differences, sex differences are basic to the structure of the industry.

7   Sewing, listening and talking are linked activities elsewhere also, of course. In 1986, in the Kathmandu area of Nepal, I visited some homes where several members of the family worked at looms or at treadle sewing machines. Noting that sometimes the women worked facing each other, I asked about the placement of the machines, and was told that the locations of the machines were determined by the door or window light (homes I visited had no electricity or only one light bulb) and by the desire of the women to talk easily to each other while they worked.

8   I thank Susan Thomas (1986 conversation), exemplary sewer and teacher, for her observations on changes in recent sewing practices.

REFERENCES

Baron, Ava and Susan E. Klepp. 1984. 'If I didn't have my sewing machine ...: women and sewing machine technology.' In Joan Jensen and Sue Davison, eds. *A Needle, a Bobbin, a Strike: Women Needleworkers in America*. Philadelphia: Temple University Press, 20-59.

Chicago, Judy. 1985. *The Birth Project*. Garden City, New Jersey: Doubleday.

Chicago, Judy, with Susan Hill. 1980. *Embroidering Our Heritage: The Dinner Party Needlework*. Garden City, New York: Anchor Books.

Cowan, Ruth Schwartz. 1983. *More Work For Mother: The Ironies of Household Technology from the Open Hearth to the Microwave*. New York: Basic Books.

Ferguson, Kathy E. 1984. *The Feminist Case Against Bureaucracy*. Philadelphia: Temple University Press.

Fields, Mamie Garvin with Karen Fields. 1983. *Lemon Swamp and Other Places: A Carolina Memoir*. New York: Free Press.

Forman, Ellen. 1986. 'Gourmet stitching.' *Working Women*. November, 79–80.

Green, Harvey with the assistance of Mary Ellen Perry. 1983. *The Light of the Home: An Intimate View of the Lives of Women in Victorian American*. New York: Pantheon Books.

Jensen, Joan M. and Sue Davidson, eds. 1984. *A Needle, a Bobbin, a Strike: Women Needleworkers in America*. Philadelphia: Temple University Press.

Juster, Norton. 1979. *So Sweet to Labor: Rural Women in America 1865-1895*. New York: Viking Press.

Levine, Louis. 1924. *The Women's Garment Workers: A History of the International Ladies' Garment Workers' Union*. New York: B.W. Huebsch.

McGaw, Judith. 1982. 'Women and the history of American technology.' *Signs: Journal of Women in Culture and Society* 7:4, 798–828.

Matthaei, Julie A. 1982. *An Economic History of Women in America: Women's Work, the Sexual Division of Labor, and the Development of Capitalism*. New York: Schocken Books.

Mies, Maria. 1982. *The Lace Makers of Narsapur: Indian Housewives Produce for the World Market*. London: Zed.

Needlework Guild of America, Inc. *Report* 1926–38. Philadelphia.

Neff, Wanda Fraiken. 1929. *Victorian Working Women: An Historical and Literary Study of Women in British Industries and Professions 1832-1850*. New York: Columbia University Press.

Parker, Rozsika. 1984. *The Subversive Stitch: Embroidery and the Making of the Feminine*. London: The Women's Press.

Reagon, Bernice Johnson. 1982. 'My black mothers and sisters or On beginning a cultural autobiography.' *Feminist Studies* 8:1 (Spring), 81–96. [This first appeared in Virginia A. Blandford, ed. 1981. *Black Women and Liberation Movements*. Institute for the Arts and the Humanities, Howard University.]

Stone, Mrs. Elizabeth [The Countess of Wilton]. 1844. *The Art of Needlework: From the Earliest Ages.* London: Henry Colburn.

Strasser, Susan. 1982. *Never Done: A History of American Housework.* New York: Pantheon.

White, Deborah Gray. 1985. *Ar'n't I a Woman?: Female Slaves in the Plantation South.* New York: W. W. Norton.

VICTORIA LETO

'WASHING, SEEMS IT'S ALL WE DO': WASHING TECHNOLOGY AND WOMEN'S COMMUNICATION

Women who had once compared their wash over back fences or the clothes lines they strung up across alleys, in a day of grueling labor that nevertheless provided the company of other women, often put non-automatic machines on porches in the summer where they could call out to friends. Those without basement space hung out even in the winter. The permanently installed automatic washer and dryer, how-ever, brought the work inside, isolating women in their houses and denying them the companionship that had once enlivened washday, compensating for the woes of the chore they hated most.

(Strasser 1982, 272)

When we think of technology, household technology is usually overlooked, yet it has certainly affected women's lives, markedly changing the traditional domestic sphere. It seems we have uncon-sciously welcomed technology into our homes without questioning its effects on our lives, effects which extend beyond simply enabling us to complete a task.

One important effect is that much technology has privatized women's work, isolating them from each other and from the rest of society. The image of the isolated suburban housewife is certainly not new. Betty Friedan (1963) and Ann Oakley (1974a) identified the phenomenon in the 1960s and early 1970s. The purpose here is to examine how technology contributes to this isolation.

To analyze how technology isolates women, we must look at specific household tasks because, while technology may not define housework in a general sense, we can clearly see how it dictates pro-cedures for specific tasks (Oakley 1974a, 98). Of all housework, laundering has received the most technological attention, with more patents than for any other process (Giedion 1948). The evolution of the completely automatic electric washer has certainly eased what was for centuries women's most dreaded chore, but in the meantime it robbed women of the companionship they gave each other as they worked out of doors (Davidson 1982).

In contrast to the long history of laundering innovations is another washing mechanism: the dishwasher. Technology came late for the dishwashing task, and while most women today no longer have to haul in and heat their water, hand washing is still common, even in the US. Dishwashing, like laundering, was once considered a social occasion where primarily women and children worked together and visited, making the best of the routine chore. Yet, even where dishwashers are not in use, women today report a loss of companionship and help during dishwashing (Strasser 1982). This latter finding suggests the need to explore other possible influences besides technology, such as social–political structures, which have made domestic work a solitary task.

Two basic questions are asked in this research: how has the development of washing technology for laundry and dishes isolated women, and what are the consequences regarding women's social interactions? To answer these questions I examined the historical development of washing technology and the social–political context in which it evolved, and I talked with women, from several countries, at a children's lunch program and at a laundry facility (both operated by a midwest USA university). Residents of a midwest town were also interviewed at commercial laundromats. In all, thirty-three women were interviewed, eighteen of whom represented twelve foreign countries. (Since this is a preliminary study and women with home laundry facilities were not as accessible, no attempt is made here to quantify results of these discussions.)

Results of this study suggest the available household technology does encourage isolation, but equally influential, if not more so, is the social–political context which fostered its growth. Together they defined not only that appliances be designed for one-person operation, but also who that person should be, and how often she should use the equipment. Granted, in more recent years, as women have taken jobs outside the home, men have begun to share domestic chores, but women still do 90 percent of the housework and still spend as much time doing it as their grandmothers did (Zimmerman 1983). Technology has curtailed important sources of social interaction for women, and the new contexts for communication which have evolved are limited, and may not be as rewarding.

THE HISTORY OF LAUNDERING: A COMMUNICATION PERSPECTIVE

Hand laundry procedures encourage socializing

The history of washing takes us back more than 3000 years, and until the 1800s, washing clothes was woman's most demanding task, taking approximately a third of her work time. Primitive washing procedures were marked by the use of cold water, where laundry was carried to the natural water source and detergents didn't exist. (For more details on the technological history, see Balderston 1923; Cowan 1983; Giedion 1948; Peet and Thye 1949.) Women would congregate at the head of the stream because they had to rely on the solvent power of the water to clean their clothes. After crouching several hours by the water to wash clothes, women spread the clean items over rocks or bushes to dry, and visited while they waited.

Unlike all other household tasks, a particular day, Monday, was designated for laundering in most countries. Davidson suggests the common day provided solidarity, or companionship, used to compensate for the hard work (1982, 149). Many countries made laundry day a holiday two or three times a year, marking the change of seasons. Women would meet at the riverside with their laundry and perhaps a picnic lunch and music to create a social occasion (Balderston 1923, 231).

Some women interviewed in the present study indicated these handwashing techniques and the associated socializing are still common in less industrialized countries. An American woman who has lived in various parts of Central America said washboards (which are considered the first mechanical step in laundering) are available there, but in the countryside women often use smooth stones to beat the dirt out. Women from Nigeria and India said that in villages without tap water, women wash together at a designated stream and then visit, or even barbecue food while their clothes dry.

Nineteenth-century improvements: more work, less socializing

Two improvements came in the 1800s: soaps were developed and water was now boiled before laundering (for a history of cleansing agents see Ahern 1941; Haefele *et al.* 1973). These improvements reflect a drastic increase in sanitation concerns during the century, and as cleanliness standards rose, laundry work became harder.

163

Figure 5   As in the early history of laundering processes, these young women wash clothes together in a stream, using smooth stones to pound out the dirt. They are Guatemalan refugees in rural Belize, Central America (1985) (picture courtesy of Eunice Buck)

A one-day operation turned into three days. Laundering now began on Saturday night when clothes were soaked, and more hot water was added on Sunday night. Clothes were individually rubbed on washboards, boiled, rinsed and wrung out several times. The first American washing machine patent was in 1846, although the only improvement from the hand process was that clothes were now wrung out by feeding them through a hand-cranked machine (which didn't become obsolete until well into the twentieth century). The James T. King cylinder washing machine of 1851 is claimed as the first automatic washer, eliminating the hand process of feeding clothes through a wringer, but it wasn't perfected until the introduction of electricity [Strasser 1982, 116].

It was now more difficult for women to work side by side, but kettles of water were often boiled outside, or women put the hand-cranked machines on their porches so they could talk with neighbors as they worked (Filbee 1980; Strasser, 1982).

The rise and fall of commercial laundries

Production of washing machines doubled between 1870 and 1890, but these were commercial machines, actually the first to make washing truly automatic with the use of costly steam-operated equipment, before electricity was developed. However, as indoor plumbing, electricity and gas became mass produced from 1890 to 1920, the electric washer, introduced in 1914, caused immediate competition by expanding the home laundry machine industry. The 1920s are considered a boom period for household technology in general, with mass production making electric washers affordable to lower classes as well. By 1929, 84 percent of the 1,134,000 machines sold were electric.

The number of commercial laundries declined. They never competed for housewives' total laundry job since usually only men's shirts and flat pieces were sent out. Household experts like Christine Frederick warned not to trust delicate items to commercial laundries due to possible unsanitary conditions and loss or damage to clothes (Cowan 1983, 7). Furthermore, advertisers promoted individual machines more because the home laundering market yielded higher profits by creating a whole network of product dependence involving manufacturers of washers, detergents, textiles, electrical parts and plumbing (Strasser 1982, 122). As a result, commercial prices went up at a time when home washers were cheapest.

Communal laundry attempts fail

Another alternative laundry technology which didn't survive in Western countries is the communal laundry. Public washhouses existed in London as early as 1832 where a poor woman would set up a washboiler, soap kettle and other needs, charging others a penny for their use. The first official public washhouse was in Hamburg in 1852, where the city provided the land and water. A woman interviewed from Zambia said communal compounds for handwashing are still popular there for the poor: 'There is always lots of talking and singing while they wash, all the while with children strapped to their backs.'

Some communal laundries hired employees to do the work. Melusina Fay Peirce's experiment with this in the 1860s lasted just one year, however, since only twelve of the forty members patronized it (Strasser 1982, 112-13). And, as late as 1918, editors of *The*

Figure 6 'Which woman would you rather come home to?' From the earliest laundry history, husbands have complained about eating cold leftovers and tolerating exhausted wives on laundry day. This 1920s advertisement tells husbands to join industrialization; machines should do the laundry, so women can fulfill their modern roles as loving wives and mothers

Ladies' Home Journal advocated communal laundries with hired help. But these attempts failed, largely because communalization was seen as socialistic and unAmerican (Cowan 1976b, 164; Cott 1977).

One innovative solution for reducing the laundry task in rural areas utilized the steam plants and water supplies which operated creameries to do laundry as well. At the Milltown Cooperative Creamery Co., in Wisconsin, the laundry of fifty families could be washed in forty-five minutes. It seems, however, these rural alternatives couldn't compete with the urban commercial laundries and these eventually gave way to self-service laundromats (Cowan 1983).

Clothes driers add convenience and more isolation

Clothes driers didn't actually become affordable until the 1940s. The main contribution of clothes driers was not efficiency as much as convenience (Warfield *et al.* 1976). Women no longer had to wait for a sunny day to wash, they could launder day or night, and this was necessary since the automatic washer raised cleanliness standards, consequently increasing the number of times women washed.

By the end of World War II, 'A job once performed at home, substantially commercialized before 1929, headed out of the household for the social realm like weaving and soapmaking and all other traditional household skills, went back home' (Strasser 1982, 120).

DISHWASHING HAS BRIEF TECHNOLOGICAL HISTORY

Indoor plumbing has provided the only major improvement to hand dishwashing methods since the 1800s, although the dish drainer has also been added (Strasser 1982, 89). The basic concept of the dishwasher was invented by 1865, but since electricity wasn't available yet, the hand-propelled machine was not efficient (for a technical description see Giedion 1948, 576-9). Electric dishwashers appeared in the 1930s, but were not widely used. As late as 1945, when *McCall's* magazine ran a 'Kitchens of tomorrow' contest, there were 11,446 responses to the contest, with only 115 of these women owning electric dishwashers (Giedion 1948, 578-9). However, by 1980 the dishwasher was considered a major appliance in almost half of American homes, with women primarily responsible for its operation (Strasser 1982, 279).

Cleaner Clothes the Easier Way

YOU know the worry and the work of having the washing done the "rub in the tub" way at home—yet your home is the place where your clothes should be washed.

Only in your own home can you personally supervise the work—know that nothing is lost, nothing mishandled, and everything washed perfectly clean.

With an Automatic Electric Washer in your home you are forever free from worry over the unreliability, the whims and the charges of laundresses.

Automatic Bench Washer No. 4
For the average family

A Clean Tubful Every 10 Minutes

The automatic is so thorough that the heaviest blankets can be washed in a few minutes, yet its action is so gentle that it cannot harm the filmiest lingerie.

Every lamp socket is a power station, ready at the snap of a switch to run your Automatic. Costs only a trifle to operate.

Plenty of Bench Room in this Electric Model No. 6

Strong, substantial and simple, the Automatic has been a leader for twelve years.

Write for two valuable booklets on household cleaning. Gladly sent free for the asking.

AUTOMATIC ELECTRIC WASHER CO.
335 Third Street   Newton, Iowa

Automatic "Washer Twins"
Belt Power Model No. 7

AutoMatic Washer

Figure 7 'Cleaner clothes the easier way' To counter the competition of professional laundresses, advertisers encouraged women to take pride in their laundry and do it themselves with the latest washing technology, the electric machine. Advertisers and domestic columnists cautioned women about the risks of having their clothes washed with the soiled clothes of strangers, that is, the exposure to contagion, and about valuable items of clothing not being handled with care (D'Arcy Collection, University of Illinois, Urbana–Champaign)

THE SOCIAL-POLITICAL FRAMEWORK OF DOMESTIC TECHNOLOGY

In Western countries during the 1920s, there were more variations in laundering methods than for any other household task. According to advertisements, washing was done by a variety of workers and methods: by handwashing, electric home washers, commercial laundries, and by laundresses who worked in the home, and those who worked out of the home (Cowan 1976b, 162). But something happened between that time and the present to prescribe who is responsible for the task and the type of technology used, not only for doing laundry, but for dishwashing (and other household tasks) as well.

To understand why some technology won out over alternatives and why the chosen appliances isolated women without proving time-efficient, we must also examine the social-political context in which the devices were created and marketed. The specific issues addressed here are the decrease of domestic help; emotionalism/professionalism of housework; and basic gender differences in relationship to predominant technology.

Growing scarcity of domestic help

In the beginning of the nineteenth century, unmarried daughters, sisters, orphans and hired girls were the 'domestic help.' By the 1830s industrialization began to affect these women's lives in two ways. It raised cleanliness standards and thus increased their workload, and it attracted many of these women to work in factories. In addition, income taxes, social security deductions and tighter immigration laws all inhibited families from employing servants (Cowan 1983; Howe 1918). As 'good' domestic help became more and more difficult to acquire, the demand for household technology increased.

Of course, this lack of servants affected only the middle- and upper-class women who could afford them. Domestic technology was used to raise their social status with, if possible, servants operating the equipment. Thus initially technology may have liberated middle-class women at the expense of the working classes. They became supervisors instead of working alongside helpers as before, leading to further alienation of women from each other (Dudden 1983, 7). It was not until the twentieth century that technology and its associated middle-class status values (discussed below) became

169

affordable for the working classes.

Emotionalism of housework imposed isolation

Before World War I, housework was largely regarded as a task to be handed over to someone else if at all possible. However, after 1918, housework became an expression of the housewife's personality, an act of love for her family (Cowan 1976b, 150; and 1974, 218). Housekeeping became homemaking. Linking the work to affection made it an emotional burden, replacing the physical one women had before the technological boom of the 1920s (Juster 1979, 94; Strasser 1982, 8). Betty Friedan (1963) later termed the phenomenon 'the feminine mystique,' where a woman's sole purpose in life became to be a 'good' wife and mother. (As many feminists have pointed out, this was primarily a white, middle-class phenomenon.)

Technology and the commercial society in which it occurred helped to propagate the emotionalism of housework, if not create it. Cleanliness standards were increased through advertisements. In the 1920s advertisers found they could be more effective by appealing to women's guilt and fear than by simply telling the ingredients or functions of their products. A soap ad in 1908 might describe the clean factory and pure ingredients used there. By 1928 a similar ad would portray the psychological trauma children experienced if they had to go to school with soiled clothes (Cowan 1976b, 165). And, due to the repetitious nature of the work, women could never purge their guilt, which could then often lead to seemingly compulsive behaviors (Hobson 1978). Jill Duffy, interviewed in Oakley's 1974 study, said in reference to laundering, 'I hate leaving it. If I did leave it, I'd stay up in the evening to do it. It'd be on my conscience.... I wish I didn't have to do it ... I wish I had the nerve just to leave it, but I don't' (Oakley 1974a, 109).

Home economists welcomed industrialism and its efforts to professionalize housework (Strasser 1982, 8). This trend began in the nineteenth century, when people such as Catharine Beecher sought to raise domestic standards by creating pride in women's work, calling for a domestic science. Her followers, in what is termed the 'domestic science movement' of the 1920s, applied industrial management efficiency techniques in the home (Bose, 1979, 298; Zimmerman 1983, 84). From the 1920s to the present, household experts have advised women to approach housework like a business: 'be goal oriented,' 'be like an engineer,' 'avoid interruptions' (Gilbreth et al. 1954; Zimmerman 1983).

The contradiction here is that women were encouraged to embrace technology and the values associated with it, while at the same time maintain the home as a separate sphere from the cold industrial society (Andrews and Andrews 1974). From the appearance of the first factories around 1820, the American home became the counter-symbol to industrial life. Advertisers, and later the domestic science movement, idealized domesticity as protecting the private haven and individual autonomy (Strasser 1982; Newman 1985, 156–64; Andrews and Andrews 1974). In discussing why individually operated technology such as the washing machine survived instead of communal operations, Ann Cowan claimed it was not due to capitalism, but to this desire to preserve family autonomy (1983, 149–50). Thus communal or commercial alternatives for doing housework were unacceptable. We can see why, by the 1940s, most women wanted to be the first on their block to own an automatic washer. They weren't as concerned with efficiency as with status symbols; technology was the sign of a well-kept home. (Andrews and Andrews 1974, 317; Bose 1979, 299; and Cott 1977, 60).

The effects of man the inventer, woman the operator

Pacey (1983) pointed out that due to the social-political constrictions of the times, inventors are always guilty of tunnel vision. Thus men, who have primarily controlled the invention of household technology, have provided tools which reinforce predominant values of patriarchical industrial capitalism: efficiency, materialism, and rationality, whereas the concerns of the primary operators, women, do not seem to reflect these dominant values. When asked about household chores, the common complaint of the women in Ann Oakley's study wasn't time expenditure but the repetitious, boring nature of the work.

The things women most disliked about being housewives were: (1) housework, monotony and repetitious work (70 percent of the women reported this), (2) constant domestic responsibility, and (3) isolation and loneliness. The most positive attribute of a given chore was being able to talk to others while doing work, such as shopping (Oakley 1974a, 43).

The technology men have created thus far has not improved social conditions for these women since it has increased the division of labor and routinization (Oakley 1981). Instead, male inventors seem to be imposing isolation on women by limiting their appliance options to machines intended for single-operator, single-household usage.

THE CONSEQUENCES FOR WOMEN'S
COMMUNICATION

Given the history of washing technology and the development of its associated values, what are the consequences regarding women's communication today? The widespread use of household technology has meant an increase, rather than a decrease, in time spent with domestic work; it has meant work isolated from others; and it has meant a change in the primary source and context of communication.

We seem to assume that technology reduces work time, but in actuality, few appliances save women time. The dishwasher and washing machine do save labor, but more than saving women's time, they require a restructuring of work, as do most other appliances (Zimmerman 1983). One set of studies, covering a forty-year time span on the electric dishwasher, showed it did reduce work time by twelve to thirty-seven minutes per day (Zimmerman 1983, 88). However, women today are more often solely responsible for this work, so while the machine may save time, compared to one person performing the work by hand, it may not be as efficient as when the task was divided among family members.

Even when appliances do save women time, this saving is simply redistributed to new tasks women took on as housekeeping became professionalized, such as teaching the children, scheduling family members' activities, providing transportation, and overseeing appliance maintenance. Oakley reported urban housewives in the United States were spending from fifty-one hours a week on housework in 1929, to seventy-eight to eighty-one hours in 1945 (1974b, 7), and this has only begun to decrease within the last few decades, since more than half the married women now hold full-time, paying jobs (Newman 1985, 161).

Technology is not responsible for this decrease; families have compromised on cleanliness standards and have begun to share domestic chores. However, results from a survey of fifty newly wed couples (married ten months or less) found that when husbands performed domestic chores, they worked with their wives; the wives performed additional chores alone (Huston et al. 1981).

A second effect domestic technology has had on women's communication is that the work environment has become isolated. Technology and the values of family autonomy have 'privatized' housework. In pre-industrial times, the kitchen was the center of activity for female companionship. Women's sphere was still primarily isolated from men's, but the domestic sphere was similar to a subculture. Nancy Cott called it the bond of sisterhood: women working together (1977, 29). Now, housewives are not only isolated from the male sphere, they are isolated from each other. By the nineteenth century, the kitchen was reorganized, becoming a smaller, service area only (Carroll 1979, 493). And even more isolated is the laundry facility of today, usually hidden away in some basement corner.

Large immobile household appliances were not designed to operate in the center of activity. Thus social interaction just became another interruption to one's work. A perfect example of this problem is the dishwasher, where the introduction of a loud machine seems to have brought a halt to after-dinner group clean-up and discussion. Susan Strasser interviewed a woman from California who said the dishwasher completely altered family relationships. 'We never get together to chat in the kitchen, because why should we be in the kitchen with the dishwasher?' Another woman reminisced about her after-dinner talks with her daughter; if she 'wanted to ask me some questions that were on the sexy side, she didn't have to look at me, because I was at the sink.... It was a nice feeling that we had when we were in the kitchen together' (Strasser 1982, 279).

If the technology alone is responsible for more isolated work, how do we explain the fact that even women without dishwashers note a change from the former socializing associated with dishwashing? Only one woman interviewed owned a dishwasher, yet several Americans reminisced about doing dishes with siblings when they were growing up, versus now when the women usually do dishes alone. One woman said, 'We had fun, sang dumb songs.' Two others, now in their thirties, did dishes with their sisters: 'they told me stories,' 'we played around, acted silly, hit each other with dishrags.' Only two women said they usually do dishes with someone (their husbands), and only one of these considered it a time to visit. The women generally described their attitudes toward the task as, 'just get it done.'

The recollections of these women could certainly have been nostalgic, and they may presently do the dishes alone because many are young mothers with husbands busy in graduate school. Some said their children would probably help when they get older; however, those who do have older children said if they help, they take turns to avoid arguments. Several said their husbands did dishes occasionally, but the task seems to be primarily women's responsibility.

There are a number of possible sociological reasons why women have taken on more domestic responsibility, such as changes in child rearing philosophies, but the bottom line is that research shows that when families purchase an appliance, women take over the task previously shared with other family members (Bose 1979). Women may assume the task to reduce chances of breakage, especially since appliances are designed to be safely operated by only one person. Or, it could be to justify the family's investment in a machine. That is, since the appliance is supposed to save mother time, she should not need others' help any more.

Where dishwashers aren't in use, but the task has still changed to become mother's sole responsibility, it seems likely that the change is due to a residual effect from the introduction of other household technologies. If, when a family purchases an appliance, the woman takes over work previously shared with others, isn't it also possible that she would be expected to take on work which does not include the operation of an appliance? In other words, if most tasks have changed to a single-person operation, it is doubtful families would distinguish between tasks which involve the operation of an appliance and those which do not. Furthermore, if women have washing machines, vacuums and garbage disposals, perhaps they are expected to then have plenty of time to do the dishes by hand.

However, it is not simply a matter of household technology isolating women's work. Alternatives for performing domestic tasks outside the home are not attractive to most women. Almost all the women I interviewed (twenty-nine out of thirty-one) preferred washing clothes at home rather than using a laundromat. Concerns for cleanliness and the privatization of housework were apparent in most of their remarks. A young single mother said, 'I don't like folding my clothes in front of strangers.' Others' comments were, 'It's not the chore that bothers me, it's having to go out. I don't like having to bring my daughter here, it's dirty,' 'I don't like fighting over space, sharing machines, you don't know who's been there.' Thus when women must use a laundromat, they commonly try to go when the facility is least crowded (Strasser 1982, 121).

A third consequence of household technology is that the quality of communication for women may be changed in terms of its sources, contexts and topics of discussion. No one would argue that we should reject current technology just because it has hurt communication. Obviously women have other contexts for communicating. Today, women have paid jobs outside the home, they have social responsibilities with associates and their spouses' associates, responsibilities with volunteer organizations and children's activities. But, how many of these occasions are seen as truly social opportunities versus social obligations, or more work for mother?

Social contacts are especially limited for women who do not work outside the home: technology seems to have contributed to severely regimenting their social space (Baxandall *et al.* 1976, 6). For full-time housewives, children are the primary source of communication, and according to Ann Oakley's study, only middle-class mothers consider their children as companions (1974a, 173). Several mothers in the present study said the primary way they meet other women is through their children's playmates: 'We visit on the playground.' One young woman commented on staying home full-time, 'I feel like my brain is just a piece of gray matter. I'm so hungry for adult conversation. Even when I do talk to other mothers at the park, all we have to talk about are the kids.' It seems that at least for this woman, the quality of communication is not what she would like it to be.

Housewife communication no longer seems work-related, and in a capitalistic society, work-related relationships might be seen as more valuable. Routine interaction certainly makes communication more immediate. Furthermore, if family autonomy is valued above other relationships (as the discussion on social-political influences suggested), then communication outside the family may be viewed as less important. Placing an emphasis on the family might mean communication within the home has improved, but, on the basis of my research, the most we can suppose is that not much communication occurs in the context of completing domestic chores.

These consequences indicate household technology, at least regarding washing processes, has not freed women, as might have been popularly assumed. Instead, it has curtailed a primary source of communication for them and changed the context in which communication now occurs. Furthermore, it has enforced the notion that communication impedes efficiency, instead of seeing it as a way to cope with monotonous work.

CONCLUSION

No one would suggest we return to the days when doing laundry was an all-day affair requiring tremendous amounts of physical exertion. But we must recognize that when we welcomed mechanization into our homes, we compromised convenience for companionship and we accepted a set of social values which have served to further isolate women. We need to examine ways to improve currently available alternatives, such as the laundromat. And more ideally, we need to examine ways to change technology and its associated social values, ways which are gender–neutral and do not promote isolation.

While the laundromat (currently the most prominent laundry alternative to home washers in the US) does not free women of work, it could return companionship as compensation for repetitious labor, as in the days before mechanization. Two women in the present study saw going to the laundromat as a social occasion. The mother and daughter meet every Saturday at 7 a.m., along with four other women who have been doing laundry at the same time for years. They bring coffee or breakfast and visit while they work. Both women interviewed have full-time jobs, and the daughter said, 'This is the one time of the week Mom and I have together.'

However, most women seem to prefer home laundry facilities, and it cannot simply be due to the emotionalism of housework; laundromats are not typically nice places to be. Laundromats are often dirty, sparsely decorated, cold environments, certainly not designed to facilitate communication. The seats are uncomfortable, the machine noise is loud, and mothers are preoccupied with containing their children since there is no place for them to safely play without bothering others. Also, the facilities are not located close enough to homes to become neighborhood gathering facilities. The women interviewed said they seldom see their neighbors at the laundromat.

Ultimately, we need to develop new household technology which truly liberates women from repetitious, time-consuming, isolated work. However, while there was a great deal of technological growth in the first half of this century, further development might be impossible without basic changes in societal values first (Ravetz 1965). We will need to recognize that cleanliness is not an absolute. We will need to redefine responsibilities for household chores, and most importantly, we will need to question what was previously seen as the natural linear order of technological progress.

REFERENCES

Ahern, Eleanor. 1941. *The Way We Wash Our Clothes*. New York: M. Barrows.

Andrews, William C. and Deborah C. Andrews. 'Technology and the housewife in nineteenth-century America.' *Women's Studies* 2, 309–28.

Balderston, L. Ray, A. M. 1923. *Laundering Home-Institution*. Philadelphia: J. B. Lippincott.

Baxandall, Rosalyn, Elizabeth Ewen and Linda Gordon. 1976. 'The working class has two sexes.' *Monthly Review Press*, 1–9.

Bose, Christine. 1979. 'Technology and changes in the division of labor in the American home.' *Women's Studies International Quarterly* 2, 295–304.

Bose, Christine and Philip L. Bereano. 1983. 'Household technologies: burden or blessing?' In Jan Zimmerman, ed., *The Technological Woman: Interfacing with Tomorrow*. New York: Praeger, 83–93.

Carroll, Kimberley, W. 1979. 'The industrial revolution comes to the home: kitchen design reform and middle class women.' *Journal of American Culture* 2, 488–99.

Cott, Nancy, F. 1977. *The Bonds of Womanhood*. Stoughton, Mass.: Alpine Press.

Cowan, Ruth Schwartz. 1974. 'A case study of technological and social change: the washing machine and the working wife.' In Mary Hartman and Lois W. Banner, eds. *Clio's Consciousness Raised*. New York: Harper & Row.

Cowan, Ruth Schwartz. 1976a. 'The industrial revolution in the home: household technology and social change in the twentieth century.' *Technology and Culture* 17, 1–23.

Cowan, Ruth Schwartz. 1976b. 'Two washes in the morning and a bridge party at night: the American housewife between the wars.' *Women's Studies* 3, 147–72.

Cowan, Ruth Schwartz. 1983. *More Work for Mother*. New York: Basic Books.

Davidson, Caroline. 1982. *A Woman's Work Is Never Done*. London: Chatto & Windus.

Dudden, Faye, E. 1983. *Serving Women*. Middletown, Conn.: Wesleyan University Press.

Filbee, Marjorie. 1980. *A Woman's Place*. London: Ebury Press.

Friedan, Betty. 1963. *The Feminine Mystique*. New York: W. W. Norton.

Giedion, Siegfried. 1948. *Mechanization Takes Command*. New York: Oxford University Press.

Gilbreth, Lillian, M., Orpha Mae Thomas and Eleanor Clymer. 1954. *Management in the Home*. New York: Dodd, Mead.

Haefele, Carl W., Richard C. Davis and Fred Fortess. 1973. *The Technology of Home Laundering*. New York: American Association for Textile Technology.

Hobson, Dorothy. 1978. 'Housewives: isolation as oppression.' In Women's Studies Group, Centre for Contemporary Cultural Studies, University of Birmingham. *Women Take Issue: Aspects of Women's Subordination*. London: Hutchinson, 79–95.

Howe, Frederic C. 1918. 'The vanishing servant girl: the problem that confronts the woman with help in her home.' *Ladies' Home Journal* 35, 48.

Huston, T. L., C. A. Surra, N. M. Fitzgerald and R. M. Cate. 1981. 'From courtship to marriages: mate selection as an interpersonal process.' In S. Duck and R. Gilmour, eds. *Personal Relationships 2.: Developing Personal Relationships*. New York: Academic Press.

Juster, Norton. 1979. *So Sweet to Labor*. New York: Viking.

Newman, Louis Michele. 1985. *Men's Ideas/Women's Realities: Popular Science 1870-1915*. New York: Pergamon.

Oakley, Ann. 1974a. *The Sociology of Housework*. Bath: Pitman.

Oakley, Ann. 1974b. *Woman's Work: The Housewife, Past and Present*. New York: Pantheon.

Oakley, Ann. 1981. *Subject Women*. New York: Pantheon.

Pacey, Arnold. 1983. *The Culture of Technology*. Cambridge, Mass.: MIT Press.

Peet, Louise Jenison and Lenore Sater Thye. 1949. *Household Equipment*. New York: Wiley.

Ravetz, Allison. 1965. 'Modern technology and an ancient occupation: housework in present–day society.' *Technology and Culture* 6, 256–60.

Rothman, Sheila A. 1978. *Woman's Proper Place*. New York: Basic Books.

Strasser, Susan. 1982. *Never Done*. New York: Random House.

Warfield, Carol, Jackie Anderson and Marjorie Mead. 1976. *Saving*

Energy in the Home: Doing the Laundry. Urbana, Ill.: Cooperative Extension Service, University of Illinois, circular 1120.

Zimmerman, Jan. 1983. *The Technological Woman: Interfacing With Tomorrow*. New York: Praeger.

LEANNE HINTON

ORAL TRADITIONS AND THE
ADVENT OF ELECTRIC POWER

A good-looking woman,
A good-looking girl,
She won't just sit around
Inside her home
Until she gets so old
That she uses a cane to get around.
A lovely bird
I want to be.
The rock slopes,
Those places,
I go from point to point.
At Hasogyavo,
I land there.
I look down,
A fancy man,
A good-looking man,
He is sitting there
Outside his home.
There I settle down,
My soul settles down there.
So it is.

(Excerpts from free translation of traditional
Havasupai women's love song)

The Havasupais live on an isolated reservation in a tributary of the
Grand Canyon. Theirs is the only American Indian reservation in
the country where the center of population and administration cannot be reached by car. A 65-mile dead-end road leads to a trailhead,
and the reservation town of Supai can be reached from there by foot
or horseback. The little town is nestled in a lovely canyon, with a
blue river threading through a forest of deep-green cottonwoods, a
wealth of fruit trees, and well-tended cornfields, all dominated by
1000-foot high cliffs. No roads are in the canyon, and no motorized
vehicles, except for a tractor and an emergency jeep. People travel
on foot around town most of the time, saving their horses for trips
out of the canyon.

Because of their isolation, the Havasupai tribe has been able to
maintain much of its cultural integrity. The Havasupai language is
still spoken by all age groups, and many old traditions are retained.
Nevertheless, in the twenty years since this author first visited the

180

reservation, many very obvious changes have occurred, which have functioned both to increase the degree of exposure of Havasupais to the outside world and to significantly change many patterns of interaction among the Havasupais themselves. I will consider here one technological change that has resulted in an increase in the amount of time spent indoors. It will be shown that this change—the coming of electric power—has had effects on interaction patterns that hasten the loss of traditional knowledge, especially certain genres of oral literature. Women and men alike are affected by this change, but since women have different ways of spending their days than men, there is some differential influence.

A hundred years ago, Havasupais migrated seasonally: summers were spent farming in the canyon, and winters were spent hunting and gathering on the Colorado Plateau. Families tended to be separated from each other in the winter, each having a large territory of its own in which to hunt. Wintertime was a time when members of an extended family unit interacted only with each other. This was the time of the telling of mythic tales, an important vehicle for the transmission of knowledge. These tales must not be told in the summertime, a restriction which meant that every family has its own tales and its own versions of widespread tales, for people outside the family rarely heard them. Each family also had its own hunting songs.

Summertime was a gathering time, when all Havasupais would live close together, tend their gardens, have group festivals, and spend a fair portion of their day visiting each other. In the words of Leslie Spier, 'Morning finds the families in the fields; the heat of the afternoon (never excessive) is spent in the sweatlodge or at some favorite spot gambling and gossiping' (Spier 1928, 99-100). This was the season of interaction between families, and a time when the non-mythic tales would be told—autobiographical tales, legends and historic accounts. This was also the time of the singing of many genres of song: the circle dance songs, men's songs, women's songs, love songs. These tales and songs, being performed in the summertime and in gatherings that consisted of people from different families, were known by the community as a whole, or by a wide selection of people within the community, in contradistinction to the winter songs and stories which were within the family domain.

In 1880, President Hayes set up a reservation for the Havasupais that essentially removed all plateau land from their jurisdiction. Unable to obtain sufficient firewood or food in the canyon, and unwilling to give up their traditional way of life, the Havasupais continued to winter on the plateau, but they were harassed by ranchers, miners, the railroad, the National Forest Service and the National Park Service to such an extent that most Havasupais eventually began to spend the whole year round on the 518-acre reservation. The establishment of a day school on the reservation in 1895 added to the pressure to remain in the canyon in winter (Smithson 1959). In 1975, after a long legal and political battle, the tribe won back about 250,000 acres of their traditional lands (Hirst 1976). Despite this great triumph, legal restrictions on land use and the adaptation of Havasupais to wage economy, schools, etc., mean that almost all members of the tribe continue to live all year round in the canyon, or else travel out of the canyon to work on ranches or in towns. (The tribe is working with a land-use plan that will probably eventually result in the development of a plateau community.)

Even though most people spend the whole year in the canyon now, there is relatively less interaction between families in winter than in summer, because fields are not being worked and the cold keeps people indoors. People see each other at the school, at the store and post office, and at work; but leisure-time visiting is limited. This has been the way of things in wintertime ever since the Havasupais were forced to forego their traditional winter residences on the plateau.

Twenty years ago, summertime interaction had many of the same qualities that it had in the days before the reservation was set up. Families would spend morning time in their fields, and would relax in the heat of the afternoon. They would often make another trip back to the fields in the cool of the late afternoon, and go to bed soon after dark. Most activities took place outdoors in the summer. The government-funded one-room wooden shacks, and the larger pre-fab homes that replaced them in the 1970s, were too hot to spend time in during the heat of the day. Most families moved beds outside in the summertime for afternoon resting; cooking was done outdoors in the summer, over a fire or a wood-burning stove which would be moved back indoors in the winter. Benches were set out in front of the store for people to relax and talk. The sweatlodge, which is a place for bathing, ritual purification and social gathering, was (and still is) utilized by the men most days.

Women often used the afternoons for leisure time, either resting or playing cards or talking together. In the later afternoon, they

182

would wash clothes at the river, and cook in their outdoor kitchens. Other activities, such as basket weaving and preparing fruit to dry, would also occur outdoors. The old people of a household, unable to get around very well, would almost always be lounging outside in the afternoons. Women spent more time at home than the men did, but the time was spent in the yard, not the house.

One aspect of daily life that resulted from this outdoor orientation was a good deal of informal interaction between people from different households. Walking to or from the fields, the store, or home from a job, people would pass by other people's yards. If someone was there in the yard, at least a few words would be exchanged, and often the person walking by would stop to visit awhile. Havasupai tradition does not demand that visitors speak, and often people would simply sit together in a comfortable silence. But more often, people would discuss the latest gossip, or listen to the old-timers talk and sing songs. This latter form of exchange is especially important: a good deal of oral history and tradition was passed from person to person during these leisurely afternoon visits (Hinton 1984).

During the past twenty years, enormous changes have occurred on the Havasupai reservation. A gigantic increase in tourism, the expansion of the school and its transferral from the Bureau of Indian Affairs to tribal authority, increased tribal interactions with the federal government, increased dependence on wage economy, increased ease of transportation away from the canyon by helicopter and car (although the parking area can still only be reached by ten miles of foot-trail), have all created great cultural changes among the Havasupais. There are a few changes which seem small by comparison to these, but which have had an important impact on the rate of erosion of Havasupai traditional knowledge. The changes I concentrate on here are those brought about through the introduction of electricity to the canyon, and which have resulted in a reduction of the amount of time people spend outdoors.

In the late 1960s, a gasoline-run generating plant was constructed at the lip of the canyon, and lines were run down for public use. Needless to say, anyone wanting electricity had to pay for it, and Havasupais, attracted like other Americans to the convenience of light and automatic heating, were drawn ever more deeply into the economy of money. At around the same time, a general sewage system was constructed, allowing the development of indoor plumbing: running water and toilets are now found in every home. The more people work for wages, the less economical it is to have a garden, and so traditional agriculture, although it will probably never disappear altogether, is less active than it used to be. Havasupai families now buy most of their food from the store or make shopping trips to Arizona cities for their groceries. Wage labor and generally increased exposure to modern ways have led to the adoption of further technologies: most families now have electric stoves, telephones and air-conditioning. Many families now have washing machines. In the last six years, even television has come to the canyon. In the past television reception was blocked by the cliffs, but now an increasing number of families own large satellite receptors.

The net result is a vast increase in indoor living. Electric stoves cannot be moved outdoors, so summer cooking is now done inside. Television provides indoor entertainment, decreasing the urge to go out. There is no need to go to the river to get water or wash clothes. No longer is it ever necessary for short trips to the outhouse. Air-conditioning has created the biggest change of all, for now the summer environment indoors is more comfortable than outdoors.

Women, especially, spend more time indoors. They still get together on a summer afternoon to play cards, but now it is inside someone's house rather than in a public place. People phone to see if a game is on, rather than just taking the chance to walk over. All the women's tasks that used to be performed outside are now done in the house. The major reasons to go out are to feed the stock and to go to the store. Both these tasks are quite often done by the men before they go to work, or on their way home.

Because people now spend summer afternoons inside the house, there is much less in the way of informal visiting between different households. The key to informal visiting has always been the initial visual contact that allows a passerby to see whether the members of a household are busy, asleep, or available for a visit. An informal visit is spontaneous, unplanned, based on a decision made after visual contact is established. It is very different from the sort of visit that must be initiated by walking through a person's yard (often past unfriendly, barking dogs) and knocking on a closed door. When people are inside, the passerby cannot know if she or he would be bothering them by coming to visit. The result is that, more often than not, the person just walks on instead.

The old and infirm especially suffer from a marked increase in isolation. No longer do they sit outside where they can see people passing by and stand a chance of receiving a visit. Instead they go to their bedrooms for afternoon relaxation. Even if a visitor does come, the old-timer is likely not to be in the room where the visit takes place. Furthermore, this group is more likely than others to be asleep in the afternoon, or perhaps not feeling well, thus making people less likely than ever to initiate a visit, out of consideration. And the presence of a television strongly decreases the amount of talking, singing, reminiscing and story telling in any case.

There are so many factors that erode the transmission of traditional knowledge in American Indian communities that it is impossible to isolate any particular one. However, it is obvious that the new technological developments adopted by the Havasupais over the last two decades have, among other things, decreased the amount of time spent outdoors, which has in turn decreased the amount of informal interaction that goes on between families, and also has changed the nature of the interaction. As a result of this change, an important forum for the passing on of traditional knowledge has been lost. Only a very few individuals know the old songs, legends and historical accounts that used to be passed on orally in the course of informal, spontaneous visits between families. Thus only the more formal interactive traditions persist, and the oral traditions associated with them. One of these is the circle dance, which takes place yearly and is attended by a portion of the Havasupai population of both sexes and all age groups. The other is the sweatlodge, which is a daily activity primarily for men. The sweatlodge procedure includes a large group of songs, the knowledge of which is eroding at a slower rate than other genres, for the songs are heard quite frequently by a large subset of men. There is no similar retention of a traditional forum for the transmission of oral literature for women.

In the summer of 1974, while I was in the canyon, a major malfunction occurred in the electric plant, and the electricity was out for almost a week. At first everyone grumbled because of the inconvenience: there were no lights, no air-conditioning, no running water. But then people unearthed their old kerosene lamps and their buckets, and moved their beds out of the houses into the shade of the cottonwoods, and within a day or two life was functioning much as it had before the advent of electricity. People went to the river to get water a few times a day, and started visiting with other folks sitting outside. There was almost a festive air in the canyon during those days. As one woman told me, 'I've seen people I

185

haven't seen in years! I wasn't even sure some of them were still alive.' A few days after that, the familiar far-off hum of the generator started up again, and everyone smiled and sighed, and moved back inside their houses.

REFERENCES

Hinton, Leanne. 1984. *Havasupai Songs: A Linguistic Perspective*. Tübingen: Gunter Narr.

Hirst, Stephen. 1976. *Life in a Narrow Place: The Havasupai of the Grand Canyon*. New York: David McKay.

Smithson, Carma Lee. 1959. 'The Havasupai woman.' Salt Lake City: University of Utah, Anthropological Papers no. 8.

Spier, Leslie. 1928. 'Havasupai ethnography.' New York: Anthropological Papers of the American Museum of Natural History, 29, Part III.

ANNE McKAY

SPEAKING UP: VOICE AMPLIFICATION AND WOMEN'S STRUGGLE FOR PUBLIC EXPRESSION

'If a woman knows her business when she tries to speak before the microphone she can create a most favorable impression.'
(Jennie Irene Mix 1924)

Devices for artificial voice amplification were developed in the last quarter of the nineteenth century. They were brought into practical application during World War I, and began to be used for public address and for radio during the 1920s. These devices—the microphone, amplifier and speaker—accomplished for the ear what the microscope and telescope did for the eye. Sounds fainter than the footstep of a fly or the voice of a woman could now be amplified and distributed to unlimited numbers of listeners.

Walter Ong (1967; 1974) has suggested that the technology of voice amplification is significant for women's advancement because it helped to open the world of public participation previously closed to them by natural vocal deficiency and reinforced by custom and lack of training. I have tested Ong's assumption by examining evidence surrounding some related questions.

(1)   Are women's voices in fact less powerful than men's? What is the cultural and sociobiological evidence? What is the evidence left by observers of women's public speaking in the era before artificial amplification?

(2)   How did women make use of amplification devices when they first appeared, and what was the response to them?

My findings, drawn largely from reports and commentary in newspapers and popular journals, suggest a familiar thesis—that when women used the new technology in support of the goals and activities of established institutions, they were applauded at best or ignored at worst. When they attempted to use it in ways that would lead to change in the traditional order and in women's customary roles, their right to use it at all was challenged.

ARE WOMEN'S VOICES NATURALLY LESS POWERFUL THAN MEN'S?

It has long been assumed that most women's voices without artificial amplification are unequal to the demands of big-time public speaking. Ong (1974) states that, 'the typical male voice can articulate words at a far greater volume than can the typical female voice'(8). Only post-pubertal males, and only exceptional ones among them, are said to have had the vocal power needed to address great open air crowds assembled on battlefields, on town squares, and inside vast churches and other public buildings.

An important consequence is that the style and form of public address and later of formal education were developed with little participation by women, and in many ways most compatible to the needs of men. Education, like public speaking, developed as an aggressive, combative, all-male activity centered on attack and defense. Both remained so in the West from the time of the Greeks until the beginnings of this century.

The roots of this style and form lie deep in the intellectual economy of pre-literate cultures—in procedures for managing knowledge, that is, for remembering hard-won information essential for continuity and survival. These procedures are 'formulaic in design and, particularly in public life, tend to be agonistic in operation' (Ong 1974, 2). The exclusion of girls from formal education meant that few had the chance to develop the required intellectual tools of public discourse, even if some had possessed the necessary vocal power.

In the nineteenth century many factors converged to provide more ladders on to public speaking platforms for women, including:

(1)   Changing roles and aspirations of women in church settings in America, partly in response to republican ideals and frontier conditions. These prepared women for active, vocal participation in the great nineteenth- and twentieth-century reform movements—temperance, abolition and suffrage (Griffith 1984).

(2)   Growth of public gatherings outside the church context, including the lyceum and Chautauqua movements. These

provided new arenas for women's public speaking, even though frequently limited to traditionally women's subjects and roles (Bode 1956; Gould 1961; Harrison and Detzer 1958; Morrison 1974).

(3) Rapid industrialization and the resultant growth of cities, promoting large-scale social movements, led and followed by women.

Direct witnesses to the public speaking of nineteenth- and twentieth-century women in response to these forces, prior to artificial amplification, provide cause to question the absolute primacy of vocal debility in accounting for women's long silence in public:[1]

Her voice was deep toned and heavy, and well suited to a public speaker. She sometimes spoke in large houses, and even in the open air; and was distinctly heard by large audiences.... In the pulpit her appearance was bold and commanding. She used but few gestures, but her manner was such as to gain the attention of those who heard. (Said of Salome Lincoln, a female preacher; in Davis 1843, 22.)

I remember being one of five thousand who listened to her in Hyde Park, and I shared the general delight in her musical voice and the force of her logic. (Said of Eleanor Marx; in Rosebury 1973, 45.)

[Her] voice is of small compass, but before an audience it is so excellently 'pitched' and is used with such clarion-like effect that every word, as it comes in soft, measured cadence, can be heard. (Said of Mrs. Russell Cooke; in Dolman 1897, 677.)

The full complement of enabling and disabling factors for pre-microphone women speakers is summed up in the following description of a talented nineteenth-century orator, Lady Henry Somerset:

As was to be expected, questions of the heart rather than the intellect, questions of moral and spiritual well-being, have been the most effective in leading women to undertake the work of the platform. But for the temperance movement, it is exceedingly doubtful whether Lady Henry Somerset, for example, would have become one of the most widely known public speakers of her time. Her ladyship first discovered that she possessed the gift of eloquence at temperance meetings held in the neighborhood of her Herefordshire estate, and it was through the British Women's Temperance Association that she soon had opportunities of addressing gatherings that numbered several thousand.... Whether she is addressing five hundred or five thousand, Lady Somerset is always audible to everyone of her audience.... Endowed by nature with a voice clear and musical, but not at all strong, her Ladyship acquired, by two or three years of constant practice, the art of making herself heard without strain or apparent effort. She would take her maid to a meeting, post her at its farthest point, and by signals learn whether or not she was succeeding in filling the hall with her voice. This is the secret of Lady Somerset's great success on the platform, coupled with a rare faculty for seizing hold of the strongest points in her case and presenting them in vivid and graphic speech. (Dolman 1897, 679-80)

Many of these women were identified with powerful, influential men. The few who were not were unusually endowed with intellectual and educational resources and with personal dynamism rare in either gender, which helped them overcome the problem which may be more critical than vocal or oratorical ability—legitimation of their right to speak publicly at all.

The anti-slavery platform perhaps provides the best evidence of the importance of such legitimation. In 1898, a professor of public speaking reminisced about his first 'teachers' on the abolition circuit:

[I] cannot remember a really poor speaker; as Emerson said, 'eloquence was dog-cheap' there. The cause was too real, too vital, too immediately pressing upon heart and conscience, for the speaking to be otherwise than alive.... [M]y own teachers were the slave women who came shyly before the audience ... women who, having once escaped, had, like Harriet Tubman, gone back again and again into the land of bondage to bring away their kindred and friends. (Higginson 1898, 188)

There, all questions of vocal and oratorical ability and of propriety were put aside by the public's intense interest in what slave women had to say.

The testimony of women who themselves became skilled in oratory is also instructive. A Mrs. Phillips was described in 1894 as one of England's brightest and most successful political speakers. At first, she says, she had a great prejudice against women on the platform. 'Now I am more than reconciled, and I fully appreciate the value of public speech. I consider that it is the revival of one of the noblest of all arts, and should take a place in education, and in recreation as well, alongside with writing books and reading them.'

Asked her advice for women who wished to follow her example, she said,

> Take trouble. I often say to women who feel it their duty to speak, but find it so difficult: 'Do you take as much trouble in trying to make a speech as you would in learning French verbs or cooking an omelette? Why should you expect to make a speech without taking the trouble and going through the drudgery which would be absolutely essential to excellence in a very much easier department of work?' (Woman as..., *Review of Reviews*, June 1894, 709)

Mrs. Phillips was herself trained in elocution but recommended study of voice production rather than elocution.[2]

Temperance leader Frances Willard (1839–1898) summed up the situation as she saw it in 1888:

> Formerly the voices of women were held to render them incapable of public speech, but it has been discovered that what these voices lack in sonorosity they supply in clearness, and when women singers outrank all others, and women lecturers are speaking daily to assemblies numbering from one to ten thousand, this objection vanishes. It is probably no more 'natural' to women to have feeble voices than it is for them to have long hair. (Willard 1888, 53)

SOME SOCIOBIOLOGICAL EVIDENCE ABOUT THE POWER OF FEMALE VOICES

Evidence gathered over the past fifty years on sexual dimorphism indicates that gender alone is often a poor predictor of general physical ability. The difficulty of abstracting gender expectations and social norms from 'scientific' evidence can be seen in a study of men's and women's voices made at Bell Laboratories in the mid-1920s.

The conclusion drawn from a series of experiments comparing voices was that women's were equal to men's in *loudness*, but significantly less *intelligible*:

> The experiments which revealed this information were designed to measure the relative difficulty with which the fundamental sounds were perceived when uttered by male and female speakers. Each speaker uttered a hundred simple English words; and observers recorded the words in the usual manner of an articulation test.... The percentage of the various vowel and consonant sounds which were correctly perceived was thus ascertained for each of forty speakers.
>
> At the same time the loudness with which the various sounds were spoken was automatically recorded.... [M]easurements ... showed that on the average a woman's voice is as loud as that of a man although individuals differ widely.... In the case of the women the enunciation, or articulation, of the vowels was on the average a few per cent less than for the men, and the consonant articulation was about ten per cent less. (Steinberg 1927, 153)

The author attributes the greater difficulty in understanding female speech to two factors.

(1)   Women's higher fundamental tone (250 cycles per second at the lowest end of the speaking range, on the average) produces only one-half as many audible overtones as a man's voice (125 cycles at the lower end of its range).

(2)   'Auditory masking,' whereby if women's speech (or any high-pitched tone) is *loud*, the higher frequencies are obliterated by the ear itself. (It is not mentioned that a similar masking occurs with low frequencies when they are loud.) The author concludes that 'It thus appears that nature has so designed woman's speech that it is always most effective when it is of soft and well modulated tone.' (Steinberg 1927, 154)

More recent studies suggest that physique may be far less important than acculturation in producing gender-specific variations in speech. In their study of the factors enabling identification of a speaker as male or female, Sachs *et al.* (1973) made some observations that are relevant here:

> There are ... some rather puzzling aspects to the actual acoustic
> disparities that exist between adult male and female speakers....
> [Reanalysis of previous studies suggests that] acoustic differ-
> ences are greater than one would expect if the sole determining
> factor were simply the average anatomical difference that exists
> between adult men and women. It is possible that adult men
> and women modify their articulation of the same phonetic
> elements to produce acoustic signals that correspond to the
> male-female archetypes. In other words, men tend to talk as
> though they were bigger, and women as though they were
> smaller, than they actually may be. (Sachs *et al*. 1973, 75)

In tests with preadolescent girls and boys, matched by size,
listeners were almost always able to correctly identify the speakers
by gender.

> If there is no average difference in articulatory mechanism size,
> the differences ... observed could arise from differential use of
> the anatomy. The children could be learning culturally deter-
> mined patterns that are viewed as appropriate for each sex.
> Within the limit of his anatomy, a speaker could change the for-
> mant pattern by pronouncing vowels with phonetic variations,
> or by changing the configuration of the lips. Rounding the lips
> will lengthen the vocal tract, and lower the formants. Spread-
> ing the lips will shorten the vocal tract, and raise the formants.
> The characteristic way some women have of talking and smil-
> ing at the same time would have just this effect. (Sachs *et al*.
> 1973, 80-81)

THE FIRST MICROPHONES AND AMPLIFIERS ('LOUDSPEAKERS')

Techniques for voice amplification are surely as old as public speaking itself. They include manipulation of physical and acoustic space,
such as in the amphitheater, and devices based on the horn, such as
the speaking trumpet and the megaphone.

The *microphone* is one of three developments based on the
transmission of sound vibrations by electromagnetism. The other
two, the telephone and the phonograph, are closely connected in the

order and method of their development.

As early as 1856, the principle of the first microphone was articulated, and primitive microphones were, of course, part of the first telephones which appeared in the mid 1870s. But their full development as instruments of public address and for radio occurred during World War I, when their value in detection of enemy bomber-dirigibles and submarines was realized (Watt 1878; Du Moncel 1879; Listening for submarines 1915; Aerial range-finding ... 1915).

Contemporary estimations of the power and impact of some of the first microphones are instructive in the light of later objections to their use by women. '[T]he steps of a fly walking on the stand are clearly heard, and give the sensation of a horse's tread; and even a fly's scream, especially at the moment of death, is said ... to be audible' (Du Moncel 1879, 146). 'It conveys speech or music, or the slightest inflections of accent and *timbre*, with perfect distinctness...' (Watt 1878, 39).

While the microphone converts soundwaves into electrical signals of corresponding wave form, the *loudspeaker* is based on devices for converting electrical signals back into soundwaves—a microphone in reverse (Tucker 1978, 1265). The acoustical problems of loudspeakers have always been very difficult because of the unpredictable and often uncontrollable effects of the environments in which they are used, such as time lag, wind effects, echos and feedback characteristics in building and outdoor spaces.

EARLY DEMONSTRATIONS OF LOUDSPEAKING EQUIPMENT USED BY WOMEN

One early display of the new public address systems occurred in New York in the spring of 1919, shortly after the end of World War I. The inclusion of women as speakers, and their cordial reception, by the mainstream press at least, is of interest.

A 'Victory Loan' drive had been organized to raise $4½ billion in bonds (Gov Smith ... 1919). A five-block stretch of Park Avenue was designated 'Victory Way,' and loudspeaking telephone equipment was installed—102 loudspeaking telephones, each with a phonograph horn, suspended from a cable stretched across the avenue. These instruments amplified the voices of speakers located on platforms along the way, or connected by telephone from remote cities, or from aircraft flying above the site. Crowds numbering 'tens of thousands' and at a distance of more than a quarter of a mile were reported to receive the signals easily (Recent novelties ... 1919, 489).

Women were very much in evidence as speakers at this event, and it is instructive to read accounts of who they were and what they said. On 'Stage Women's War Relief Day,' one highlight was an address made long-distance from Washington. *The New York Times* reported,

URGES NOTE PURCHASES AS A THANKSGIVING:
Mrs. Baker Spurs Buying Here by a Speech Over the Telephone.

Speaking by telephone from the Capitol in Washington, Mrs. Newton D. Baker, wife of the Secretary of War, urged the crowds thronging Victory Way yesterday to buy bonds in the same spirit as they returned thanks to God for the nation's victory. She said that the Victory Loan was in reality a Thanksgiving Loan.

Mrs. Baker's words were carried, clear and distinct, to the electric megaphones hanging over the heads of the crowds in Victory Way. When she had finished, such a great burst of applause greeted her remarks that ... she could hear the cheering where she was in Washington. (26 April 1919, (6, cols 4–5)

On 22 April, 'Mothers and Wives' Day' on Victory Way, the featured long-distance speaker was Mrs. Carter Glass, wife of the Secretary of the Treasury. *The New York Times* reported,

Mrs. Glass spoke over the long-distance telephone from the Capitol and her words were distinctly transmitted to every person on the way.... 'No one knows better than the housewives of the country the necessity of paying bills, since the Government is housekeeping on a gigantic scale. The women of the United States appreciate fully the Government's problems and its purpose in the Victory Liberty Loan.... [W]e women will do all in our power to further the process of the Victory Liberty Loan.' (23 April 1919, 4, col. 4)

No difficulties in amplification of the women's voices on Victory Way were reported. The context of the event may account for the unanimous approval; it was an intensely patriotic situation in which women were speaking principally to other women, in support of the policies of powerful men.[3]

Figure 8   Collecting book donations to be sent to World War I soldiers.
Women speaking loudly in public during World War I seem to have
been well accepted when it was in support of the war effort (National
Archives)

The National Republican and Democratic Conventions of 1920 provided another opportunity for implementation of the new loudspeaking technologies (Will carry voices to all ... 1920). A count of women speakers at conventions prior to and after 1920 may indicate the importance of voice amplification in promoting women's participation. However, the effect of the microphone was no doubt mixed with impetus from the suffrage movement, which culminated in passage of the Nineteenth Amendment shortly after the conventions that same year.

The indexes of the Official Proceedings for both parties show that for the five held between 1900 and 1916, the only female speaker was at the Democratic Convention of 1900. She addressed the assembly in some fifty-five words, seconding the nomination of William Jennings Bryan for President. (*Official Reports*, Democrats, 1900, 148).

In 1920, sixteen Democratic and eight Republican women are listed as speakers, usually seconding a nomination. From that year through 1936, there are always females listed for both groups, averaging around 10 percent of the total number of speakers.

Women speakers at the National Political Conventions, 1900-1936

year	Democratic Party, women speakers	Republican Party, women speakers
1900	1	0
1904	0	0
1908	0	0
1912	0	0
1916	0	0
1920	16	8
1924	13	3
1928	4	4
1932	10	6
1936	13	5

Source: *Official Reports of the Proceedings*[4]

I have found no assessments of how the first amplified speeches in 1920 were received. The 1924 Conventions were, however, broadcast on radio, and comments of a skilled observer will be discussed in the following section.

WOMEN ON EARLY RADIO

Women's voices amplified by radio caused controversy from the beginning. The intimacy of the medium perhaps proved startling to women and men alike, particularly when women performed as announcers.

Then, as now, the job included extempore speaking as well as reading of program information and news. The announcer is the 'presiding officer,' and it should be recalled that only seventy-five years prior to the beginning of radio broadcasting, in 1848 at the women's rights convention at Seneca Falls, the organizers dared not preside over the meeting themselves, but delegated that honor to their husbands (Griffith 1984, 55).

The transition, from the necessarily exaggerated style of the platform to the one-on-one of radio, was not achieved overnight. Men as well as women announcers were accused of monotony in pitch, of poor diction and grammar, and of being either too *chummy* and offensively cordial or too cold and distant (Mix, August 1924, 334; September 1924, 392).

Women nevertheless came under particularly intense fire. Cheris Kramarae (1984) has documented the story of Mrs. Giles Borrett, the British Broadcasting Corporation's first female announcer at the BBC. Though highly praised for her performance during a three-month 'trial' in 1933, her contract was abruptly terminated. Reasons were never specified exactly, but speculations ranged along a familiar gamut, from allegations of listeners' objections to a woman's voice in the announcer's role to objections that, as a married woman, she was taking a man's job.

Attitudes parallel to those in Britain were prevalent in the United States. NBC's first female announcer was appointed in 1935. She was Elsie Janis, an 'actress, writer, and imitator,' described by *Newsweek* as 'mature but still merry.' The only woman among twenty-six announcers, her employer said that he was not

quite sure what type of program her hoarse voice is best suited for, but he is certain she will read no more Press-Radio news bulletins. Listeners complained that a woman's voice was inappropriate. For any other sort of announcing job, however, Miss Janis is well equipped. 'I can even push all the buttons on the control board,' boasted the 44–year-old ex-vaudevillist. (Radio announcer ... 1935, 24)

THE RADIO BROADCAST DEBATE WITH JENNIE
IRENE MIX

A debate about women's voices was conducted in the pages of *Radio Broadcast* magazine, a popular journal featuring technical and consumer information for non-specialist radio enthusiasts. Jennie Irene Mix wrote a column called 'The listeners' point of view' from April 1924 until her death in April 1925.

Mix was described as a woman of 'striking personality,' and her column was the 'first attempt to present sound radio program criticism in any magazine.' Her qualifications were impressive. Well trained in music, she was a published critic and a correspondent from major European and American cities to a number of American newspapers. The column included her remarks on programs and personalities and analysis of the 'new world of radio' (The listeners' ... July 1925).

One topic she took on with gusto was the suitability of women's voices for announcing. The discussion began in June of 1924 and continued even after her death, when the column was written by men. It is clear from her remarks that women performed many roles in early, pre-network radio, including that of announcer.

A reader had written to her on his experience as a dealer in phonograph records; he reported that the public refused to buy recordings of women talking. Manufacturers lost several thousands of dollars, he wrote, before they learned that the public will not pay money to listen to the talking record of a woman's voice. His interpretation was that the voice of a woman when she cannot be seen 'is very undesirable, and to many, both men and women, displeasing.'

Mix responds, 'This is interesting. And when one stops to consider the matter it is impossible to recall a phonograph record of a monologue by a woman. Yet, some of the highest paid women in vaudeville are the women heard only in monologues' (Mix, August 1924, 332).

She invited reader's comments. One station director observed that,

For certain types of radio work I consider that a woman's voice is very essential; but for announcing, a well modulated male voice is the most pleasing to listen to. I have absolutely nothing against a woman's announcing, but really do believe that unless a woman has the qualifications known as 'showman's instinct,' it really does become monotonous. As a general thing, a woman's voice is considerably higher pitched than a man's voice and sometimes becomes distorted. (Mix, September 1924, 393)

A manager of two New York stations complained about the quality of transmission of the female voice but acknowledged the utility of women announcers who knew their subject:

We use, of course, just as every other station, a great many women speakers on various subjects, but in no case does the female voice transmit as well as that of the man. As a general thing it does not carry the volume of the average male voice. As far as women announcers are concerned, we have never used them with the exception of Miss Bertha Brainard, who occasionally broadcasts theatrical material or announces a play being broadcast directly from the stage. In this case she is used because she knows a great deal about the theater. (Mix, September 1924, 393)

Another associate of a Pittsburg station writes that,

[A] woman speaker ... is rarely a success, and ... I would permit few women lecturers to appear [on radio]. The reason is that their voices do not carry the appeal, and so, whatever the effect desired, it is lost on the radio audience. One of the chief reasons for this is that few women have voices with distinct personality. It is my opinion that women depend upon everything else but the voice for their appeal. Their voices are flat or they are shrill, and they are usually pitched far too high to be modulated correctly.

Another reason is that women on the radio somehow don't seem able to become familiar with their audiences, to have that clubby feeling toward the listeners which is immediately felt and enjoyed. (Mix, September 1924, 391-2)

William Cunningham, writing in *Colliers* at the same time, called the radio microphone itself the 'veiled lady'—the centerpiece of a padded room, the object of near veneration. 'It's the ... suggestion of thousands of silent listeners out beyond her somewhere, ready and able to hear the very breath you draw, that chills the feet and shackles the speech of the broadcasting neophyte no matter how facile or voluble he may be from the lecture platform' (Cunningham 1924, 24).

The ideal radio voice, according to Cunningham, was a baritone. Tenors and female singers reproduced less satisfactorily, but so did basses, who could 'run into wolf tones.' Vocal power, he thought, was not the problem. 'The operator on the roof can supply the power. What the operator can't supply is life, color, vivacity and tone. These are the things the microphone demands' (24, 48).

Jennie Irene Mix made her own position clear in a review of the radio broadcasts of the 1924 political conventions:

> Speaking before the microphone during those conventions were many men (far too many), all of whom should have proved that they knew something about the use of the voice and about diction when addressing an audience.... But the large majority of them pitched their voices too high and adopted a booming aggressive tone ... [that was] intolerable to hear.... Many of them gave the impression that they were talking through whiskers that had been allowed to go uncut since the last election. But the moment someone rose to speak who had even a halfway idea of enunciation, and how to poise the tones, that speaker ... was as plainly understood as if he had been in the very room where the listeners sat.
>
> Which brings us back to women radio speakers. At these conventions some of them had it all over the men. Occasionally one heard a woman who talked through the top of her head.... But there were others who came near to being ideal orators. Voices perfectly poised, flexible in pitch, and faultless diction.... These conventions proved conclusively that if a woman knows her business when she tries to speak before the microphone she can create a most favorable impression. (Mix, September 1924, 394-5)

When Mix died the following April, the subject was initially dropped, to be revived briefly by one of her successors who gave a report of a survey.

Men vs. Women as Announcers.

[F]urther light has been cast upon the subject by a questionnaire conducted by WJZ. A canvass of 5000 listeners resulted in a vote of 100 to 1 in favor of men as announcers....

It is difficult to say why the public should be so unanimous about it. One reason may be that most receiving sets do not reproduce perfectly the higher notes. A man's voice 'takes' better. It has more volume. Then, announcers cover sporting events, shows, concerts, operas and big public meetings. Men are naturally better fitted for the average assignment of the broadcast announcer.

[P]erhaps the best reason suggested for the unpopularity of the woman's voice over the radio is that it usually has too much personality.... Only male announcers, and only a few of them, have been able to strike the right key, equally remote from the majesty of Hamlet's father's ghost and the sweetness of a night club hostess. (Wallace 1926, 44-5)

'RADIO FOR WOMEN'

At the same time, 'radio for women' was gaining in popularity, both as a retailing and as a programming strategy. The idea was to interest women in listening to and buying radios (Wood 1924; Radio for women 1925). *Radio Retailing* magazine began a nation-wide campaign in 1925. Part of the plan included 'radio teas' to gather groups of women to be addressed by radio. Radio dealers gave demonstrations in homes and stores at the times when special women's programs were on the air. The magazine states that, 'This plan presents a great and important opportunity for the radio industry to accomplish a long-desired aim—to get women equally interested in radio reception as are men.' The programs produced for this campaign included speakers of both sexes, but women speakers were frequently limited to 'women's subjects.'

Women and men alike had to learn to perform effectively on radio. But the statement that the equipment was not suited for women's voices was nearly always coupled with remarks about other personal qualities that were far more important in disqualifying them.

THE RADIO SOPRANO

The soprano did, it seems, present the first radio engineers with difficult technical problems. *Scientific American* addressed the issue in 1928. An elderly gentleman is described, demanding adjustment of his new radio set over which he was hearing 'nothing but screeching sopranos.' A survey is cited, showing 'a general dislike for the radio soprano.' Three reasons are given. Dr. J. C. Steinberg of Bell Laboratories is quoted, stating that, first,

> women are found to talk less distinctly than men. Secondly, the speech characteristics of women, when changed to electrical impulses, do not blend with the electrical characteristics of our present day radio equipment. Thirdly, the demand of the radio public for radio equipment to meet their aural fancy had led to design of equipment that impairs the reproduction of a soprano's voice. (Rider 1928, 334)[5]

CONCLUSION

Does the development of voice amplification devices deserve as much credit for promoting women's advancement as Walter Ong suggests? It is certain that these devices helped to complete the transformation of public speech from a formal, combative, argumentative style to a more pacific, intimate and informal mode, better aligned with female conditioning. Nevertheless, it seems clear that even with the microphone on the platform, women have had to continue to struggle for legitimation of their right to speak publicly, particularly when their topics or roles have been in conflict with those of men of influence.

NOTES

1   While Ong points out that 'there has been no female William Jennings Bryan or Everett Dirksen,' he acknowledges in a brief note the inhibiting association of women vocal in public with promiscuity (Ong 1974, 8, 12: note 30).

2   *Elocution* was a form of oral reading which developed in the 1870s and 'concentrated on dramatic presentation of the written word, using a spectrum of set-piece poses to emphasize various phrases in a memorized passage.' The elocution movement is considered to be the last attempt of the old-style oratory, as Ong describes it, to hold the stage (*This Fabulous Century* 1970, 147).

3   That this technique cannot have been altogether trouble-free in execution is evidenced by a single report of the address by the Secretary of the Navy, from a ship anchored in the Hudson River, to

crowds assembled in Times Square. Interference from atmospheric conditions and from other electrical apparatus in the Square completely blocked the transmission. What did come through, however, was an angry exchange between radio operators on the ship and those atop the *New York Times* building who were trying to receive and broadcast the message (Foreign waves dim message ..: 1920).

4   *Official Reports of the Proceedings of the Democratic National Conventions*, 1900, 1904, 1908, 1912, 1916, 1920, 1924, 1928, 1932 and 1936 and *Official Reports of the Proceedings of the Republican National Conventions*, 1900, 1904, 1908, 1912, 1916, 1920, 1924, 1928, 1932 and 1936. The *Proceedings* for the Republicans in 1912 did not include an index; a review of the text itself turned up no women speakers.

5   A tone consists of a fundamental tone plus related higher tones—overtones or harmonics. The quality of any particular tone is the result of the relative intensity and amplitude of the fundamental tone and its associated harmonics. 'Remove all the harmonics and the tone has been changed to a sound devoid of mellowness, sweetness and richness.' In the higher range of a soprano's voice, fewer harmonics are produced, and apparently the higher of these were not faithfully transmitted and reproduced by the equipment of the day. The problem, Rider says, was further exacerbated by the regulation of the time, which limited transmission to 5,000 cycle sidebands. Harmonics of a high C would be over 8,000 cycles per second and would not have been transmitted (Rider 1928, 335).

REFERENCES

'Aerial range-finding with electrical "ears": a microphone system of detecting invisible airships and determining ranges.' 1915. *Scientific American*, 30 October, 377.

Bode, Carl. 1956. *The American Lyceum: Town Meeting of the Mind*. New York: Oxford University Press.

Cunningham, William. 1924. 'How the veiled lady scares 'em.' *Colliers, The National Weekly* 7:24 (25 October) 24, 38.

Davis, Almond H. 1843. *The Female Preacher or Memoir of Salome Lincoln, Afterwards the Wife of Elder Junia S. Mowry*. Providence: Elder J. S. Mowry.

Dolman, Frederick, 1897. 'Women speakers in England.' *Cosmopolitan* 22:6 (April), 676–80.

Du Moncel, Theodore A. L. 1879. *The Telephone, the Microphone* *and the Phonograph*. New York: Harper & Brothers.

'Foreign waves dim message.' 1920. *The New York Times*, 2 May, section 1, 14, col. 3.

Gould, Joseph E. 1961. *The Chautauqua Movement: An Episode in the Continuing American Revolution*. New York: State University.

'Gov. Smith buys 1st loan note in new campaign.' 1919. *The New York Times*, 21 April, 1, col. 1.

Griffith, Elisabeth. 1984. *In Her Own Right: The Life of Elizabeth Cady Stanton*. New York: Oxford University Press.

Harrison, Harry P. and Karl Detzer. 1958. *Culture Under Canvas: The Story of Tent Chautauqua*. New York: Hastings House.

Higginson, Thomas Wentworth. 1898. "On the outskirts of public life." *Atlantic Monthly* February, 188–99.

Kramarae, Cheris. 1984. 'Resistance to women's public speaking.' English version of 'Nachrichten zu sprechen gestatte ich der Frau nicht: Widerstand gegenüber dem öffentlichen Sprechen von Frauen.' In Senta Trömell–Plötz, ed. *Gewalt durch Sprache*. Frankfurt: Fischer Taschenbuch Verlag, 203–28.

'The listeners' point of view.' 1925. *Radio Broadcast*, July, 343.

'Listening for submarines.' 1915. *The Literary Digest* 51:26 (25 December), 1473–4.

Mix, Jennie Irene. 1924. 'The listeners' point of view.' *Radio Broadcast*, August, 332–8; September, 391–7.

Morrison, Theodore. 1974. *Chautauqua: A Center for Education, Religion, and the Arts in America*. Chicago: University of Chicago Press.

'Mrs. Glass's appeal heard on Victory Way.' 1919. *The New York Times*, 23 April, 4, col. 4.

Official Reports of the Proceedings of the Democratic National Convention. 1900, 1904, 1908, 1912, 1916, 1920, 1924, 1928, 1932 and 1936. Indianapolis: Bookwalter–Ball–Greathouse Printing.

Official Reports of the Proceedings of the Republican National Convention. 1900, 1904, 1908, 1912, 1916, 1920, 1924, 1928, 1932 and 1936. Philadelphia: Dunlap Printing.

Ong, Walter J. 1974. 'Agonistic structures in academia: past to present.' *Interchange* 5:4, 1–12.

Ong, Walter J. 1967. *The Presence of the Word: Some Prolegomena for*

Cultural and Religious History. New Haven: Yale University Press.

'Radio announcer: The "sweetheart of the AEF" joining NBC.' 1935. *Newsweek*, 12 January, 24.

'Radio for women.' 1925. *Literary Digest*, 28 November, 20.

'Recent novelties in public speaking.' 1919. *Scientific American*, 10 May, 489.

Rider, John F. 1928. 'Why is radio soprano unpopular?' *Scientific American*, 28 October, 334–7.

Rosebury, Aaron. 1973. 'Eleanor Marx, daughter of Karl Marx: personal reminiscences.' *Monthly Review* 24:8 (January), 29–49.

Sachs, Jacqueline, Philip Lieberman and Donna Erickson. 1973. 'Anatomical and cultural determinants of male and female speech.' In *Language Attitudes: Current Trends and Prospects*. Washington, DC: George Washington University Press, 74–84.

Steinberg, John C. 1927. 'Understanding women.' *Bell Laboratories Record* 3:5 (January) 153–4.

This Fabulous Century: 1870–1900. 1970. New York: Time-Life Books.

Tucker, D. G. 1978. 'Electrical communication.' *A History of Technology*. Vol. 7. Trevor I. Williams, ed. Oxford: Clarendon Press, 1220–67.

'Urges note purchases as a thanksgiving.' 1919. *The New York Times*, 26 April, 6, cols 4–5.

Wallace, John. 1926. 'The listeners' point of view.' *Radio Broadcast*, November, 44–5.

Watt, Alexander. 1878. *The Microphone, With Notes on the Telephone and Phonograph*. London: Houlston & Sons.

'Will carry voices to all: sound amplifying devices to enable delegates to hear speakers.' 1920. *The New York Times*, 4 June, 2, col. 2.

Willard, Frances E. 1888. *Woman in the Pulpit*. Boston: D. Lothrop.

'Women as public speakers: advice to beginners,' by Mrs. Phillips. 1894. *Review of Reviews* 9 (June), 709.

Wood, Lewis. 1924. 'Making radio attractive to women.' *Radio Broadcast*, January, 221–2.

LANA F. RAKOW

WOMEN AND THE TELEPHONE: THE GENDERING OF A COMMUNICATIONS TECHNOLOGY

'I never answer the phone at home. It carries over. The way I talk to people on the phone has changed. Even when my mother calls, I don't talk to her very long. I want to *see* people to talk to them.'
(Telephone receptionist, in Studs Terkel (1974), *Working*. [New York: Ballantine Books, 58.])

The telephone has been presumed to have been a blessing and a liberator for women. Early commentary on the telephone, repeated by contemporary authors, extolled the virtue of the telephone in reducing women's loneliness and isolation and freeing their time from unnecessary travel. John Brooks (1976), for example, claims that by the end of the 1880s, 'telephones were beginning to save the sanity of remote farm wives by lessening their sense of isolation' and 'they were beginning to bring women in cities "out of the kitchen" by reducing the time required for shopping' (94). Sidney Aronson (1971) states, 'Since farmers' wives were especially susceptible to feelings of loneliness and isolation, the telephone here too helped to allay personal anxiety' (278).[1] Ithiel de Sola Pool (1983) notes that the telephone's role in reducing isolation and insecurity was thought to be particularly relevant to women (131).

The role of the telephone in social change and social life has never received much attention from the academic community. It has only been during the past decade and a half that a few sociologists and communications researchers have begun to think about the telephone as a serious object to study. It is not unusual in this literature for the authors to comment upon the neglect of attention to the telephone, offering various explanations: researchers and funding sources have been interested in the mass media rather than point-to-point telecommuniations (Hudson 1984,5); the place of the telephone in our lives is habitual and unconscious (Boettinger 1977,200); the telephone has no deleterious effects but adds to human freedom and choice of action (Pool 1977:4).

Even contemporary scholars who have focused their attention specifically on the telephone, however, have neglected or trivialized one of the most significant aspects of the telephone and another possible reason the telephone has not been taken seriously by scholars: the role of the telephone in women's lives and the association of the telephone with women's talk. Ironically, clues to the significance of the telephone for women and to popular and scholarly attitudes about women and the telephone are embedded in this recent literature.

Frequently mentioned by contemporary US authors, as their own opinion or their perception of popular opinion of the past, is that women talk a great deal, if not too much, on the telephone. Sidney Aronson (1977) claims that, following the expiration of Bell patents in 1894, 'the telephone became widely available to women and adolescents—two groups who, according to telephone folklore, distinguished themselves as talkers' (31). John Brooks (1977) cites an 1880 piece by Mark Twain as introducing to Americans 'the persistent hero of subsequent telephone literature, the woman user, and its dominant theme, her special love of the instrument and special ways of using it. The piece might almost have been written in the 1970's' (211). Ithiel de Sola Pool (1983) notes that in early telephone trade journals and in popular literature 'one of the most common remarks about women and the telephone is to allege a peculiar addiction on their part to its use' (131). Women's telephone talk has been referred to in recent literature as gossip (Pierce 1977,173), chitchat (Pool, 1977:133), and chatter (Pool 1983:49).

One of the few recent authors to suggest that women's relationship to the telephone is a significant topic for serious consideration is Brenda Maddox (1977). Though Maddox's research concerns women's employment in the telephone industry, she notes other ways in which the telephone has had a particular significance for women, such as providing a link to their mothers and friends and providing an instrument for male advances and harassment. She cites a Bell System study that discovered three reasons women use the telephone: their fear of crime in the streets, their confinement at home with small children, and their physical separation from relatives.

Following Brenda Maddox's lead, what can be said about women's relationship to the telephone? Why would women have developed a particular attachment to the telephone? Did it open up new possibilities for women's speaking and new ways of creating and sustaining relationships or free time from household responsibilities? Has the telephone been widely available for women to use for any purpose? The story of the telephone bears re-examination.

GEOGRAPHIC AND SOCIAL CHANGE

There is almost unanimous agreement among commentators on the social effects of the telephone that the telephone was an important agent of modernization. Pool's comments exemplify the effects attributed to the telephone:

> Among the most significant impacts of the telephone were those in modifying the pattern of human settlement. It made farm life less isolated, made suburbs more practical, helped break up single industry neighborhoods, allowed offices of industrial companies to move away from the plant into downtown office buildings, and made skyscrapers economic. (Pool 1983, 11)

If the telephone was indeed implicated in the development of suburbs, the separation of homes and businesses, and the decline of neighborhoods, it was also implicated in the physical separation of women's private sphere and men's public sphere and the isolation of the home and of individual women in them.[2] That is, the telephone may have been implicated in creating the very conditions from which it was praised for having rescued women. Susan Strasser's description of how the isolation of the housewife increased with industrialization fills in what remains unsaid in most discussions of the telephone:

> While other workers went to work in groups, however thoroughly supervised, full-time housewives lost the growing daughters and full-time servants who worked for them at home, the iceman and the street vendors who came to their houses, the sewing circle and the group of women around the well. That isolation, combined with the illusory individualism of consumerism, intensified the notion that individuals could control their private lives at home, protected behind the portals

209

of their houses from the domination of others: the central legacy of the doctrine of separate spheres. (Strasser 1982,9)

By the time Helen Lynd and Robert Lynd (1929) conducted
their US study of 'Middletown,' this isolation was readily apparent,
particularly in the lives of working-class women. One woman
commented to researchers, 'I don't see my friends at all. That is really true—I never see them unless I run into them somewhere occasionally or they come over to dinner. It was different with my
mother. She and her friends were always in each other's homes.'
Another said, 'I do very little visiting—mostly keep in touch with
my friends by telephone' (275). As for the role of the telephone in
relieving women of unnecessary travel, such as shopping, women
may have greeted such a function with mixed feelings. For some
women, shopping may have been one of their few outlets. One
Middletown woman admitted, 'I'd go anywhere to get away from
the house. I went to the store last night. I've been out of the house
only twice in the three months since we moved here, both times to
the store' (310).

Ann Oakley (1974) discovered the same loneliness and isolation in
her more recent study of London housewives. According to Oakley, 'Research has shown that loneliness is an occupational hazard
for the modern housewife, who is often cut off not only from community life but from family life—in the wider sense—also' (88). The
telephone does not seem to compensate for a lack of personal contact, though it may be valued for the kind of link it does provide.
'The only person I really see is my neighbour,' one woman told
Oakley. 'My mother comes once a week, for the day. She phones
me every other day' (89). Oakley suggests that for some women the
superficiality of the few social contacts they have may be a reminder
of the deep and meaningful relationships they lack.

The isolation of US farm women, as well as their long hours of
drudgery at household and farm work, were not cured by the appearance of the telephone, despite frequent claims to that effect (e.g.
US Bureau of the Census 1910,78), but may well have been better
helped by different government farm policies and by the kind of
community cooperative enterprises suggested by Florence E.
Ward's report (1920) for the US Department of Agriculture.
Despite the fact that 72 percent of the 9,748 farm homes in the
Department of Agriculture survey conducted by Ward had telephones (a very high percentage, suggesting an unrepresentative

sample of farm families), the isolation and burden of the farm women remained unsolved. The report suggested farm families should pool their individual interests in common community enterprises such as canning kitchens, buying centers, markets, laundries, salvage shops, and sewing rooms, as well as social centers for lectures, community sings, dramatics, and games, which, if properly handled, overcome the isolation of country homes and make possible the accomplishment of many otherwise difficult tasks with a saving of time and labor for the housewife.' (12)

Farm women were also accused of being particularly addicted to eavesdropping on their party lines. A 1914 *McClure's Magazine* article claimed, 'Some farmers' wives sit with their ears glued to the receiver all the long dreary afternoon, taking in their neighbors' secrets' (Hendrick 1914,48). Realistically, few farm women would have had time for such luxuries. In the 1910s they were working on average more than thirteen hours a day in the summer and more than ten hours a day in the winter, according to Ward (1920,7). If there had been a genuine interest in easing farm women's isolation, telephone sets would have been designed differently so that women could talk together while they worked. In the 1920s one farm woman resorted to peeling potatoes with the telephone receiver lying in the bottom of a large aluminum pan, which reflected the voices of the telephone conversation back up to her at her seat on a stool (Wisconsin State Telephone Association 1985,96).

Women's 'peculiar' addiction to the telephone is a more complex phenomenon than early and contemporary telephone literature has led us to believe. To understand women's relationship to the telephone, we must ask why women were isolated and lonely and how the telephone fit into a changing Western landscape of public and private spheres.

WOMEN'S TELEPHONE WORK

Women's work as telephone operators has been perhaps the most explored topic related to women's relationship to the telephone in popular and academic literature. Operators were popular heroines in stories, songs, and telephone industry literature in their day. More recently attention has been directed to their labor organizing activities. (Maurine Weiner Greenwald (1980) describes the US situation, for example, and Elaine Bernard (1982) describes that in British Columbia.) The full significance of the role and talk of operators, however, has not been explored.

Women worked and still work as telephone operators all around the world. A 1913 international trade journal refers to the employment of women as operators in Germany, Australia, Tasmania, Austria, Hungary and Sweden (*Telecommunications Journal* 1975). A history published by the International Telecommunication Union (1965) shows early pictures of women operators in England, Germany and the Netherlands, as well as at the switchboard of a contemporary international exchange. This transcultural use of women as operators has not been adequately examined. In the case of the US, the assumption has been that women were hired as telephone operators to replace boys because the women were more polite and mannerly (see, for example, Greenwald 1980; and Brooks 1976). Maddox (1977) points out, however, another more important reason: women's work was cheap. Women earned from one-half to one-fourth of men's wages (266). A 1906 *Journal Télégraphique* article summarized women's role in the telegraph service around the world, which suggests that women's telegraph work was the precedence for their low-paid telephone work (*Telecommunications Journal* 1975). Countries such as Italy, Hungary, France, Norway and Switzerland used women extensively in telegraph work, reporting substantial financial savings by doing so.

The employment of women at low wages does not explain why young, attractive and single women should have been hired, another common transcultural practice. The explanation for this phenomenon is multifaceted, but, at least in the US, part of the explanation might lie in the fact that the time period of the manual operator coincided with the transition to the new economic and social relations of the late nineteenth and early twentieth centuries. The voices of young women, supplemented by visual images of operators as 'All American Girls' made popular by telephone industry advertising and public relations, may have provided an important bridge in the increasing gap between public and private spheres. A Bell System advertisement in 1915 illustrates this symbolic function of operators (the advertisement is reproduced in Boettinger 1977,10). The operator is referred to as a 'weaver of speech' in the advertisement; the illustration shows an operator holding lines coming down from a telephone pole, the lines passing through her hands and out into the world, connecting homes, cities and factories. The cultural myth of the telephone operator, embodying new and old values and mediating new social relations over the telephone wires, may have functioned as a reassuring expression of the

Improved Long Distance Service to New York

An improved and much faster telephone service between Chicago and New York was recently put into effect by the Bell System. Under normal conditions during last month the records show:

75% of calls disposed of in 5 minutes or less

In less than 3% it took more than 10 minutes to make the connection.

That's Speed! The kind of speed every business man will appreciate, and can use to increase volume of sales, reduce selling expense, expedite deliveries, obtain last minute orders, and keep in close touch with the needs of customers.

Long Distance will be pleased to serve you

 ILLINOIS BELL TELEPHONE COMPANY
BELL SYSTEM
One Policy - One System - Universal Service

Figure 9   In this 1925 advertisement, the young woman operator connects the businesses of Chicago and New York. The visual images of operators in ads during the early days of telephone service were 'All American Girls' mediating (primarily men's) relationships (from D'Arcy Collection, University of Illinois, Urbana–Champaign)

new social order in an uneasy transition from the old. These young women were to be both innocent and efficient, desirable yet unattainable, businesslike but adept as soothing the harried and demanding captain of industry of the public sphere as well as the stereotypically portrayed petty and demanding matron of the private sphere.

The importance of the operator's voice and restrictions on her speech were hallmarks of operator selection and training in the US, Canada and France, as well as in other countries. Part of the examination of operator applicants usually included an evaluation of the women's ability to speak clearly and 'without an accent.' Once hired, operators underwent stringent training in what to say and how it was to be said. They learned set phrases and proper inflection, deviations from which could result in punishment. A 1921 article in a US women's labor magazine described how the training room sounded like an operatic rehearsal as operators in training learned how to sing out phrases, sweetly, with the proper inflection (The Pilgrim 1921,14). An early federal investigation of the US telephone industry, though clearly sympathetic to the industry and its need for efficiency in the name of public service, described the operator's frustration with these restrictions. When a subscriber scolds her for being kept waiting,

> She is not allowed by the rules of most companies to answer this, but may only repeat 'Number please' until the caller gives the number so that she can make the connection. For with most companies the operator may not 'talk back' no matter how much she is abused by a subscriber; the only words she dare use over a phone are the set phrases printed in her book of instructions. (US Bureau of Labor 1910,56)

Operators in Canada and France underwent similar training and were subject to such restrictions as well, according to Elaine Bernard (1982,42) and Pierrette Pézerat and Danièle Poublan (1985,32). One operator in France remarked, 'In order to talk PTT [Postes, Télégraphes et Téléphones], one is forbidden to be oneself' (Pézerat and Poublan 1985,33). Yet the voice of the operator, in accordance with the operator myth of a number of countries, was deemed to have special powers, widely acclaimed in popular and telephone industry literature, illustrated by these comments: 'The dulcet tones of the feminine voice seem to exercise a soothing and calming effect upon the masculine mind, subduing irritation and suggesting gentleness of speech and demeanor; thereby avoiding unnecessary friction' (McCluer 1902,31).

The telephone work that women have been performing in businesses and offices since the turn of the century has received little analysis, yet is an area that could provide useful insights into the gendered hierarchy of communication. Despite the fact that the telephone has long been hailed as a great social leveler (e.g. in recent literature see Cherry 1977; and Ball 1968), business and social practices immediately arose to embed hierarchical social relations into the use of the telephone. A.H. Hastie, leader of the Association for Protection of Telephone Subscribers, for example, suggested in 1898 that 'The telephone should be primarily answered by a servant' to screen intrusions, just as a gentleman would have a servant answer the door to keep out unwanted guests (1898,894).

Despite the decline of servants to answer the telephone and the door, social relations remain embedded in telephone access and use. Martin Mayer (1977) points out that a central difference between white-collar and blue-collar workers in US society is that white-collar workers have access to telephones on the job (244). A primary means, however, by which hierarchical distinctions are made through telephone use is by gender, a social hierarchy presumably readily recognizable by sound. The employment of women in offices as 'telephonists' was undoubtedly related to the particular economic and social forces of the time, but was likely also to have been related to the usefulness of women's voices in establishing hierarchies among men, an explanation often masked by appeals to women's 'natural' suitability to telephone office work. Henry M. Boettinger (1977) illustrates this 'natural' argument: 'Few devices are so well matched [as the telephone] to the needs and style of women. The instrument seems particularly suited to their voice range and timbre' (15).

More likely, women's voices have been particularly suited to the needs of their employers. Secretaries and receptionists, charged with answering the telephone and placing telephone calls, convey the importance of the caller or the person being called, screen callers, and relieve others from interruptions and the detail work of looking up telephone numbers, dialing and taking messages. Being responsible for answering the telephone restricts movement and concentration. Office telephonists are often restricted in what to say, and instructed in telephone etiquette. Receptionist Sharon Atkins has related how the telephone was a constant source of inter-

Figure 10   In this 1922 advertisement, the woman secretary and
telephone operator is 'making friends' not for herself but for her boss.
Women were employed to answer business phones because supposedly
they not only had friendlier voices, but they were more patient with
callers than men operators would be (D'Arcy Collection, University of
Illinois, Urbana-Champaign)

216

ruption and how she was often required to lie for others (Terkel 1985,57–60). Much has been made in social mythology of the power of the secretary over telephone access to important people (usually men), but little has been made of women's voices as commodities bought to achieve just such an effect.

Women's work accounts for another area of socially significant but unrecognized and unpaid telephone labor. This work was anticipated and encouraged from the outset of the telephone. An 1878 advertising circular in New Haven, Connecticut advised men, 'Your wife may order your dinner, a hack, your family physician, etc., all by Telephone without leaving the house or trusting servants or messengers to do it' (Fischer 1984,5–6). By 1948, a study of telephone use in rural Indiana reported that men and women in the study both agreed that women used the telephone most frequently. 'Many men said they did not like to use the phone, so they had the women call for them' (Robertson and Amstutz 1949,18).

The responsibility for maintaining family and social relations and home–business transactions which was relegated to women was apparently, then, quickly extended to the use of the telephone. Today, women arrange visits with family members and dinner parties with friends, remember birthdays and anniversaries, and 'keep in touch.' With primary responsibility for the household and family, women most likely take the majority of responsibility for telephone calls with plumbers, optometrists, veterinarians, music teachers, dentists, pharmacists, babysitters and the like. (Many of these interactions, of course, will be with women on the other end of the line, hired by men to talk to other women.) For women working outside the home, the logistics of making these calls can be difficult, particularly if her place of employment has restrictions on employees' personal telephone calls (more likely to be the case with hourly workers). Little is known about women's networks and women's use of the telephone in carrying out church and school work, such as making arrangements for providing food at funeral services and planning community meetings, or their work in canvassing, fundraising, and political organizing. Finally, women may do a majority of home telephone work answering surveys and listening to salescalls. It is little wonder that Martin Mayer (1977) reports, 'the most important single factor [determining how many calls a household will make] is the presence of a woman between the ages of 19 and 64' (23).

Figure 11 'Co-operators!' The young woman provides the connection
for the older businessmen in this 1917 advertisement. At this time the
New York Telephone Company was inviting applications from women
between 16 and 23; the recruitment advertisements promised telephone
operators good locker space, comfortable and safe areas for breaks, and
good food at low cost. The ads did not mention the salary (D'Arcy
Collection, University of Illinois, Urbana-Champaign)

UNIVERSAL ACCESS AND AVAILABILITY

Availability of telephone service varies widely around the world. Sweden, the US, Switzerland, Denmark and Canada all have over sixty telephones per 100 population, for example, while Brazil, Columbia, Turkey, Iran and India have fewer than ten (AT&T 1982,16). While it is obvious that access to and use of telephone service will be much more restricted in countries with fewer telephones, it should not be assumed that the mere presence of greater numbers of telephones per capita ensures its universal access. This assumption marks early predictions and later assessments about the telephone service in the US, which has been thought to have been quickly diffused throughout the country and universally available. Telephone service was soon available to anyone who wanted to use it to talk to anyone they desired, according to popular and academic writers (see Pool 1983,86 for a sample of such comments). Pool (1983) states that early expectations about a low-cost universal service became a self-fulfilling prophecy (24). Boettinger (1977) extols the telephone's democratic functions: 'The privately owned American system arrived at the greatest public market and the widest use of the telephone, a reflection of a democratic mind.... Bell, Watson and Vail were indifferent to class or ideology. The telephone itself did not discriminate against race, creed or color. It served lords and "commoners" equally' (98).

The story of the diffusion and availability of the telephone in the US is not quite so simple. As Claude S. Fischer (1984) explains, the diffusion of telephones did not follow a steady, chronological, upward trend. Forty-two per cent of all households had telephones by 1929, but in 1940, only 32 per cent had telephones (4). The shrinkage of the number of telephones in service during the Depression led Bell Telephone to expand its marketing approaches to include encouraging the social use of the telephone, a use the exchanges had seemed to frown on until then. Indeed, women's 'gossip' on local lines when a flat local area rate was charged added little to telephone company coffers, suggesting one reason women's telephone talk was ridiculed or discouraged. Two non-Bell companies in Indiana and Oregon went so far as to take their cases to the public service commissions in their states to ask for extra service charges for each call. Women gossiping at length were detrimental to their business, they claimed. When the Indiana Public Service Commission held its hearing, according to one account, 'the whole countryside turned out. Many telephone subscribers testified that they had no objection to the women talking at any length they wished, so the commission ruled it could do nothing.' The Oregon commission ruled similarly, though it denounced gossiping (MacMeal 1934,224). Bell Telephone, meanwhile, began placing greater emphasis on the social uses of the telephone after the Depression (Fischer 1984,9), presumably in order to increase installations.

If diffusion was not evenly spread across time, it was also not evenly spread across classes and geographic location, raising questions about who had access to telephones. The Lynd and Lynd survey (1929) found that all forty of the business class families they interviewed had telephones, but only 55 per cent of the working-class families did (173). When forced to make cutbacks in a time of unemployment, five of twenty families having a telephone had it taken out (62). A survey by R.O. Eastman, Inc. (1927) showed a correlation of income with telephone ownership. Not surprisingly, the higher the income, the more likely a family was to have a telephone. Urban zoning of residential and industrial areas, popular around the turn of the century, was supported by telephone companies and utilities because the companies were uninterested in business in poor or deteriorating neighborhoods (Pool 1983,46). Telephone service, consequently, was less likely to be available to lower-income families. Diffusion of telephone service in rural areas was also highly uneven. States such as Iowa and Wisconsin had early and vigorous development of private and community telephone exchanges. However, many rural communities and farm families in other states and in isolated areas had to wait until the Rural Electrification Administration made loans for rural telephone development beginning in 1949. Commentators on the social effects of the telephone have been too ready to assume a homogeneous diffusion and effect among the population. The experiences of poor, rural, working-class, non-white and non-native born women may have varied widely in terms of telephone access and use.

Even today about one in twenty homes in the US has no telephone, homes disproportionately likely to be those in which older and poorer people are living, people who are likely to be most in need of telephone service. Lewis Perl (1978) has concluded that a household's access to telephone service is positively related to income, age and education and inversely related to number of persons per household (4). Only recently has the New York City Welfare Department permitted welfare recipients to have telephones, presumably because welfare recipients tend to live in dangerous neighborhoods (Keller 1977,284, 286). We do not know how the telephone functions in the delivery of social services or in the lives of those who need them. Nor should we forget that having a telephone does not solve problems of isolation or loneliness if we have no one to call (Keller 1977,294), nor can it solve personally experienced problems of poverty, unemployment or fear of crime if there is no one we can call who will or can help.

In addition to limits on the availability of telephone service, women may experience other restrictions on their use of the telephone. Maddox (1977) reports that women call their mothers, sisters and mothers-in-law, but regard the calls as frivolous, feeling guilty when the telephone bill comes (264). Since AT&T offers residential rate discounts after 11 p.m. weekdays and on weekends, women may feel restrictions on when they call long-distance relatives and friends. The US trend toward 'usage sensitive pricing,' where the caller is charged for each local call, and away from flat local pricing, may be creating new economic restrictions on women's telephone use. Women in Great Britain, for example, which has a system of charging for each call, may experience guilt feelings and hesitation about making calls for non-business reasons. Party lines, which were once prevalent in rural areas and still remain in some rural areas, also probably acted to restrict talk, despite popular folklore. One Canadian study reported that 11.2 per cent of the respondents had party lines. Survey respondents indicated they restricted their talk because of the possibility of being overheard and indicated the telephone was often unavailable when they wanted to use it (Singer 1981,56).

Social etiquette from the outset of the telephone industry dictated against girls and women calling boys and men, among other rules for proper telephone behavior. The telephone industry was active in prescribing proper telephone use, as this comment from a telephone trade journal illustrates:

> The etiquette of calls holds good in the matter of telephone calls between men and women. It is not good form for a young woman to call up a man, either at his home or at his office.... It is sure to be an interruption; it is quite likely to be embarrassing, and above all this is the fact, that a tactful girl will avoid all appearance of pursuing the man of her acquaintance. (*Telephony* 1907,138)

A woman waiting by the telephone for a call became a stock cultural image based on the experiences of real women. Dorothy Parker's 'A Telephone Call' (1942), about a woman agonizing over a man's call that does not come, illustrates vividly that the telephone did not free women to call whom and when they pleased nor did it eliminate for women the hierarchy of gender relations.

Telephone directories and unlisted numbers suggest that women are not accessible to others in the same manner that men are. Telephone directories exist in principle so that people listed can reach any of the others as a right of 'membership,' Colin Cherry points out (1977,138). Women's names are often absent from telephone directories, subsumed under the names of their husbands because their name is considered less important or because additional listings involve a telephone company charge. Women do not apparently share the same rights of membership as men, and if telephone directories 'represent a symbolic map of a community's members' (Boettinger 1977,206) women's unequal appearance in telephone directories suggests women's symbolic cultural status. If a number published in a directory is a cue for interaction (Latham 1975,35), women are less accessible than men. Of course, accessibility is a double-edged sword for women in a patriarchal culture. Women resort to using initials in telephone directories rather than first names in order to disguise their gender. They resort to unlisted numbers in an attempt to prevent unwanted calls.

PRIVATIZED OPPRESSION

Marshall McLuhan (1964) labeled the telephone an 'irresistible intruder in time and space' (238), an observation to be echoed by later commentators on the telephone. For example, Garry Mitchell (1984) notes, 'The event of a ringing telephone is an intrusion into personal privacy and individual predictability. Few can ignore this imperious summons' (251). But the kind of intrusion and violation that the telephone made possible for men against women has been little noted or studied.

It was apparently a combination of the spread of automatic switching and private lines and the social disorder of the 1960s that either increased abusive calling in the US or at least brought it to the attention of the Bell Telephone Company and federal officials. With automatic rather than operator switching and with private rather than party lines, abusive callers apparently felt less likely to be found out (Pool 1983,133; John Brooks 1976,286). The weakening of social norms in the 1960s was supposed to have increased such 'antiso-cial' behavior. John Brooks (1976), melodramatically, describes the problem as one of social deviation rather than of an intensified ex-pression of cultural misogyny: 'The venom of the poisoned, the bad blood of society, was spread through the national blood vessels of the telephone network' (286). AT&T expressed its official concern about such calls in its annual reports in the mid-1960s, undertook an 'education' campaign advising callers how to deal with such calls, and began offering a device that enabled the company to track call-ers (Brooks 1976,287).[3]

AT&T's actions were likely to have been spurred by US Senate hearings on abusive and harassing telephone calls held in 1965 and 1966. The record of the May and June 1966 hearings, however, sug-gest that the Senate Commerce Committee, Subcommittee on Communications, chaired by John Pastore of Rhode Island, was more concerned about malicious calls to the families of Vietnam ser-vicemen than about abusive calls to women. The Bell System re-ported receiving 375,000 complaints a year; the Bureau of Police-women of the New York Police Department was reported to have received a 30 per cent increase in complaints of obscene calls over 1964. Yet the testimony, all by men, reflected little concern for women by either AT&T or senators:

Senator Pastore. '[About the question of sexual perversion,] how many would you say were men as against women in these cases that you prosecuted?'

Mr. Kertz [Herbert Kertz, operating vice president, AT&T]. 'The majority are men.'

Senator Pastore. 'The majority are men?'

Mr. Kertz. 'Yes, sir. Now, when I said that, you qualified, Mr. Chairman, the type of cases. There are a great many cases that in-volve domestic squabbles where the woman is the offender.'

Senator Pastore. 'I see.'

Mr. Kertz. 'But going to your pervert, the majority of it is men.'

Senator Cotton [Norris Cotton, New Hampshire]. 'It is practically impossible for a woman to put in a telephone call and not talk; is it not?' [laughter]

Mr. Kertz. 'The strength of our business, Senator.' [laughter] (US Senate 1966,45)

A bulletin by the US Independent Telephone Association, placed into the record, reveals how the telephone industry was likely to view abusive calls as a 'customer service problem' because they were 'irritating' to customers (US Senate 1966, 48-9). The bulletin cited the problem of growing non-published and non-listed service resulting from abusive and commercial solicitation calling.

Liz Stanley and Sue Wise, conducting research on their personal experiences in England of abusive telephone calls, have begun to shed light on the culturally telling nature of abusive calls and the complex experience of oppression faced by women in Western countries. They received abusive calls every day over a period of several years when their home telephone number was advertised as a contact for several local lesbian groups (Stanley and Wise 1979). By unflinchingly publishing the transcripts of some of these calls, they have exposed the virulent side to women's oppression and the everyday violations to which women can be subjected. Their categorization of different types of calls and callers, their analysis of responses to their experiences from feminists and male homosexuals, and their self-scrutiny of their own feelings and strategies (see Stanley 1984) suggest this topic has received too little serious attention.

COMMENTS

This review of the received story of the telephone should suggest that women's relationship to the telephone has been much more complex than popular and academic literature has led us to believe. The telephone opened up new possibilities for women's talk and women's relationships, but may have been implicated in closing off others. It may serve as a lifeline to women isolated in a private sphere and cut off from family and friends, but the telephone may have helped bring that isolation about. The telephone did not level and democratize all social relations, but arrived embedded in them and was used to perpetuate and create hierarchies. Women's speech was commoditized, controlled, and restrained for business purposes at an early stage. The telephone was not and is not available for all women for all purposes, even in countries where telephone service is widespread. The telephone has been used by some men to bring oppression through abusive and harassing calls into the most private spaces women occupy.

The story of the history of the telephone cannot be told without accounting for the gender relations within which a telephone system developed. The telephone, in turn, was used to construct and maintain gender differences and hierarchies. The story of the telephone teaches us the lesson that communications technologies in a gendered society are not gender-neutral.

NOTES

1 The wording of these comments—'sense of isolation' and 'susceptibility to feelings of loneliness and isolation'—are interesting. The implication is that the isolation of these women was not as serious as they felt it to be or that their feelings resulted from their own weakness.

2 Claims about the telephone's cause and effect relationship to these changes should be weighed carefully, however. See Fischer (1985) for a discussion of the complexity of technological assessment.

3 The sincerity of then AT&T's chief executive officer, Frederick R. Kappel, in wanting to do something about calls against women cannot be taken at face value. The following incident raises questions about his feelings toward women. According to one account, at an annual AT&T meeting in Detroit in 1966, 'after a wrangle with Mrs. Wilma Soss of the Federation of Women Shareholders, he silenced her by summarily having her floor microphone turned off' (Brooks 1976,280).

REFERENCES

Aronson, Sidney. 1971. 'The sociology of the telephone.' In Gary Gumpert and Robert Cathcart, eds. *Inter/Media*. 2nd edn New York: Oxford University Press, 1982, 272-83. Reprinted from *International Journal of Comparative Sociology* 12:3 (September 1971).

Aronson, Sidney. 1977. 'Bell's electrical toy: what's the use? The sociology of early telephone usage.' In Ithiel de Sola Pool, ed. *The Social Impact of the Telephone*. Cambridge, Mass.: MIT Press, 15-39.

AT&T. 1982. *The World's Telephones*. Morris Plains, New Jersey.

Ball, Donald. 1968. 'Toward a sociology of telephones and telephoners.' In Marcell Truzzi, ed. *Sociology and Everyday Life*. Englewood Cliffs, New Jersey: Prentice-Hall, 59-75.

Bernard, Elaine. 1982. *The Long Distance Feeling: A History of the Telecommunications Workers Union*. Vancouver: New Star Books.

Boettinger, Henry M. 1977. *The Telephone Book: Bell, Watson, Vail and American Life, 1876-1976*. Croton-on-Hudson, New York: Riverwood.

Brooks, John. 1976. *Telephone: The First Hundred Years*. New York: Harper & Row.

Brooks, John. 1977. 'The first and only century of telephone literature.' In Ithiel de Sola Pool, ed. *The Social Impact of the Telephone*. Cambridge, Mass.: MIT Press, 208–24.

Cherry, Colin. 1977. 'The telephone system: creator of mobility and social change.' In Ithiel de Sola Pool, ed. *The Social Impact of the Telephone*. Cambridge, Mass.: MIT Press, 112–26.

Eastman, R.O., Inc. 1927. *Zanesville and Thirty-six Other American Communities: A Study of Markets and the Telephones as a Market Index*. New York: Literary Index.

Fischer, Claude S. 1984. 'Educating the public: selling Americans the telephone, 1876–1940.' Unpublished revision of paper presented to the Social Science History Association, Washington, D.C., October 1983. Berkeley: University of California, Department of Sociology.

Fischer, Claude S. 1985. 'Studying technology and social life.' In Manuel Castells, ed. *High Technology, Space, and Society: Emerging Trends*. Urban Affairs Annual Reviews, Vol.28. Beverley Hills: Sage Publications.

Greenwald, Maurine Weiner. 1980. *Women, War, and Work*. Westport, Conn.: Greenwood Press.

Hastie, A.H. 1898. 'The telephone tangle and the way to untie it.' *Fortnightly Review* 70, 893–900.

Hendrick, Burton J. 1914. 'Telephones for the millions.' *McClure's Magazine* 44 (November), 45–55.

Hudson, Heather E. 1984. *When Telephones reach the Village: The Role of Telecommunications in Rural Development*. Norwood, New Jersey: Ablex Publishing.

International Telecommunication Union. 1965. *From Semaphore to Satellite*. Geneva: ITU.

Keller, Suzanne. 1977. 'The telephone in new (and old) communities.' In Ithiel de Sola Pool, ed. *The Social Impact of the Telephone*. Cambridge, Mass.: MIT Press, 281–98.

Latham, Robert F. 1975. 'The telephone and social change.' In Benjamin D. Singer, ed. *Communications in Canadian Society*, 2nd rev. ed. Vancouver: Copp Clark, 19–39.

Lynd, Robert S. and Helen Merrell Lynd. 1929. *Middletown*. New York: Harcourt, Brace.

McCluer, C.E. 1902. 'Telephone operators and operating room management.' *the American Telephone Journal* 6:2 (12 July), 31–2.

McLuhan, Marshall. 1964. *Understanding Media*, 2nd ed. New York: Mentor.

MacMeal, Harry B. 1934. *The Story of Independent Telephony*. Chicago: Independent Pioneer Telephone Association.

Maddox, Brenda. 1977. 'Women and the switchboard.' In Ithiel de Sola Pool, ed. *The Social Impact of the Telephone*. Cambridge, Mass.: MIT Press, 262–80.

Mayer, Martin, 1977. 'The telephone and the uses of time.' In Ithiel de Sola Pool, ed. *The Social Impact of the Telephone*. Cambridge, Mass.: MIT Press, 225–45.

Mitchell, Garry. 1984. 'Some aspects of telephone socialization.' In Sari Thomas, ed. *Studies in Mass Communication, Vol. 1*. Norwood, New Jersey: Ablex, 249–52.

Oakley, Ann. 1974. *The Sociology of Housework*. New York: Pantheon.

Parker, Dorothy. 1942. 'A telephone call.' In *The Collected Stories of Dorothy Parker*. New York: Random House, 41–50.

Perl, Lewis J. 1978. *Economic and Demographic Determinants of Residential Demand for Basic Telephone Service*. New York: National Economic Research Associates.

Pézerat, Pierrette and Danièle Poublan. 1985. 'French telephone operators past and present: the ambiguities of progress.' *Oral History Journal* 13:1 (Spring), 28–42.

Pierce, John. 1977. 'The telephone and society in the past 100 years.' In Ithiel de Sola Pool, ed. *The Social Impact of the Telephone*. Cambridge, Mass.: MIT Press, 159–96.

Pilgrim The. 1921. 'Pilgrim's progress in a telephone exchange.' *Life and Labor*, Part I, 11:1 (January), 11–14; Part II, 11:2 (February), 48–52.

Pool, Ithiel de Sola, ed. 1977. *The Social Impact of the Telephone*. Cambridge, Mass.: MIT Press.

Pool, Ithiel de Sola. 1983. *Forecasting the Telephone: A Retrospective Technology Assessment*. Norwood, New Jersey: Ablex.

Robertson, Lynn and Keith Amstutz. 1949. *Telephone Problems in Rural Indiana*. Agricultural Experimental Station Bulletin no.548, Lafayette, Ind.: Purdue University.

Singer, Benjamin D. 1981. *Social Functions of the Telephone*. Palo

Alto, Cal.: R&E Research Associates.

Stanley, Liz. 1984. 'Open secrets: what they are and what we should do about them.' In Olivia Butler, ed. *Feminist Experience in Feminist Research*. Manchester: University of Manchester, 117–39.

Stanley, Liz and Sue Wise. 1979. 'Feminist research, feminist consciousness and experiences of sexism.' *Women's Studies International Quarterly* 2, 359–74.

Strasser, Susan. 1982. *Never Done: A History of American Housework*. New York: Pantheon.

Telecommunications Journal. 1975. *Journal Télégraphique* 42:12 (December), unnumbered.

'Telephone good form.' 1907. *Telephony* 14:3 (September), 138.

Terkel, Studs. 1985. *Working*. New York: Ballantine Books.

US Bureau of the Census. 1910. *Telephones: 1907*. Washington, DC.

US Bureau of Labor. 1910. *Investigation of Telephone Companies*. Washington, DC.

US Senate. 1966. *Abusive and Harassing Telephone Calls*. Washington, DC.

Ward, Florence E. 1920. *The Farm Woman's Problems*. Circular no. 148. Washington, DC: US Department of Agriculture.

Wisconsin State Telephone Association. 1985. *On the Line ... A History of the Telephone Industry in Wisconsin*. Madison: WSTA.

NOTES ON CONTRIBUTORS

Ellen Balka, who is conducting research for unions about how technology is affecting union jobs, is a graduate student at Simon Fraser University in Burnaby, British Columbia. She is designing, using and evaluating educational materials used to teach women workers about technological change. She plans soon to be working full-time on implementing the women and technology network discussed in the essay she co-authored with Judy Smith.

Margaret Benston teaches jointly in the Computing Science Department and the Women's Studies Program at Simon Fraser University in Burnaby, British Columbia, and does research on women and technological change. Her publications include 'The political economy of women's liberation' (article in the *Monthly Review*), 'Feminism and the critique of scientific method' and 'The myth of computer literacy' (in *Canadian Women's Studies*). She has been active in the women's movement since 1968, including participation in a feminist singing group that teaches feminist, labor and anti-war songs to anyone interested.

Margery W. Davies is the author of *Woman's Place Is At the Typewriter: Office Work and Office Workers, 1870-1930* (Temple University Press, 1982). She has worked as an editor of the journal *Radical America* and has been an active volunteer in both day care and the public schools. Presently she is doing research on the social history and sociology of breast and bottle feeding in the United States. She lives in Cambridge, Massachusetts, with her husband and four children.

Leanne Hinton teaches in the Linguistics Department at the University of California at Berkeley. Her graduate work was in anthropology, ethnomusicology, ethnography and linguistics; she has done extensive work with the Havasupais in these research areas. She has also done fieldwork with Hualapai, Diegueno, Mixtec and others. Her publications include *Havasupai Songs: A Linguistic Perspective and Spirit Mountain: An Anthology of Yuman Narrative and Song* (co-edited with Lucille Watahomigie).

Cheris Kramarae teaches sociolinguistics in the Department of

229

Speech Communication at the University of Illinois at Urbana-Champaign. She is author of *Women and Men Speaking*, editor of *The Voices and Words of Women and Men*, and co-editor of several books including *Language, Gender and Society* (with Barrie Thorne and Nancy Henley) and *A Feminist Dictionary* (with Paula Treichler and with the assistance of Ann Russo).

Victoria Leto, a postgraduate student in Speech Communication at the University of Illinois at Urbana-Champaign, researches the sociological influences of gender roles and racism in interpersonal communication. She is currently studying the role of questions and answers in marital discussions and sex differences/similarities in preferences for how a conversation should occur.

Anne Machung is a former typist, secretary and word processing operator, and author of *The Politics of Office Work* (Temple University Press, forthcoming). She recently completed the Work and Family Research Project for the Women's Center at the University of California at Berkeley, and is currently a visiting scholar at the Institute for the Study of Social Change on the Berkeley campus.

Anne McKay is a freelance consultant working in telecommunications policy and market research, planning and implementation of new communications technologies, and video production. She has been a teacher in Spain, Mexico, New Zealand, Zambia and California, and holds degrees in interactive telecommunications from New York University, in Spanish from the University of Eastern Washington, and in home economics from the University of California. She currently lives in Brooklyn.

Lana Rakow teaches in the communication program at the University of Wisconsin-Parkside, Kenosha. She is interested in bringing feminist theory and methodology to the study of communications. Her most recent research project is an ethnographic study of the history of women's relationship to the telephone in a small community.

Virginia Scharff is writing a dissertation in history at the University of Arizona, on American women and the automobile in the early car culture. She has written about women and technology, and about the history of women in the American West. Scharff has directed and participated in a number of public humanities programs, including spending several summers touring with Chautauqua troupes. She lives in Tucson and teaches in American history and Women's Studies.

Mark Schulman heads the Department of Communications, Film and Video at the City College of the City University of New York. His most recent publication is the chapter on 'Language and communication' in the 1985 edition of *Good Reading*. He recently completed an action-research project to guide the on-air preparation for WHCR-FM, a community radio station for New York City's Harlem neighborhood.

Judy Smith, coordinator of the Women and Technology Project in Missoula, Montana, is involved in a variety of educational projects, on campuses and in communities, that focus on feminist assessment of technology, technoliteracy for women, computer equity, and the development of appropriate technology. She is a member of the Northwest Women's Studies Science and Technology Caucus, and the Women and Technology Computer Network.

Sherry Turkle teaches in the Program in Science, Technology and Society program at Massachusetts Institute of Technology. She is the author of *Psychoanalytic Politics: Freud's French Revolution* (Basic Books, 1978; MIT paperback) which traces the reversal of the long-standing French hostility to Freudian ideas in the years following the student uprising of 1968 and the development of a 'French Freud,' of poeticized, politicized, uniquely Gallic psychoanalytic culture. Her most recent book, *The Second Self: Computers and the Human Spirit* (Simon & Schuster, 1984; Touchstone paperback) looks at the relationships that people form with computers and the ways in which these relationships affect values, ways of thinking about the world, and ways of seeing oneself and other people.

Women and Transport Forum was a group of women who worked on transport and related issues at the now defunct (March 1986) Greater London Council (GLC). They came together to share ideas and their research on women's mobility. This work entails promoting public transport since this is the means of mobility most used by women in London: Kate Oliver, who worked in the Public Transport Campaign Unit and is now a Senior Transport Planner with the London Strategic Policy Unit (LSPU), wrote the chapter for this volume. The other members of the Forum provided much of the information and helped with editing. They are Claire Barrett, from the Public Transport Campaign Unit; Benedicte Foo, an architect who works with Matrix women's architecture cooperative and used to work on planning and transport issues in the Women's Committee Support Unit; Christine Hemming, the race relations advisor in the Transport and Development Department; Maureen Mackintosh, an economist, and Tina Mackay, a researcher in occupational health, both from the GLC's Industry and Employment Unit; Jane Smith, in the Transport and Development Department, who directed the survey on Women's Transport needs and analysed the data and who now works at Social and Community Planning Research; and Beverley Taylor, who was the Equalities Officer in the Transport and Development Department and is now a team leader in the Planning Group of the LSPU. Thanks are also due to Richard Hallé and Nick Lester of the Public Transport Campaign Unit for their comments, and to all the women in the GLC's Word Processing Centre who typed the paper.

INDEX

233